The Cross and the Kaleidoscope: Substitutionary Atonement and Our Relationships

Alex Early & Enoch Wan

Relational Paradigm Series of CDRR

The Cross and the Kaleidoscope: Substitutionary Atonement and Our Relationships

Copyright 2021© Western Academic Publishers

Alex Early & Enoch Wan

ISBN: 978-1-949201-07-9

TABLE OF CONTENTS

LIST OF FIGURES

LIST OF FIGURES

FORWARD

This book demonstrates that opposites not only attract – they are essential to each other's existence. Authors Alex Early and Enoch Wan adeptly weave the historic, theologically orthodox doctrine of Penal Substitutionary Atonement (PSA) together with their vision of "the relational paradigm," which, the authors contend, is essential to effective ministry in the 21st century.

The genius of this move may not be fully appreciated without knowing why the doctrine of PSA and relationality in any form might be construed as conceptual opposites. Critics of the doctrine of PSA are of help here. The most cogent argument against PSA is the claim that it conceives of Jesus' sacrificial death on the cross as little more than a *legal transaction*, devoid of any relational content. Jesus' sacrifice, according to PSA, fulfills God's justice based on a payment that is recognized as sufficient by the "law" – the substitution of another victim. Critics of PSA argue that penal substitution, thus conceived, amounts to little more than the payment of a penalty. In this sense, the argument goes, when justification is based on a payment (substitutionary or otherwise), there is no basis or need for forgiveness. There is no actual place for *relationship* because salvation is achieved by *forensic transference*, not by forgiveness. Redemption, in other words, is *transactional*, not *relational*.

One such critic puts this succinctly:

The biblical idea of forgiveness resulting from obedient and faithful response to the covenant stipulations of God's relationship to humanity is thus replaced by the forensic emphases of justice, guilt, penalty, and legal satisfaction by carrying out the terms of the legal sentence. One may either serve a sentence to satisfy the 'law,' or be pardoned and forgiven, but not both (R. Larry Shelton, *Cross & Covenant: Interpreting the Atonement for 21st Century Mission* [Paternoster, 2006], 198).

If such a criticism has any merit, it is due mainly to the *emphasis* that certain protagonists of PSA ascribe to the forensic nature of the metaphor, which has the (unintended) effect of eclipsing the interpersonal aspects of the Atonement.

In bringing together the doctrine of PSA and their relational paradigm, Early and Wan safeguard the potential excesses to which certain advocates of PSA might press the forensic character of Jesus' death by providing an essential counterpoint, highlighting the scriptural truth that atonement is about *both* the satisfaction of God's righteous requirements embodied in the Law and the relational reconciliation that Jesus' atonement effects for all those on the receiving end of his propitiatory achievement on their behalf.

From beginning to end, Early and Wan underscore the centrality of relationship as the principal connection with God, which was uniquely established at the beginning of creation with the breath of God in human nostrils and then broken by sin through Adam and Eve's willful disobedience. From that point forward, the relational deficit between

God and humanity (and between humans as a whole) comprises *the all-consuming loss* that every instance of atonement was intended to repair, culminating in the once-for-all sacrifice of Jesus Christ on the cross. Not a single case of sacrifice and atonement in Wan and Early's envisioning of God's covenantal dealings occur apart from his (relational) mercy and grace. And through the outworking of God's love, made fully efficacious through the atoning sacrifice of Jesus Christ, believers now experience a progressive transformation in their relationship with God (vertically) and in their relationships with fellow contemporaries in this life (horizontally). While on this side of eternity such progression is gradual, and though it will never be fully complete in this temporal existence, our redemption and sanctification point to complete restoration at the End of the Age, when we will become God's full image bearers.

Thus construed, the doctrine of PSA *informs* and *enriches* our conception of relationality rather than nullifying it. Through penal substitution, Jesus averts God's wrath, which opens the way for God's love to be fully extended to his chosen people. God's enemies are family again. For Wan and Early, Jesus' atonement and resurrection pave the way for the entirety of God's salvific work, which is superintended by the Holy Spirit:

The work of Good Friday and Easter Sunday are what provide the context for which we can construct a relational paradigm that functions both vertically and horizontally. This opens the door and beckons us to consider the Person and Work of the Holy Spirit because he not only *informs* the horizontal relationships, but is himself the grounding, the energy, the active agent who applies the work of Christ–extending his peace in the ministry of reconciliation (2 Cor. 5:17-21) (p. 48).

The authors show that the substitutionary atonement of Christ not only reestablishes redeemed humanity's vertical relationship with the Triune God, effecting our adoption as his children (Gal. 4:6), but also brings into existence God's covenant people, who at the horizontal level kaleidoscopically manifest *doxology*, *service*, and *forgiveness* (see pp. 122-124).

Moreover, the relationality of Jesus' penal substitution informs our vision for ministry, be it evangelism, preaching, or pastoral care. Regarding evangelism, for example, Early and Wan's relational paradigm enables us to see that human beings "are not merely projects to be maintained but image bearers to be redeemed by the God who sent his Son…to reconcile his people to himself." Thus, we are "to lovingly, winsomely, and intelligently communicate the gospel in a way that is both faithful to Scripture and contextualized to the hearer" (p. 189).

In the final analysis, the authors deliver on their promise to offer a fresh take on theological research into the biblical doctrine of PSA and its inextricable (and biblical!) connection to relationality. This book is a valuable resource to everyone who wishes to enrich their appreciation for the practical implications of Jesus' atonement and its centrality for ministry in the 21st century.

Charles J. Conniry, Jr., PhD
President, Western Seminary

CHAPTER 1

INTRODUCTION

Purpose of the Book

The purpose of this book is to integrate the doctrine of Penal Substitutionary Atonement with the relational paradigm for Christian ministry in the 21st century employing a kaleidoscopic perspective.

Background of the Book

It has been somewhat over a decade since many evangelical Christians started questioning and, for many, *denying* the long-held trust in the doctrine of Penal Substitutionary Atonement (PSA). The questioning and denials of PSA did not only occur in scholarly circles, rather also in the local church amongst the clergy and her members. This occurred largely because more popular authors, pastors, and speakers began taking their musings outside of private reflections and dialogues and into public squares and ecclesial spheres. For example, writers such as Steve Chalke in the United Kingdom and Brian McLaren and Rob Bell in the United States in particular carried tremendous influence.

I (Alex)[1] was pursuing my MA in *Aspects of Biblical Interpretation* at the London School of Theology (2008) immediately after the school held a large symposium on this now very *controversial* doctrine. To date, my time at LST was the most ethnically and theologically diverse experience I have encountered. Fellow classmates from Brazil, the Congo, Taiwan, Vietnam, Iceland, Singapore, Pakistan, and many other places around the globe all challenged me in ways that continue to benefit me to this very day. In fact, I suspect this will be the case for the rest of my life.

Having been raised in a conservative evangelical home and church, and considering myself *Reformed* in my soteriological thinking, I was intrigued by the controversy surrounding what I had always assumed to be what all Christians in all places had always believed. The nature and character of God are of utmost importance in Christian thought. Words like "wrath" and "love" were not foreign to my Christian vocabulary. Yet, I had never considered that these two concepts might be contradictory; or better, how they can *both* be true. Is "divine child abuse" actually occurring in the death of the Son of God or are the Father and Son cooperatively accomplishing the redemption of the children of God? Does PSA pit one member of the Trinity *against* another? If yes, what am I to make of the passages that speak about Christ as a propitiatory sacrifice? For me personally, these and many more questions surrounding PSA soon demanded further study. While these questions surged something else happened to me; in addition to a love for academic theology an even greater love and desire to serve the local church was born. Therefore, I studied systematic theology in London under the supervision of Dr. Graham McFarlane, then later expanded my doctoral research into relational theology and missiology under the supervision of Professor Enoch Wan in

---

[1] The reference "I" is used throughout this book to be more personal and readable.

Portland Oregon at Western Seminary. To be more precise, the purpose of taking the research into this present book is two-fold: the first is to help Christians think correctly and articulate themselves well regarding this precious aspect of the atonement. Secondly, Professor Wan's many years of missiological research and writing assists in directing the reader towards developing a more robust relational theology, ethnohermeneutic, and missiology that takes doctrine from the academy directly to the mission field and local church. Years of collaboration led to the joint authorship of this volume.

Definition of Key Terms

Penal Substitutionary Atonement

The doctrine of PSA states that Jesus Christ, the second member of the Trinity, died in the place of sinners on his cross and thereby satisfied and averted the just wrath of God. His *propitiatory* death paid the full price of every human for whom he died.

Christian Ministry

Christian Ministry is an act of service carried out in the name of Christ by those who profess to follow him as his disciples.

Figure 1 – The five-step (STARS) interdisciplinary approach proposed by Enoch Wan:[2]

Listed below are simple explanations of each of the five points in Figure 2:

Five-step interdisciplinary approach	#
Scripturally Sound: Not proof-text; rather the "whole counsel of God" (Acts 20:26-27)	S
Theologically Supported: Not mere pragmatism/expedience; but sound theology	T
Analytically Coherent: Not to be self-contradictory; rather to be coherent	A
Relevantly Contextual: Not to be out of place; instead, fitting for the context	R
Strategically Applicable: Not only good in theory; also, may be put into practice	S

1. Scripturally Sound
   a. As evangelicals, Scripture is to be the basis and guide of Christian faith and practice. It is axiomatic for evangelical Protestants to base one's convictions on the grounds of *"sola scriptura."*
2. Theologically Supported

---

[2] Enoch Wan, "Inter-disciplinary and integrative missiological research: the 'what,' 'why,' and 'how,'" *Global Missiology* (July 2017), www.GlobalMissiology.org. An earlier version of the "STARS" approach by Wan was published as the Featured Article in "Core values of mission organization in the cultural context of the 21st Century," *Global Missiology* (January 2009), www.GlobalMissiology.org.

a. Merely basing a thought on pragmatism/expedience is insufficient; sound theology is essential and required.
3. Analytically Coherent
a. Not to be self-contradictory; rather to be both consistent and coherent.
4. Relevantly Contextual
a. Not to be out of place; instead it is required to be fitting for the context.
5. Strategically Practical

It is good to have scriptural/theological support with coherent theory and cultural relevance; also, may be strategically put into practice.

Figure 2 – Comparisons Between "Biblical" and Scriptural"[3]

#	BIBLICAL	SCRIPTURAL
1	Descriptive: Recorded/reported in the Bible	Prescriptive: Prescribed by the Incarnate and "enscriptured" Word
2	Precedent in the Bible	Principle of "the whole counsel of God"
3	Particular: time and place specific	Universal: transcending time and space
4	Culturally and contextually specific	Neither culturally nor contextually limited

The Bible is full of "description" (#1 in the figure above) of behavior and practice of major figures in biblical times; this is not necessarily "prescriptive" for us today in a modern context. For example, the Bible recorded/reported patriarch Abraham and King David as polygamists; it is prescriptive for us to be monogamists by the teaching of Jesus (Matt. 19; Mark 10; Luke 16) and consistent teaching (elsewhere in Scripture – Gen. 2:24; Deut. 24:1-3; Mal. 2:15).

Let us use another example to illustrate this point. The selection of a substitute for Judas after his suicide was by "casting lots" (Acts 1) so this way of selecting a leader is merely "biblical" (#2 in Figure 2). Should the Christian church follow that manner in identification and selection of leaders today? In other words, casting lots as a form of decision-making as recorded/reported in Acts 1 is "biblically accurate" yet is not "scripturally binding" for us to follow today.

There is a popular Christian hymn based on Psalm 51:10-11, the psalm of confession written by King David after his adulterous relationship with Bathsheba. However, though the hymn is "biblical" ("do not take your Holy Spirit from me" based on Ps. 51:10-11), it is theologically incorrect and inapplicable to us. The reason is that David's confession is "particular," being "time and place specific" (#3 of Figure 2); it is not "universally" applicable to us because Jesus promised that the Holy Spirit will "be

[3] Enoch Wan, ""Core Values of Mission Organization in the Cultural Context of the 21st Century," *Global Missiology* (January 2009), 6-7, www.GlobalMissiology.org.

with you forever" (John 14:16). King David's confession and the hymn based on Psalm 51 though being "biblical" is not "scriptural." The ceremonial law and sacrificial system of the OT is "biblical" as revealed by God in the OT and taught in the Pentateuch. The writer of Hebrews expounded the "scriptural meaning" of the old covenant and related Jewish traditions (#4 in Figure 2) for us – the NT Christians. The "scriptural teaching" of Hebrews is binding for all people at all times.

Figure 3 – Directional Understanding of Being "Biblical" and "Scriptural"

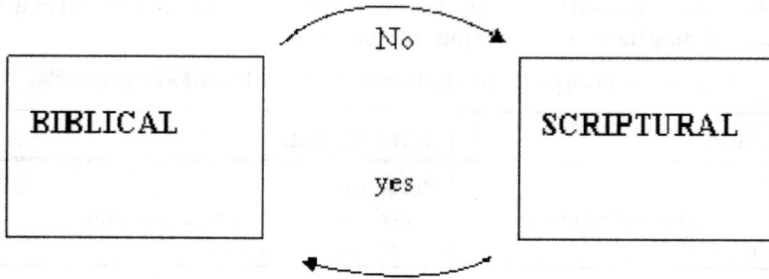

Note: Not all men are husbands; nonetheless, within the context of "traditional Christian marriage," all husbands are male.

Likewise, whatever is "biblical" is not necessarily "scriptural," nevertheless, whatever is "scriptural" should also be "biblical." Not only are "biblical" and "scriptural" different in meaning and usage, the proper order and the correct direction are also important. For example, when Jesus was tempted, Satan quoted verses from the OT so he is no doubt being "biblical." However, his use of the Scripture is not "scriptural" at all. Jesus responded to Satan also by quoting verses from the OT (being "biblical"); but his usage is very different from that of Satan because He is both "biblical" and "scriptural" at the same time.

To illustrate the significance and importance of the sequential order of the five elements in "The five-step (STARS) integrative approach," the mistake of reversing the order will be explained first, followed by the example of the proper sequential order. The use of terrorist means by "Jihad Muslims" to propagate their faith may be practically effective and expediently feasible (point #5 in Figure 2). However, the "terrorist way" cannot be used by evangelical Christians in their statements of mission, vision, core values, and strategic goals. It cannot be an option for evangelical Christians for several reasons:

- The message of their gospel is "God so loved the world" according to the Scripture – point #1 in Figure 2;
- The God they proclaim is the "God of love" theologically – point #2;
- The Christian faith and practice is to be consistently and coherently characterized by "love" – the Great Commandment of "love God" and "love thy neighbor" – point #3 in Figure 2.

The "Gospel of wealth and health" and "the positive thinking" approach are popular these days because of "cultural relevance" of our time (point #4 in Figure 2) and expedient/practical (point #5) with desirable outcomes quantitatively. However, evangelical Christians cannot ignore the importance of the points #1, #2, and #3 and should not "conform to this world" (Rom. 12:1-2). No statements of mission, vision, core values, and strategic goals of evangelical Christians should be embraced if these only measure up to points #4 and #5 yet fail in #1, #2, and #3 in Figure 2.

The organization of the book

Following the five-step (STARS) interdisciplinary approach of Enoch Wan, arrangement by chapter (except "introduction" and "conclusion") as listed below:

STARS	CHAPTER	TITLE
S	Chapter 2	Biblical-historical foundation for PSA
T	Chapter 3	Preliminary theological understanding: the "image of God"
A	Chapter 4	Theological foundation for PSA
I	Chapter 5	The theoretical integration of PSA and relational paradigm
I	Chapter 6	PSA and the horizontal relational paradigm
R	Chapter 7	The theoretical integration of PSA with "honor and shame" from a relational perspective
S	Chapter 8	Practical implications for Christian ministry in North America

CHAPTER 2

BIBLICAL-HISTORICAL FOUNDATIONS FOR PSA

Introduction

Hugh Rayment-Pickard's recent work entitled *50 Key Concepts in Theology* is one example of contemporary theological thinkers as they seek to condense enormous theological concepts down to a pop-theology quick reference book. And yet, their (like everyone) theological presuppositions influence and inform how they go about defining various doctrines. For example, they state that the "earliest doctrines of the atonement, prevalent among the Church Fathers and in the centuries up to the first millennium, were so-called 'victory' or 'ransom' theories."[4] They continue by saying that "it was St. Anselm, writing a thousand years after the birth of Christianity, who proposed a revised understanding of the atonement, offering a *new theory* based upon God's need to punish someone for the sins of humanity."[5] It is precisely this line of thinking that seeks to persuade people to believe that the penal view of the atonement is simply a late product of a certain time and place and is neither demonstrated in Scripture nor amongst the theologians of the early church. In this chapter, it shall be demonstrated that the penal understanding of the atonement *is* found and affirmed both in the biblical records as well as in early church history as being a major tenant of orthodox Christian thought.

Contemporary biblical-historical positions on the atonement are debated amongst both the academy and within the local church. For instance, some propose that there is no concept of the wrath of God being exercised in the work of the crucifixion of Jesus.[6] This is nothing new. In 1739, Thomas Chubb in *The True Gospel of Jesus Christ Vindicated* wrote, "God's disposition to show mercy ... arises wholly from his own innate goodness or mercifulness, and not from anything external to him, whether it be the sufferings and death of Jesus Christ or otherwise."[7] Rather, others ascribe to ransom, example, and victor theories of the atonement and dismiss the penal view altogether for

---

[4] Hugh Rayment-Pickard, "Atonement," in *50 Key Concepts in Theology* (London, England: Darton, Longman, and Todd, 2007), 4.

[5] Rayment-Pickard, "Atonement," 5, italics mine.

[6] Joel Green and Mark Baker, *Recovering the Scandal of the Cross: Atonement in New Testament and Contemporary Contexts* (Downers Grove, IL: InterVarsity Press, 2011), 32, 42, Charles Dodd, *Epistle of Paul to the Romans* (New York, NY: Harper and Row, 1932), 32, Tom Smail, *Once and For All: A Confession of the Cross* (London, England: Darton, Longman, and Todd, 1998), 87. Steve Chalke and Alan Mann, *The Lost Message of Jesus* (Grand Rapids, MI: Zondervan, 2003),182.

[7] Charles Hill, "Atonement in the Old and New Testaments," in *The Glory of the Atonement: Biblical, Historical, and Practical Perspectives: Essays in Honor of Roger Nicole,* ed. Charles E. Hill, and Frank A. James, III (Downers Grove, IL: InterVarsity Press, 2004), 24.

reasons such as primitive thinking,[8] nothing more than the result of social conditioning,[9] or because of the sheer masochism that one would accredit to the character of God.[10] Such conclusions are made through skewed hermeneutics and theology and are the result of improper reading strategies. As such, any conclusions are only partial representations of God's action in, through, and as Christ.

Vanhoozer reminds us that "for every action there is an equal and opposite reaction." With this physical law in mind he claims that it could serve our morality "equally well."[11] These theological conclusions must be recognized as intelligent decisions (though some react quite passionately against them) and at the same time they appear to leave the reader with one particular question unanswered, namely, "Is there indeed a *penalty* for sin and if so, how is it recognized before God?" For, if the crucifixion is a demonstration of love without a penalty being paid, then how is God still *just* if in his grace he acquits the guilty and chooses to simply leave sin unaddressed while he triumphs in victory? It will first serve well to look into atonement laid out in the Bible and history.

Atonement in the Bible – the Necessity

Despite being made in the image of God, Scripture conveys humanity as fallen in Adam (Gen. 3:17-19; Rom. 5:12-14), inclined towards sin (Gen. 6:5), and therefore subject to the judgment of a holy and just God (Rom. 2:5, 3:23; Eph. 2:1-3).[12] However,

---

[8] Tom Smail, "Can One Man Die for the People?" in *Atonement Today: A Symposium at St. John's College, Nottingham,* ed. J. Goldingay (London, England: SPCK, 1995), 85. Also Derek Kidner, "Retribution and Punishment in the Old Testament, in Light of the New Testament," *Scottish Bulletin of Evangelical Theology* 1 (1983), 7.

[9] Green and Baker, *Scandal,* 127. Elsewhere Green and Baker state, "The Scriptures as a whole provide no ground for a portrait of an angry God needing to be appeased in atoning sacrifice," 51. Also, they state that "Anselm's model of the atonement arose out of and reflects a particular socio-historical moment relatively foreign to us," 94.

[10]Joanne Carlson Brown and Carol R. Bohn, eds., "For God So Loved the World," in *Christianity, Patriarchy, and Abuse: A Feminist Critique* (New York, NY: Pilgrim Press, 1989), 26.

[11] Kevin Vanhoozer, "The Atonement in Postmodernity: Guilt, Goats, and Gifts," in *The Glory of the Atonement,* ed. Hill and James III, 376-77.

[12] Umberto Cassuto, *A Commentary on the Book of Genesis,* part 1, *From Adam to Noah* (Jerusalem, Israel: Magnes Press, 1961), 168. See also Gordon J.Wenham, *Word Biblical Commentary,* vol. 1, *Genesis 1-15* (Waco, TX: Word Books, 1987), 82-3. See also John Goldingay, *BCOTWP,* vol. 2, *Psalms 42-89,* ed. T. Longman III (Grand Rapids, MI: Baker Academic, 2007), 144-47. See also Douglas Moo, *NICNT: The Epistle to the Romans* (Grand Rapids, MI: Eerdmans, 1996), 134-36, 512. The writer is aware that not all Christians are in agreement on this issue. For example, Pannenberg objects that "It is impossible for me to be held jointly responsible as though I were a joint cause for an act that another did many generations ago and in a situation radically different from mine." See Wolfhart Pannenberg, *Anthropology in Theological Perspective,* (Edinburgh, England: T&T Clark, 1985),124. See also Charles Carter, ed., "'Harmartiology': Evil, the Marrer of God's Creative Purpose and Work," in *A Contemporary Wesleyan Theology: Biblical, Systematic, and Practical,* 2 vols. (Grand Rapids, MI: Zondervan, 1983), 1.267. And yet, the question must be

not all Evangelicals have in mind what the more traditional understanding of these passages mean (especially in the West). For example, Green and Baker argue that "the 'wrath of God' is, for Paul, not an effective response on the part of God, not the striking out of a vengeful God."[13] Humans are merely reaping the consequences for their sin and *this* should be understood as the wrath of God.[14] To quote these scholars, "sinful activity is the result of God's letting us go our own way – and this 'letting us go our own way' constitutes God's wrath."[15] Certainly this is part of the equation and should not be quickly dismissed. However, to the first parents, God declared that the *penalty* for sinful transgression was death (Gen. 2:17).[16] This is repeated throughout the Christian Bible: "The soul that sins shall die" (Ezek. 18:4, 20); "The wages of sin is death" (Rom. 6:23, cf. 5:12) and therefore, "Without the shedding of blood there is no forgiveness of sins" (Heb. 9:22).[17]

Hill recalls Jesus' question, "What can a man give in exchange for his soul?" (Matt. 16:26) and concludes that this clearly implies that some kind of exchange is justly required by God. And yet, as the psalmist lamented, "Truly no man can ransom himself'" (Ps. 49:7, cf. Mic. 6:6-7).[18] This aids in paving the path towards articulating a case for penal substitutionary atonement (PSA).

---

asked of those who follow in Pannenberg's line of thinking, "If you will not allow Adam to represent you in the Fall 'many generations ago,' why is it that you will allow Christ to represent you 'many generations ago'?"

[13] Green and Baker, *Scandal*, 95.

[14] For example, Dodd, *Romans*. Vanhoozer points out that those that embrace such an understanding use a verse such as Galatians 6:7 regarding sowing and reaping is nothing more than "a kind of wisdom statement about the consequences that naturally flow from human acts in a morally structured created order, not a promise (or threat) that God will personally intervene to reward or punish human acts." Vanhoozer, "Postmodernity," 376.

[15] Dodd, *Romans*, 55. See also where Stephen Travis argues that "He (Paul) understands both salvation and condemnation primarily in relational terms: people's destinies will be a confirmation and intensification of the relationship with God or alienation from him which has been their experience in this life." Stephen Travis, "Christ as Bearer of Divine Judgment in Paul's Thought about the Atonement," in *Jesus of Nazareth: Lord and Christ: Essays on the Historical Jesus and New Testament Christology*, ed. Joel Green and Max Turner (Grand Rapids, MI: Eerdmans, 1994), 332.

[16] Jewish scholar Nahum Sarna and Protestant Reformer John Calvin agree that humankind was not created in an immortal condition. Sarna holds that upon transgressing the command of God, mankind would "incur immediate capital punishment." See Nahum M. Sarna, *The JPS Torah Commentary: Genesis,* בראשית (New York, NY: The Jewish Publication Society,1989), 21. Calvin believed that humankind fell from happiness and suffered alienation from God. See John Calvin, *A Commentary on Genesis,* two volumes in one, trans. by J. King (London, England: Banner of Truth, 1965),127. However, others such as David Jobling hold that Gen. 2:17 means that "on the day you eat of it you will become mortal," in "A Structural Analysis of Genesis 2:4b-3:24," *SBLSP* 1 (1978): 64.

[17] Charles Hill, "Atonement," 24.

[18] Charles Hill, "Atonement," 24-25.

Sin

The very concept of atonement primarily beckons the questions, "For what?" and, "Why is this even necessary?" John Goldingay rightly states, "There is a sense in which no Christian doctrine can be discussed in isolation from all the others, for Christian belief is a coherent whole rather than an assembly of unconnected modules."[19] Therefore, it is of highest priority to briefly address the biblical teaching on sin and the consequences that follow in order to provide the stage upon which the doctrine of PSA can be introduced.

Old Testament Concept of Sin

Sin is commonly understood as "failure, rebellion, transgression, trespass, turning from the right road, stain, infidelity."[20] Both Jewish and Christian scholars can agree that from the very opening chapters of the book of Genesis, the world and human condition becomes radically distorted due to the human decision to rebel against God in the Garden of Eden (Gen. 3).[21] However, Fromm and Fox understand this account quite differently. Fromm does not believe that original sin was anything more than humans becoming ultimately free. He states,

> The act of disobedience set Adam and Eve free and opened their eyes ... Original sin, far from corrupting man, set him free; it was the beginning of history. Man had to leave the Garden of Eden in order to learn to rely on his own powers and to become fully human.[22]

Fox echoes this in his work, *Original Blessing*, arguing that the doctrine of original sin has been given far too much prominence and that God's original blessing of the earth is what truly defines our humanity.[23] Rather than beginning with a doctrine of original sin he chooses to focus on God's blessing of the world. This leads him to conclude that a religious tradition that begins with sin and centers its energies on sin, and being redeemed from it, is distorted and salvation loses its meaning.[24]

---

[19] John Goldingay, "Your Iniquities Have Made a Separation Between You and Your God," in *Atonement Today*, ed. J. Goldingay, 39.

[20] Goldingay, "Iniquities," 39.

[21] See N. Sarna's *Genesis* בְּרֵאשִׁית; commenting on Genesis 3:6. Sarna states that "egotism, greed, and self-interest now govern human action," 25. Regarding the same verse, J. Calvin states that "after [her] heart had declined from faith, and from obedience to the word, she corrupted both herself and all her senses, and depravity was diffused through all parts of her soul as well as her body." See Calvin, *Genesis,* 151.

[22] Erich Fromm, *On Disobedience: And Other Essays* (New York, NY: Seabury Press, 1984), 2.

[23] See Matthew Fox, Original Blessing: A Primer in Creation Spirituality Presented in Four Paths, Twenty-Six Themes, and Two Questions, (Santa Fe, NM: Bear & Company, 1983).

[24] Fox, *Original,* 118. See also that John Milbank, when speaking of divine *impassibility* implies that God goes unoffended by sin and thus there is no sacrifice necessary to satisfy his holy wrath or justice. See John Milbank, *Being Reconciled: Ontology and Pardon* (London, England: Routledge, 2003), 49-62.

While this is certainly true, that the Bible does *not* begin with sin and sinners but with *God* bringing everything into creation and specifically creating human beings for fellowship with himself and one another, this does not discount what is recorded in Genesis three. Rather the rebellion of humanity is all the more intensified. Everything in creation was originally good but it is no longer good and is rather "cursed." Creation is longing to be restored (Rom. 8) and humans are in a state of hostility before God apart from his sovereign intervention, atoning work, and regeneration. To focus exclusively on original goodness to the neglect of all that follows is an error. As stated above by Goldingay, theology is not simply isolated events, rather a series of connected modules—connected to the original blessed creation before the fall of mankind.[25] By choosing to focus on one doctrine and exclude another, Fox gives a distorted view of both Scripture and God. He does not see that anything is wrong with mankind's moral corruption and therefore a penal substitution would be condemned under such thinking as simply unnecessary.

While Fox and Fromm believe that sin entering the world is something that is to be celebrated, as we become *more* human, Goldingay calls attention to the alternative understandings regarding the creation of man. The surrounding Mesopotamian cultures, during the time of the writing of Genesis, believed that the earth and humans were created out of cosmic struggle between the gods—anger and violence brought about the human race by a recycling of the corpses of the gods who lost in this conflict.[26] Therefore, this new race was placed on the earth to serve the victorious gods and to provide food for them. Goldingay declares that the OT is in sharp contrast to this way of thinking. Rather, Genesis declares that everything created was created "good" which includes the *absence* of sin. And that humankind is created in the *"image"* of God, therefore dignified.[27] The writer of Genesis tells us that sin enters the universe through humankind's sinful decision to rebel under the deceitfulness of the serpent.

Old Testament Metaphors for Sin

The Bible does not leave one wondering "what is sin?" or "what is sin like?" Rather, there are multiple ways in which the Bible seeks to address, define, and explain what sin is, its origins, and what God has done in Christ to cleanse, redeem, and heal us from sin and its consequences. John Goldingay collected seven biblical metaphors used throughout the OT that he says describe "what our sin is like."[28] The metaphors are: 1) Disloyalty to friendship (Jer. 5:11), 2) Ungrateful forgetfulness of a child (Hosea 11), 3) Getting dirty (Isa. 6:5; Lam. 1:9), 4) Wandering (Isa. 53:6; Jer. 3:21), 5) Trespassing (Josh. 22:16-31), 6) Transgressing law (Hosea 4:1-6), and 7) Failure to achieve something (Judg. 20:24-26; Prov. 19:2).[29] These metaphors reveal that according to the OT, humankind is not found to be in a righteous relationship with YHWH any longer but

---

[25] Goldingay, "Iniquities," 39.

[26] Goldingay, "Iniquities," 46.

[27] Wenham, *Genesis,* 37.

[28] Goldingay, "Iniquities," 41-44.

[29]Goldingay, "Iniquities," 41-44.

is found lacking before YHWH. Thus, the *relationship* has been breached and humanity is solely dependent on the mercy and grace of God for reconciliation with and to God. Sin is not merely transgressing a principle or law. Sin is an offense to the personal nature of God.

Old Testament Consequences of Sin

More recently, Chris Wright has noted eight specific consequences that were brought about as a result of the sinful choices made by human beings. God has declared that the entire earth was filled with the wickedness of humanity and that every intention of the thoughts of the human heart was only evil (Gen. 6:5). Indeed, the sin of humankind brought about sorrow in the heart of God in the opening chapters of Genesis and therefore God is recorded saying "I will blot out man whom I have created from the face of the land ... for I am sorry that I have made them" (Gen. 6:7).[30] God finds it appropriate to respond to sin by exercising his just wrath and therefore chooses to exterminate the human race, sparing Noah and his family.

Chris Wright shows that because of sin: 1) A relationship has been broken (relational aspect), 2) Shalom has been disrupted (social aspect), 3) A rebellion arises against authority (covenantal aspect), 4) Punishment is necessary (legal aspect), 5) Humankind is unclean (ritual aspect), 6) Shame and disgrace is on oneself and/or on God (emotional aspect), 7) Both past and future are contaminated (historical aspect), and 8) Death and destruction are inevitable (final aspect).[31]

It is particularly helpful to note Wright's fourth point that *punishment is necessary*. Not only is YHWH's wrath declared to arise from sorrow but also from anger towards sin. As early as Deuteronomy 32, *forensic* language is used as YHWH is pictured as the judge and Israel is the defendant. I would like to call attention to the fact that in this chapter, YHWH is provoked "to anger" (v.16), "spurns them" (v.19), "hides (his) face" (v.20), is "jealous" (v.21), "angry" (v.22), "will heap disasters upon them" (v.23), is "vengeful" (v.35), etc.[32] It is demonstrated this early in the Scriptures that there is indeed *penalty* for sinful behavior and that God does not simply dismiss unrighteousness as he is depicted as one who is *just*. Green rightly states, "In the Old Testament, anger appears as God's response to sinful acts rather than as a description

---

[30] Westermann declares that "the wickedness of people had risen to such an intolerable degree as to threaten their very existence." See Claus Westermann, *Genesis 1-11: A Commentary,* trans. John J. Scullion SJ (London, England: SPCK, 1974), 407. The writer is aware that opponents of PSA could cite Sarna, "God's decision is made in sorrow, not anger." See Sarna, *Genesis,* 47.

[31] Christopher Wright, "Atonement in the Old Testament," in *The Atonement Debate: Papers from the London Symposium on the Theology of Atonement,* ed. D. Tidball, D. Hilborn, and J. Thacker (Grand Rapids, MI: Zondervan, 2008), 70-71.

[32] Tigay declares that this is an impassioned God (Deut. 5:9). "Etymologically, *kanna* is similar to "fervent" and "incensed," which come from words referring to heat and fire." See Jeffery Tigay, *The JPS Torah Commentary: Deuteronomy* (Philadelphia, PA: JPS, 1996), 65. Greenberg declares that this term particularly refers to "the resentful rage of one whose prerogatives have been usurped by, or given to, another." See Moshe Greenberg, *The Anchor Yale Bible Commentaries: Ezekiel 1-20* (New Haven, CT: Yale University Press, 1983), 115. Therefore, "God resolved to bring all of His destructive forces against Israel." See Tigay, *Deuteronomy,* 308.

of God's general disposition toward humanity" (citing Exod. 34:6 and Num. 14:8).[33] However, it ought to be noted that this in no way should paint a picture of an "emotion-laden" God "that is ever on the verge of striking out."[34]

New Testament Concept of Sin

The New Testament follows in succinct fashion as the writers also address and engage with sin in the same manner as the prophets of the Old Testament.[35] No fewer than 173 times is the word for *sin* used in the NT (ἀμαρτία). The most common definition implies a "failure to achieve a standard (whether culpable or unintentional) in the broadest sense both as deed and as the nature of the deed."[36] The second most commonly used word is παραβάται. This literally means "to trespass."[37] The NT also provides many metaphors that speak to the problem of sin. For sin either leads to or is a form of 1) bondage (Heb. 12:1), 2) enslavement (John 8:34; Rom. 7:14, 23), 3) imprisonment (Gal. 3:22), 4) death (Rom. 6:23, cf. 5:12; Eph. 2:1; Col. 2:13), 5) execution (Rom. 7:11), and 6) disease (Matt. 9:2,5; Mark 2:5,9; Luke 5:18-20, 23; 1 Pet. 2:24).[38]

Later this chapter will seek to demonstrate that within the earliest sub-apostolic and patristic writings there are indeed numerous notations of the PSA view of the atonement already in place. These understandings did not arise at the exclusion of Scripture nor were they merely reflections of their (or some other!) culture alone. Rather these are conclusions that were reached by thorough careful exegesis of both Old and New Testaments. Therefore, it will serve well to examine both the Biblical and historical understandings of PSA.

PSA in the Old Testament

Green and Baker argue in their chapter, "Removing Alienating Shame," that the Japanese culture of today is much closer to actually understanding the work of the cross because it shares the common *Eastern* worldview that is oftentimes in direct contrast to

---

[33] Joel Green, "Must We Imagine the Atonement in Penal Substitutionary Terms?: Questions Caveats and a Plea," in *The Atonement Debate,* ed. D. Tidball, D. Hilborn, and J. Thacker, 162.

[34] Green and Baker, *Scandal,* 53.

[35] James Dunn notes how, in the first five chapters of Romans, Paul "exposes man's need of this divine initiative [as he] had drawn heavily on the Genesis account of Adam's fall - man's refusal to acknowledge God as God, to recognize his own creatureliness, resulting in the diminution of his humanity, his fitness to be a companion of God, a plight embracing not only Gentile idolatry and immorality, but also Jewish presumption of a favored status before God." See James Dunn, "Salvation Proclaimed: VI, Romans 6:1-11: Dead and Alive," *Evangelical Today,* 93 (1981-82), 259.

[36] Paul Fiedler, "*Amartia,*" in *Exegetical Dictionary of the New Testament,* vol. 1, Ἀαρών- Ἐνώχ, ed. H. Balz and G. Schneider (Grand Rapids, MI: William B. Eerdmans Publishing Company, 1980), 66.

[37] Leland Ryken, James Wilhoit, and Tremper Longman III, eds., "Sin," in Dictionary of Biblical Imagery: An Encyclopedic Exploration of the Images, Symbols, Motifs, Metaphors, Figures of Speech, and Literary Patterns of the Bible (Downers Grove, IL: IVP, 1998), 792.

[38] Ryken, Wilhoit, and Longman III, eds., "Sin," in *Dictionary,* 793.

the Western worldview.[39] According to these scholars, "recent work in applying what we have learned about cultural anthropology and social psychology to the Scriptures reveals how much more at home the Bible is in the Japanese context than in a Western society."[40] This is largely due to the honor and shame culture that is still in effect today as opposed to the guilt and punishment culture of the West. In many ways, they are correct.

However, as mentioned above, Chris Wright states "as early as Deuteronomy 32, the metaphor of the law court is used to portray the sin of Israel."[41] This early on in the covenant with YHWH, Israel understands that YHWH is Israel's judge exacting penalty for sin. Thus, Wright asserts "forensic metaphors are used. This way of describing sin is also common in the prophets using the language of offense, transgression, guilty, and retributive justice."[42] As the sinful condition of humanity collides with the justice of a holy God, the attribute of God's wrath is brought to the light.

Wrath of God

The book of Genesis never states that God gets angry.[43] This characteristic of God, however, does begin to surface early on in the Scriptures. For instance, the verb *kipper* is best understood as "made by an act that purifies something in such a manner that the outbreak of YHWH's holy wrath is either arrested or prevented, whichever is appropriate in a particular situation."[44] YHWH has the reputation in the Old Testament as being one of upholding justice. On some occasions, God's justice is provoked by sinful behavior and therefore retribution is wrought. The wrath of God is ignited in numerous places throughout the Old Testament. For example, in Numbers 14, where Israel lacked the faith to go up and possess the land; YHWH caused a generation to suffer the consequences.[45] Another occasion is in Joshua 7 in which the sin of Achan resulted in God striking Israel with defeat under Ai.[46]

Some Objections to Divine Retribution

This concept of divine retribution, however, is highly contested in certain strands of Western thought today. For example, there are other forms and ways in which the legal system is considering and practicing going about reforming the criminal. To many

---

[39] Green and Baker, *Scandal,* chapter 7, 153-70.

[40] Green and Baker, *Scandal,* 162.

[41] Christopher Wright, "Atonement," 70.

[42] Christopher Wright, "Atonement," 70.

[43] John Goldingay, *Old Testament Theology,* vol. 1, *Israel's Gospel* (Downers Grove, IL: IVP Academic, 2003), 140.

[44] Alan Groves, "Atonement in Isaiah 53: 'For He Bore the Sins of Many,'" in *The Glory of the Atonement,* ed. Hill and James III, 66. See also James Garrett, *Systematic Theology: Biblical, Historical, and Evangelical,* vol. 1 (Grand Rapids, MI: William B. Eerdmans Publishing, 1990), 223.

[45] Phillip Budd, *Word Biblical Commentary,* vol. 5, *Numbers* (Waco, TX: Word Books Publisher, 1984), 161.

[46] Christopher Wright, "Atonement," 74-75.

people, retribution appears to be inherently vindictive, "a kind of thinly disguised vengeance."[47] Or as Kidner puts it, retribution is viewed as a way of "rationalizing the primitive urge to hit back."[48] Fiddes has argued that "what justice demands is not payment but repentance; it is finally 'satisfied' not by any penalty in itself but by the change of heart to which the penalty is intended to lead."[49] Smail believes that the justice of God is much more focused on being *restorative* in nature and that God "is concerned less with punishing wrong relationships than with restoring right ones."[50] Travis argues that "God's mercy *constantly* overrides his retributive justice."[51]

Advocates of the penal view *do* have responsible theological responses to these types of statements. Brunner states that "the idea that God is angry is no more anthropopathic than the thought that God loves."[52] It is simply theologically inconsistent to embrace the love of God alone and ignore the wrath of God. Scripture never gives the impression that any of God's attributes were temporary in nature. If one banishes all emotional responses from God, it must be recognized that this is not the product of responsible Christian thinking, rather the result of modern "rational" thought.[53] Further responses will be addressed below.

Passover and PSA

The Passover is central to constructing a theology of PSA within the Old Testament. According to early Israelite theology, the Passover was a blood rite that sought to connect the sacrifice with remembrance of the Exodus.[54] It has been recently noted by PSA advocates that in the Passover, there is something quite unique between the first nine plagues and the tenth–namely that the tenth plague had a *condition* to it. For, a lamb must be slaughtered, and the blood applied to the door of the home *in order for* the firstborn to be spared. "Thus the lamb becomes a substitute for the firstborn son, dying in his place."[55] Therefore, "the effect of blood sacrifice in the averting of judgment is clear."[56] Because of the atoning sacrifice made by the Israelites, many of the other terms highlighted by Averbeck come into effect such as forgiveness, cleansing,

---

[47] Steve Jeffery, Michael Ovey, and Andrew Sach, *Pierced for Our Transgressions: Rediscovering the Glory of Penal Substitution* (Nottingham, England: IVP, 2007), 250.
[48] Kidner, "Retribution," 7.
[49] Paul Fiddes, *Past Event and Present Salvation: The Christian Idea of Atonement* (London, England: Darton, Longman, and Todd, 1989),104.
[50] Smail, *Once,* 95.
[51] Travis, "Christ," 11, emphasis mine.
[52] Emil Brunner, The Mediator: A Study of the Central Doctrine of the Christian Faith (London, England: Lutterworth Press, 1949), 478.
[53] Emil Brunner, *Mediator,* 478.
[54] Christopher Wright, "Atonement," 73.
[55] Jeffery, Ovey, Sach, *Pierced,* 37.
[56] Christopher Wright, "Atonement," 73. In this light, the penal dimension can be seen in the Passover.

consecration, or redemption,[57] all of which are profoundly *relational* in nature. Yet, "in each case the bottom-line connotation of the result [atonement] is the same: preventing the outbreak of YHWH's wrath."[58]

Passover, Propitiation, and "When I *See* the Blood"

The Passover account in Exodus 12-13 describes the blood sacrifice of a lamb that was to be shed and applied to the doorposts of the homes of the Hebrew people. This action was done by those who placed faith in God's instructions to Moses as it would serve the redemptive purpose of sparing the firstborn sons' certain *death.* Following the promise of the tenth plague that was to ensue, YHWH declares, "The blood shall be a sign for you, on the houses where you are. And when *I see the blood,* I will pass over you, and no plague shall befall you to destroy you, when I strike the land of Egypt" (Exod. 12:13).[59]

Undoubtedly, the slaughter of the lambs highlights the nature of the substitutionary sacrifice involved in the saving and delivering of the people of God.[60] "It was the God who *'passed through'* Egypt to judge the firstborn, who *'passed over'* Israelite homes to protect them."[61] In his passing through and passing over, God is both Judge and Savior. Yet, questions are raised regarding the *nature* of the slaughtered lambs. Does this sacrificial substitute in fact directly bear the penalty of sin? Is it propitiatory? If so, in what way is the slaughtered lamb to function in a propitiatory manner? Because we are examining more than substitution, rather specifically *penal substitution,* the question at hand is extremely important for both establishing what is meant by PSA from the Scripture as well as noting the *relational* implications. To begin identifying PSA in the

---

[57] See Richard Averbeck in *New International Dictionary of Old Testament Theology and Exegesis*, vol. 2 (Grand Rapids, MI: Zondervan, 2012), 689-710.

[58] Groves, "Isaiah," 66.

[59] Waltke writes of the lambs to be slaughtered, "The stipulations regarding the selection of the lamb pertain to its perfection. It is to be selected on the tenth day, and it is to be a year-old male (because, unlike a female, it is without unclean blood) without physical defect. Corporately, its slaughter and sprinkled blood shows the Passover lamb is both substitutionary and propitiatory. It nullifies God's wrath against sinful people because it satisfies God's holiness. The supper that night shows it is sufficient for all the firstborn of an entire household and individually sufficient for each Israelite. But since it is their substitute for God's divine wrath, it must be completely roasted, and whatever is not eaten must be burned with purifying fire." See Bruce Waltke, *An Old Testament Theology: An Exegetical, Canonical, and Thematic Approach* (Grand Rapids, MI: Zondervan, 2007), 382.

[60] Johnstone writes that in "Exodus 12 the Passover is a lay domestic rite which is thus necessarily entirely distinct from the specialized priestly rites of the sanctuary: the victim is 'slaughtered,' not 'sacrificed.'" See William Johnstone, "Exodus," in *Eerdmans Commentary on the Bible*, ed. James D. G. Dunn and John W. Rogerson (Grand Rapids, IL: Zondervan, 2003), 85.

[61] John Stott, *The Cross of Christ* 2nd ed. (Downers Grove, IL: IVP, 2006), 140, (emphasis mine). Hillyer writes that the lamb "was not primarily expiatory or redemptive; it was sprinkled on the doorposts that the destroyer angel might 'pass over' the house (Exod.12:13." See Norman Hillyer, "'The Lamb' in the Apocalypse," *Evangelical Quarterly* 39 (1967): 228-36, esp. 230.

Passover we must first begin with God's promise to Abraham to build a covenantal community.

The People of God Enslaved

In Genesis 12 we read,

> Now the Lord said to Abram, "Go from your country and your kindred and your father's house to the land that I will show you. And I will make of you a great nation, and I will bless you and make your name great, so that you will be a blessing. I will bless those who bless you, and him who dishonors you I will curse, and in you all the families of the earth shall be blessed." Then the LORD appeared to Abram and said, "To your offspring I will give this land." So he built there an altar to the LORD, who had appeared to him ... "I will surely bless you and I will surely multiply your offspring as the stars of heaven and as the sand on the seashore," (Gen. 12:1-3, 7, 22:17).

In this well-known account God initiates the covenant with Abraham indicating a blessed people that will come after him. Those brought into this covenantal relationship will not be few but will be multiplied greatly. However, what we find in the Exodus account is that though the Hebrews have indeed multiplied greatly in number, they were in fact, enslaved by Pharaoh in Egypt. Moses records, "But the people of Israel were fruitful and increased greatly; they multiplied and grew exceedingly strong, so that the land was filled with them" (Exod. 1:7).[62]

Just as God had promised Abraham, the people increased and yet were enslaved by the Egyptians (cf. Gen. 15:13). As YHWH responds to the cries of his covenantal people and engages Moses in the burning bush (Exod. 3:7-22), he does so out of his saving love though certainly not at the expense of his justice. In the burning bush account, YHWH calls attention to the Hebrews "sufferings" (v.7), "afflictions" (v.7), and "oppression" (v.9). YHWH would no longer allow the Hebrews to know their identity as the people of God and yet remain in a place controlled by Pharaoh who forbade them to enjoy their worshipful *relationship* of God. Hence, this explains YHWH's frequent references in the plagues, "That they may *worship me.*"[63]

---

[62] "And he does not word it as might be expected, that is, that as their growth increased, they naturally experienced more oppression; rather, it was as they experienced more oppression that their growth increased." Douglas K. Stuart, *The New American Commentary*, vol. 2, *Exodus* (Nashville, TN: Broadman & Holman Publishers, 2006). Moreover, John Durham notes that this scenario has a way of "dramatizing the need of Israel, and thus increasing the reader's concern that something must be done." John Durham, *Word Biblical Commentary*, vol. 3, *Exodus* (Waco, TX: Word Books, 1987), 6.

[63] Jeffery, Ovey, and Sach, state that "Exodus 7:16, 8:1, 20, 9:1, 13, 10:3 cf. 3:12, 4:23, 5:1, 10:7, 8, 11, 24, 12:31 implies that they were unable to worship God, i.e., enjoy the fullness of *relationship* with him, while in Egypt" (italics mine) in *Pierced*, 35, fn. 2. Thus, this speaks to the relational paradigm that will addressed below. Douglas Stuart reminds readers that "The demand of Yahweh ('Let my people go, so that they may worship me') will be repeated verbatim again in 8:1, 20, 9:1, 13, 10:3. It is the standard expression of God's demand to Pharaoh through Moses, and a

Each plague sent by YHWH upon the Egyptians did not go without warning. "... each begins with God giving Pharaoh an opportunity to repent before striking him, continues with a warning to remember the preceding blow and a promise of a greater blow, and culminates in a third blow without warning."[64]

Plague Ten: Conditional

There are numerous references in Exodus 7 through 14 to God hardening Pharaoh's heart (i.e., causing it to be impenitent).[65] Other occasions reveal that Pharaoh was responsible for the hardening of his own heart toward God and the Israelite people. Interestingly, the first nine plagues pose no threat to the Hebrews in captivity as YHWH pours out his judgment specifically on Egypt. And yet, the tenth plague is very interesting in that it is *conditional,* requiring the sacrifice of a lamb in order to spare the firstborn sons of *Israel.*[66] In each plague the judgment that falls upon the Egyptians is made abundantly clear. Yet, why and how does the sacrifice of the Passover lamb serve in a *propitiatory* manner for the Hebrews? In what way had the Hebrews sinned? Were they deserving of the judgment of God as well? This is where the discussion at hand regarding the propitiatory nature of the Passover sacrifices begins to surface.

In Exodus 11:4-8, YHWH "makes a distinction between Egypt and Israel" (v.7), stating that even the dogs of Egypt "shall not growl against any of the people of Israel" (v.7). The sin of the Hebrews while still in captivity was extremely offensive to God for, they too were caught up in the worship of false gods. Ezekiel expounds upon this roughly 1,000 years later as he writes:

> "... and say to them, Thus says the Lord GOD: On the day when I chose Israel, I swore to the offspring of the house of Jacob, making myself known to them in the land of Egypt; I swore to them, saying, I am the LORD your God. On that day I swore to them that I would bring them out of the land of Egypt into a land that I had searched out for them, a land flowing with milk and honey, the most glorious of all lands. And I said to them, Cast away the detestable things your eyes feast on, every one of you, and do not defile yourselves with the idols of Egypt; I am the LORD your God. But they rebelled against me and were not willing to listen to me. None of them cast away the detestable things their eyes feasted on, nor did they forsake the

---

slight but significant variation on the previous wordings (5:1, 'Let my people go, so that they may hold a festival to me in the desert,') and 7:16, 'Let my people go, so that they may worship me in the desert.' At this point, the bargaining-style reference to holding a festival/worship in the wilderness ceases, and the demand is thus more nearly explicitly one of full, permanent release. The Hebrew verb translated 'worship' by the NIV ('*bd*) could as easily be translated 'serve,' reminding Pharaoh that the God of the people he had forced to serve him as slaves was demanding their release to serve freely and permanently a new master, himself." See Douglas K. Stuart, *Exodus,* 278.

[64] Waltke, *Old Testament,* 379. See also Paul A. Wright, "Exodus 1-24 (A Canonical Study)" (unpublished Ph.D. diss., University of Vienna, Austria, March 1993), esp. 132.

[65] Waltke, *Old Testament,* 380.

[66] Jeffery, Ovey, Sach, *Pierced,* 34.

idols of Egypt. Then I said I would pour out my wrath upon them and spend my anger against them in the midst of the land of Egypt" (Ezek. 20:5-8).

As Ezekiel reflects on the Passover, he reveals that "the Israelites participated in the idolatry of their Egyptian masters; they too were guilty and were no less deserving of God's judgment. Only by God's gracious provision of a means of atonement, a substitutionary sacrifice, were they spared."[67]

Averting the Wrath of God

There are some, such as Nahum Sarna, who argue that YHWH's deliverance of his people was based solely on his divine elective purposes and the blood referenced does not serve as a means of averting wrath at all. Sarna comments, "There is no warrant for the theory that it [the blood on the door post] played a magic, apotropaic role, that is, as a means of averting or overcoming evil or danger. The deliverance of Israel is ascribed solely to divine decision."[68]

Certainly, the blood is not "magical." However, what is being enforced is by the virtue of a blood sacrifice offered *in faith* that they are spared their just punishment during the passing through of the destroyer.[69] Thus, while the lambs to be sacrificed would not be the *direct* recipients of the wrath of God, they do serve to *avert* his wrath; for when he "sees the blood"[70] he would *"pass over."* Again, the blood served to "make a distinction" (Exod. 12:7, 13) between the people of God who exercise faith in God and the Egyptians who refuse to submit to the will of YHWH. Thus, in the Passover the wrath of God is *averted,* and the *anger* of God is appeased in the substitutionary death of the slaughtered lambs.

Stuart helpfully writes,

> The blood on the doorposts showed acceptance of God's plan for *rescue* and *trust* in his word. After all, the sight of dried blood by itself had no power to deter death; it was only as the dried blood painted on the top and sides of the door was a testimony to the *faith* of the inhabitants *in Yahweh* that it had its efficacy. Thus the

---

[67] Jeffery, Ovey, and Sach, *Pierced,* 38.

[68] Nahum Sarna, *The JPS Torah Commentary: Exodus* (New York, NY: The Jewish Publication Society, 1991), 55.

[69] Waltke writes, "Deliverance rests solely on Israel's trusting God's Passover provision. Israel is delivered because *a death that satisfies God's wrath has been made and applied by faith."* Indeed, in the *aversion* of God's wrath we observe that the lambs slaughtered function in a propitiatory manner. See Waltke, *Old Testament,* 381, emphasis mine.

[70] Emile Nicole states that the sign for God and for you is significant. "Even in the paschal rite, when blood was not to be poured on an altar but put on the door frames of each individual house (Exod. 12:7) and is presented as "a sign *for you"* (Exod. 12:13), it would nevertheless be a sign *for God:* "when I see the blood, I will pass over you." Israelites would not be protected by a power of life, which could avert the peril of death, but by a sign intelligible by God." See Emile Nicole, "Atonement in the Pentateuch: 'It Is the Blood that Makes Atonement for One's Life,'" in *The Glory of the Atonement,* ed. Hill and James III, 46 fn. 38.

statement, "When I see the blood, I will pass over you"—in other words, I will spare all those who show that they have placed their faith in me.[71]

It is faith in the substitutionary slaughter of the lamb that would *avert* the wrath of God during the Passover and in that sense the death of the lamb is propitiatory.

Propitiation and the Day of Atonement

In speaking of the first three books of the Torah, Unger writes, "Genesis is the book of beginnings, Exodus the book of redemption, and Leviticus the book of atonement and a holy walk. In Genesis, we see man ruined; in Exodus, man redeemed; in Leviticus, man cleansed, worshiping, and serving."[72]

Similar to the section above regarding the Passover and the propitiatory nature of the slaughtered lambs (*aversion*, not the *absorption* of the wrath of God), the discussion at hand now turns to the Day of Atonement. Propitiation should not only be read in light of the wrath of God, but that it serves a *cleansing* purpose as well. Indeed, the entire Day of Atonement revolves around both the cleansing of *place* and *people*. "For on this day shall atonement be made for you to *cleanse* you. You shall be *clean* before the LORD from all your sins" (Lev. 16:30).

Not only had the people become defiled through sin but their sinful actions even defiled the tent of meeting (Lev. 16:5b, 12-20a, 27, 33).[73] The purpose of the Day of Atonement sought "the propitiation of the God against whom they had sinned, together with the consequent blessing of his forgiveness and of reconciliation to him."[74] The

---

[71] Stuart, *Exodus*, 278, emphasis mine.

[72] Merrill F. Unger, *The New Unger's Bible Handbook* (Chicago, IL: Moody, 1984), 85.

[73] Consider the more recent work by Darrin Belousek. Belousek presses away from a propitiatory sacrifice presented in the Day of Atonement passages and is convinced that rather than finding penal substitution here, one finds expiation. He is correct in that the doctrine of expiation is most certainly present. He also highlights the altar and sanctuary in need of *kippur*. He asks "Why? What offense have they committed? How could the sanctuary or altar have transgressed and so provoked God's wrath? What could it mean to satisfy retribution on behalf of places or things?" However, Leviticus 16:16 says, "Thus he shall make atonement for the Holy Place, because of the uncleanness of the people of Israel and because of their transgressions, all their sins." He continues by saying, "The anomaly grows when we consider atonement rituals concerning cleansing or purification (Lev. 12-15). Childbirth (12:6-8), leprosy (14:10-32), and bodily discharge (15:13-15, 25-30) all require making atonement (*kipper*) by blood sacrifice. In each case, the worshipper offers a burnt offering and a sin offering, and the priest makes atonement on her or his behalf. Again, why? Neither childbirth, nor leprosy, nor seminal emission, nor menstruation is sin; none of these are transgressions against the covenant. Why– if, in fact, making atonement propitiates God by satisfying retribution – is God wrathful against a woman for having given birth or a man for having a skin lesion? These sacrificial rituals make no sense in terms of penal substitution." Darrin Belousek, *Atonement, Justice, and Peace: The Message of the Cross and the Mission of the Church* (Grand Rapids, MI: Eerdmans, 2012), 177.

[74] J. B. Payne and W. Möller, "Atonement, Day of," in *The International Standard Bible Encyclopedia,* rev. ed., vol. 1, ed. G. W. Bromiley (Grand Rapids, MI: Wm. B. Eerdmans, 1988), 1:360.

reconciliation experienced by the people could not be experienced apart from the necessary cleansing that was wrought through blood sacrifice. Indeed, there was no atonement applied apart from the shedding of blood. "Indeed, under the law almost everything is purified with blood, and without the shedding of blood there is no forgiveness of sins" (Heb. 9:22)

The Death of Aaron's Sons

In the chapter immediately following the Day of Atonement passage Moses records, "For the life of the flesh is in the blood, and I have given it for you on the altar to make atonement for your souls, for it is the blood that makes atonement by the life" (Lev. 17:11). Moreover, "the aim of [*kipper*] ... always is to *avert* evil, especially punishment."[75] Again, *aversion* of wrath is key in understanding propitiation in the Day of Atonement. Leviticus 16 begins in the wake of the *death* of Aaron's two sons after offering unauthorized fire before the Lord; their transgressions resulted in *death* (Lev. 10:1-20, cf. 16:1-2). "The LORD spoke to Moses after the death of the two sons of Aaron, when they drew near before the LORD and died, and the LORD said to Moses, 'Tell Aaron your brother not to come at any time into the Holy Place inside the veil, before the mercy seat that is on the ark, so that he may not die'" (Lev. 16:1-2).

The *deaths* of these two men serve as "a stark reminder of the holiness of God and its incompatibility with human sinfulness."[76] In the death of the two sons we must stay mindful of the fact that God was not suddenly breaking out in wrath, seeking to judge the sons. Were that the case, the Scriptures would indicate as much. The sons died as a result of approaching God in a relational manner that he himself forbade and thereby were judged, suffering the penalty for their sin.

God instructs Moses as to how the sins of the people will be atoned for through the blood sacrifice of various animals. First, Aaron is to offer a bull to God as a sin offering and a ram for a burnt offering for himself (Lev.16:3):

> "Aaron shall offer the bull as a sin offering for himself and shall make atonement for himself and for his house. ... Aaron shall present the bull as a sin offering for himself and shall make atonement for himself and for his house. He shall kill the bull as a sin offering for himself. And he shall take a censer full of coals of fire from the altar before the LORD, and two handfuls of sweet incense beaten small, and he shall bring it inside the veil and put the incense on the fire before the LORD, that the cloud of the incense may cover the mercy seat that is over the testimony, so that he does not die. And he shall take some of the blood of the bull and sprinkle it with his finger on the front of the mercy seat on the east side, and in front of the mercy seat he shall sprinkle some of the blood with his finger seven times" (Lev. 16:6, 11-14).

---

[75] L. Koehler and W. Baumgartner, *Lexicon in Veteris Testamenti Libros* (Leiden, Netherlands: Brill Academic Publishers, 1953), 452, emphasis mine.

[76] William D. Barrick, "Penal Substitution in the Old Testament," *TMSJ* 20, no, 2 (Fall 2009), 11.

In addition to the atoning sacrifices that Aaron is to offer on his own behalf, he is also to do so on behalf of the people, taking from the congregation of the people of Israel two goats for the sin offering and one ram for the burnt offering (Lev. 16:5).

"Then he shall take the two goats and set them before the LORD at the entrance of the tent of meeting. And Aaron shall cast lots over the two goats, one lot for the LORD and the other lot for Azazel. And Aaron shall present the goat on which the lot fell for the LORD and use it as a sin offering, but the goat on which the lot fell for Azazel shall be presented alive before the LORD to make atonement over it, that it may be sent away into the wilderness to Azazel" (Lev. 16:7-10).

Two Goats, One Offering

On the Day of Atonement, "One goat was offered as a sin offering and another goat had the High Priest transfer to it the sins of the people, which were carried with it into the wilderness, to a land of no return."[77] John Stott writes in his landmark book, *The Cross of Christ,* that "some commentators make the mistake of driving a wedge between the two goats, the sacrificed goat and the scapegoat, overlooking the fact that the two together are described as 'a sin offering' in the singular (Lev. 16:5)."[78] Moreover, he references Thomas Crawford who suggests that perhaps the animals offered on the Day of Atonement each "embody[ied] a different aspect of the same sacrifice."[79] Crawford holds that one goat exhibits the means and the other goat renders the results.[80] This is certainly helpful in that the doctrines of propitiation and expiation are both placed on display in the offering of the goats in the cleansing of both the Holy Place and the people.

---

[77] Baruch Levine, *The JPS Torah Commentary: Leviticus,* (New York, NY: The Jewish Publication Society, 1989), 106. Levine also affirms that the second goat (scapegoat) is continually referred to as "the live goat," thus highlighting the distinction between its function and the function of the sin offerings, which were slaughtered. Furthermore, it is not too narrow of a reading to interpret this as being strictly "penal." C. Wright says "that the fact remains that it is costly and involves the death of a victim that would otherwise have been spared," Christopher Wright, "Atonement," 60. See also Gordon Wenham, "The Theology of the Old Testament Sacrifice" in *Sacrifice in the Bible,* ed. Roger Beckwith and Martin Selman (Eugene, OR: Wipf & Stock, 2004), 75-87.

[78] Stott, *Cross,* 144.

[79] Stott, *Cross,* 144.

[80] Stott, *Cross,* 144, See Thomas Crawford, *Doctrine of the Holy Scripture,* (Edinburgh, England: W. Blackwood, 1871), 225. See also "The Day of Atonement," chapter 3 in Leon Morris's *The Atonement: Its Meaning and Significance* (Downers Grove, IL: IVP, 1983), 68-87. Geerhardus Vos says similarly, that in both goats what we observe is "in reality one sacrificial object; the distribution of suffering death and of dismissal into a remote place simply serving the purposes of clearer expression in visible form, of removal of sin after expiation had been made, something which the ordinary sacrificial animal could not well express, since it died in the process of expiation." See Geerhardus Vos, *Biblical Theology: Old and New Testaments* (Grand Rapids, MI: Eerdmans, 1997), 163.

The First Goat: Cleansing of the Holy Place

It is important to note in what way the death of the first goat is propitiatory. The Scriptures do not indicate that the wrath of God actively went directly to the goat presented in the sin offering. Aaron was responsible for the slaughter of the goat because the people were sinful and in need of reconciliation with God (the purpose of the sin offering). The place to which they were to go was defiled (see references above). Yet, what we do observe is that were the goat not offered, the Israelites would remain with their sin intact, under the judgment of God (i.e., death). Thus, in the first goat being slaughtered in the sin offering, the wrath of God is *averted* because his just anger is appeased and the Holy Place is cleansed.

The Second Goat: Cleansing of the People

The second goat, the scapegoat, was to "carry on itself all their sins" (Lev. 16:22). Milgrom does not see this goat as propitiatory in any way because the animal is not sacrificed or punished.[81] He states that the scapegoat's "expressed purpose... is to carry off the sins of the Israelites transferred to it by the High Priest's confession."[82] Yet, the laying on of both hands (Lev. 16:21) of the priest is clearly a signal of substitution, for the sins are being *transferred* from the people to the head of the animal.[83]

Moreover, throughout Leviticus we find that to be excluded, or *"cut off,"* from the camp of Israel was to experience God's *punishment* for sin (Lev. 7:20-27; 17:4, 9-14; 18:29; 19:8; 20:3, 5-6, 17-18; 22:3; 23:29).[84] The second goat mentioned in Leviticus 16:22 is unique in that it is the subject of the verb and therefore "the judicial fate of the Israelites is transferred to the animal in such a way that they do not bear it themselves. The natural reading in this case is that the animal bears the sin and guilt of the people *in their* place and they are thereby released from this burden."[85]

The second goat, like the first, does not *directly* bear the wrath of God but is banished to die in the wilderness as it bears the sins of the people (16:21-22). Yet, in the cutting off and suffering the punishment as in the sins listed above, the goat functions in a propitiatory manner.[86] Thus, both the slaughtered goat and the banished goat function in a penalty-bearing way but expiatory because of the *cleansing* they provide of both place and people.

---

[81] Jacob Milgrom, Anchor Yale Bible Commentary Series, vol. 3, *Leviticus 1-16* (New York, NY: Doubleday, 1991), 1021.

[82] Milgrom, *Leviticus,* 1021.

[83] Thomas Schreiner, "Penal Substitution View," in *The Nature of the Atonement* (Downers Grove, IL: IVP, 2006), 84.

[84] Jeffery, Ovey, and Sach, *Pierced,* 49.

[85] Jeffery, Ovey, and Sach, *Pierced,* 49.

[86] The "scapegoat depicted in Leviticus 16 as bearing the sin, guilt, and punishment of the people, and being condemned to death in their place." See Jeffery, Ovey, and Sach, *Pierced,* 50.

The Burnt Offering

After the first goat is slaughtered and the second goat is banished, both the High Priest (Aaron) and the designated man who led the scapegoat into the wilderness were required to bathe (16:24, 26). Aaron was to offer (16:5b), "the burnt offering of the people and make atonement for himself and the people" (v.24). The bull and goat offered in the sin offering that first cleansed the Holy Place was then to be "carried outside the camp. Their skin and their flesh and their dung shall be burned up with fire" (v.27). This all speaks profoundly to the relationship that God has with his people. His holiness goes uncompromised and yet, in his grace, he communes with his covenantal people. This will be more fully explored in the relational paradigm chapters below.

Isaiah 53

Although the verb *kipper* is not used within Isaiah 52:13-53:12[87] it is still necessary to glance in this direction at this stage. Hofius *defends* the penal aspects of Isaiah 53 even though he deems the notion of it completely unacceptable.[88] N. T. Wright struggles to find the penal understanding in Isaiah 53 as he understands the Servant to be the sanctuary (v.5), or the suffering of the Messiah at the hands of the enemies (vv.7, 9, 11), or the tribulation of the exiles (52:14; 53:3-4, 8), or the remnant that would be purified (v.10).[89]

Wright concedes, however, that in the Targum's reading of verse12, "there is a different note" for "it seems to be the Messiah who 'delivered his soul unto death.'"[90] Even though the Torah understood the atonement as the only means by which the wrath of YHWH against sin and uncleanness could be quenched, it did not encompass that which Isaiah envisioned with universal and permanent purification.[91] Such an extraordinary purification required a newer "atonement of equally extraordinary and radical nature."[92] Isaiah argued that the way in which this atonement would come about would not simply be by means of the traditional medium of atonement (Levitical sacrifice; see Isa. 1:11-15).[93] It also would not come by means of repentance (Isa. 6:10) nor Israel's suffering in the Babylonian exile.[94] For, it is not to be found in Scripture that

---

[87] Groves, "Isaiah," 64.

[88] Otfried Hofius, "The Fourth Servant Song in the New Testament Letters," in *The Suffering Servant: Isaiah 53 in Jewish and Christian Sources,* ed. Bernd Janowski and Peter Stuhlmacher, trans. Daniel P. Bailey (Grand Rapids, MI: Eerdmans, 2004), 163-172.

[89] N. T. Wright, "The Reasons for Jesus' Crucifixion," in *Stricken by God?: Nonviolent Identification and the Victory of Christ,* ed. Brad Jersak and Michael Hardin (Grand Rapids, MI: William B. Eerdmans Publishing, 2007), 128.

[90] N. T. Wright, "Reasons," 128.

[91] N. T. Wright, "Reasons," 88.

[92] N. T. Wright, "Reasons," 88.

[93] N. T. Wright, "Reasons," 89.

[94] N. T. Wright, "Reasons," 89.

exile was in some way redemptive.[95] Rather, it is blood sacrifice that is the means that God has ordained for his rebellious people to be reconciled.[96]

"The opening section (52:13-15) speaks about things previously 'never told' and 'never heard' (v.15b). But this is hardly to be limited to the Servant's unique fate: it relates directly to the substitution of existence that occurs in that fate."[97] This event would make an atonement that is sufficient to satisfy the wrath of God and accomplish the global, permanent purification revealed in Isaiah's vision."[98]

Focusing in upon the theology and hermeneutics of the atonement will come below. However, in light of Isaiah 53, one scholar who does not find the penalty position in this section of scripture is Whybray. He argues, rather, that the Servant does not function as a *substitute* in the *place of* sinful people, but rather he suffers *alongside*, as a *representative*.[99] PSA need not dismiss representation theology nor should representation theology negate the doctrine of PSA.

PSA in the New Testament

The term for *punishment* occurs six times in the NT (Matt. 24:43-51, 25:46; Luke 12:45-48; 2 Thess. 1:9; Heb. 10:29; 2 Pet. 2:9).[100] Therefore, those who are opposed to the penal understanding of the work of the cross can quickly site the rarity of the word in order to promote alternative understandings and downplay those who hold to penal substitution. Yet, rarity does not bring the sum total to zero.[101]

---

[95] Jeffery, Ovey, Sach, *Pierced*, 57.

[96] John Oswalt, *NICOT: The Book of Isaiah, Chapters 40-66* (Grand Rapids, MI: Eerdmans, 1998), 385.

[97] Hoffius, "Fourth," 168.

[98] Hoffius, "Fourth," 168.

[99] Richard Whybray, "Thanksgiving for a Liberated Prophet: An Interpretation of Isaiah Chapter 53," *Journal for the Study of the Old Testament Supplement Series,* vol. 4 (Sheffield, England: JSOT Press, 1978), 61-62. Harry Orlinsky argues that the suffering servant suffered "on account of and along with the people at large, the latter because of their own sins, the former because of his unpopular mission." See Harry Orlinsky, *Supplements to Vetus Testamentum, Studies on the Second Part of the Book of Isaiah: The So-Called "Servant of the Lord" and "Suffering Servant" in Second Isaiah* (Leiden, Netherlands: E. J. Brill, 1967), 3-133. Also the language of *"for"* or *"because of"* in verse 5 carries significant weight in this passage. See Brevard Childs, *Isaiah: A Commentary* (Louisville, KY: Westminster John Knox Press, 2001), 407. See also Walter Bruggemann, *Isaiah, 40-66* (Louisville, KY: John Knox Press, 1998),145.

[100] Richard France, *NICNT: The Gospel of Matthew* (Grand Rapids, MI: Eerdmans, 2007), 945, 967, Frederick Bruner, *Matthew: A Commentary,* vol. 2, *The Church Book: Matthew 13-18* (Grand Rapids, MI: William B. Eerdmans Publishing, 1990), 542, 579. See also Norval Geldenhuys, *Commentary on the Gospel of Luke,* (London, England: Marshall, Morgan, and Scott, 1950), 364, Frederic Godet, *A Commentary on the Gospel of St. Luke,* vol. 2 (Edinburgh, England: T&T Clark, 1957), 107, Richard Blight, *An Exegetical Summary of 1 and 2 Thessalonians* (Dallas, TX: Summer Institute of Linguistics, 1989), 152-53.

[101] Marshall reminds us that "in English versions sometimes words more expressive of judgment are translated by terms for punishment since the judgment implies condemnation and

Jesus states clearly that he has come to fulfill the OT Law (Matt. 5:17). Grogan notes that the death of Jesus fulfilled the OT themes presented in passages like Exodus 12,[102] Leviticus 16,[103] the suffering Psalms,[104] as well as Isaiah 53,[105] which are all used to interpret the purposes of the crucifixion and thus arranged by penal advocates to support this position.[106] Jesus readily acknowledges the sinful condition of mankind and that the wrath of God is something that is to be reckoned with. Jesus states that "whoever believes in the Son has eternal life; whoever does not obey the Son shall not see life, but the wrath of God remains on him" (ὀργὴ τοῦ θεοῦ μένει ἐπ᾽ αὐτόν) (John 3:36). This "wrath" is commonly understood by textual scholars as a "strong indignation directed at wrong doing with focus on retribution."[107] Ridderbos states, "'remains' is a present reality (cf. Rom. 1:18)."[108]

Hill argues in the line of thought of this book, giving primacy, seeing the anchoring color in the kaleidoscope, to the doctrine of PSA. "The shedding of Jesus' blood occurred

---

subsequent sentence." See Howard Marshall, *Aspects of the Atonement: Cross and Resurrection in the Reconciling of God and Humanity* (London, England: Paternoster, 2007), 12.

[102] "The setting of Passover and the Feast of Unleavened Bread … proved the background to Jesus' atoning passion, recalling that eating this meal is a symbol that 'saves the believer from the righteous wrath of God' (Exod. 12:1-14)." See Royce Gruenler, "Atonement in the Synoptic Gospels and Acts: Poured Out for the Forgiveness of Sins," in *The Glory of the Atonement,* ed. C. Hill and F. James, 103.

[103] Emile Nicole, "Pentateuch," 45.

[104] Referring to Psalm 22 Campbell says, "these sufferings were *penal.*" See J. Campbell, *The Nature of the Atonement* (Grand Rapids, MI: William B. Eerdmans Publishing, 1996), 209. McKnight also relates Psalm 22 and Isaiah 53 to Mark 9:12, Scot McKnight, *Jesus and His Death: Historiography, the Historical Jesus, and Atonement Theory* (Waco, TX: Baylor University Press, 2005), 213.

[105] Jeffery, Ovey, and Sach, *Pierced,* 52-67, Anthony Thiselton, *Hermeneutics of Doctrine* (Grand Rapids, MI: Eerdmans, 2007), 333-34, Joachim Jeremias, *The Central Message of the New Testament* (London, England: SCM, 1965), 36-37.

[106] Geoffrey Grogan, "The Atonement in the New Testament," in *The Atonement Debate,* ed. D. Tidball, D. Hilborn, and J. Thacker, 95.

[107] Frederick Danker, "ὀργὴ," in *Greek-English Lexicon of the New Testament and Other Early Christian Literature,* 3rd ed (BDAG), (Chicago, IL: The University of Chicago Press, 1957), 720. Furthermore, Robert Yarborough states "that at a time when humanity has come to be seen as basically good, the concept of divine wrath seems obscene. The nobly intentioned affirmation of God's goodness and therefore of the absence of wrath from his being are of a piece with post-Christian theories of the innate innocence of humanity and the minimal significance of sin in human nature." See Robert Yarborough, "Atonement," in *New Dictionary of Biblical Theology,* ed. T. Alexander and B. Rosner (Downers Grove, IL: InterVarsity Press, 2000), 390.

[108] Herman Ridderbos, *The Gospel of John: A Theological Commentary,* trans. J. Vriend, (Grand Rapids, MI: William B. Eerdmans Publishing, 1997), 151. Charles Kingsley Barrett writes, "Judgment is pronounced upon men in terms of, and through, their relation to Jesus, and when that relation has been established the judgment abides either for eternal life or for wrath." Charles Kingsley Barrett, *The Gospel According to St. John: An Introduction with Commentary and Notes on the Greek Text,* 2nd ed. (London, England: SPCK, 1978), 227.

not merely to demonstrate the heinousness of sin-,[109] or to give us an example of self-giving, (or of the renunciation of violence),[110] or even simply to remind us of the depths of divine love (1 John 4:9;[111] Rev. 1:5[112])."[113] Rather, Hill rightly reminds us that Jesus himself said that his blood would be "poured out for many for the forgiveness of sins" and that Paul repeatedly notes this (for example, 1 Cor. 15:3[114] and Gal. 1:4[115]).[116] Again, this does not take away from other models of the atonement, rather grounds them as the holiness and justice of God is preserved through demonstrating wrath toward sin and yet simultaneously loving, providing atonement for, a reconciliation to the sinner. Blocher reminds us not to overemphasize one doctrine at the exclusion of another, that "various presentations should be interpreted as convergent and complimentary and not opposed. And theological 'hygiene' should banish dichotomies between Biblical themes (e.g., initiative of love/appeasement of wrath)."[117] In an effort to be mindful of theological hygiene, it would be imperative to seek the nature, the intention, the purpose, and most certainly the *authority* of Jesus in his death.

The Authority of Jesus in His Death

Concerning the death of Jesus, questions arise as to whether he suffered exclusively as a victim of a band of religious people who won the day through persuading Pilate or, what role, if any, did God the Father play in the death of his Son. As the second person of

---

[109] Jeremiah continually likens Israel's sin to that of a *whore* (2:20; 3:1-5,6,9; 13:27).

[110] Such as in Girardian thought. See Rene Girard, *Things Hidden Since the Foundation of the World,* trans. Stephen Bann and Michael Metteer, (United Kingdom: The Athlone Press, 1987), 181.

[111] Georg Strecker, Hermeneia: A Critical and Historical Commentary on the Bible, The Johannine Letters: A Commentary on 1, 2, and 3 John (Minneapolis, MN: Fortress Press, 1996), 151. See also Colin Kruse, The Pillar New Testament Commentary: The Letters of John (Grand Rapids, MI: William B. Eerdmans Publishing, 2000), 157-58.

[112] "John reminds us that the love of Jesus, shown in his passion at one moment in history is continuous. So he uses the present tense in the participle ἀγαπῶντι (lt. [to the one] 'loving'). John's revelation is, above all, a triumphant disclosure of God's love, expressed through his judgment." See Stephen Smalley, The *Revelation to John: A Commentary on the Greek Text of the Apocalypse* (Downers Grove, IL: IVP, 2005), 35. See also Stephen Smalley, *Thunder and Love: John's Revelation and John's Community* (Franklin, TN: Authentic Lifestyle, 1994), 147-49. See also Ben Witherington III, *Revelation* (Cambridge, England: Cambridge University Press, 2003),76.

[113] Charles Hill, "Atonement," 28.

[114] Anthony Thiselton, *1 Corinthians: A Shorter Exegetical and Pastoral Commentary* (Grand Rapids, MI: William B. Eerdmans Publishing, 2006), 266. Fred Fisher, *Commentary on 1 and 2 Corinthians* (Waco, TX: Word Books, 1975), 236.

[115] James Dunn, Black's New Testament Commentaries: The Epistle to the Galatians (London, England: A & C Black, 1993), 34-35. See also Mark Sefrid, New Studies in Biblical Theology: Christ, Our Righteousness: Paul's Theology of Justification (Leicester, England: Apollos, 2000), 91.

[116] Charles Hill, "Atonement," 28.

[117] Henri Blocher, "Atonement," in *Dictionary for Theological Interpretation of the Bible,* ed. C. Bartholomew, D. Treier, and N. T. Wright, gen. ed. Kevin Vanhoozer (London, England: SPCK, 2005), 75.

the Trinity, did Jesus have authority in his death? Many scholars are pressing "Toward a human Jesus who is just like one of us, who holds values, that are very close to our ideological commitments, ... a Jesus who, as a real human person, can stand as an example and inspiration for worthy causes."[118] This would not imply that Jesus had any authority in his death. However, the Gospel of Mark continually calls attention to Jesus having "authority." "The term is found nine times in Mark–six with reference to Jesus (1:22, 27; 2:10; 11:28, 29, 33), twice of the Apostles (3:15; 6:7), and once in the simile of the man who "gave authority over his house to his servants" (13:34), which doubtless is an allusion to the disciples of Jesus."[119]

Jesus declared that he would give his flesh for the life of the whole world (John 6:51).[120] The sovereignty and unmistakable plan of God in the death of Christ is expressed in all four gospels.[121] Geoffrey Grogan states that "Calvary was no afterthought but fulfilled the divine purpose."[122] Very early on in his ministry, Jesus declared that he would be taken from his disciples as he says "the days will come when the bridegroom is taken ..." (Mark 2:20).[123] In both Mark 8:31[124] and John 12:27 Jesus declares that the cross was the focal point of his ministry ("*for this purpose* I have come" John 12:27).[125] Indeed, Jesus was keenly aware of the wrath of God, the bitter cup that he must drink and spoke of it often (Luke 12:49-50; Mark 10:38).[126]

It is not too early here to mention the relationality of the Trinity; the reality that the Father and Son are never at odds with one another. Indeed, wrath without enmity. There is no concept of an abusive Father, but rather the Father and Son *working together* to accomplish the redemption of the world with both divine love and divine wrath present and active. The tender relationship that Jesus shares with his *"Abba"* is

---

[118] Helmut Koester, "Jesus the Victim," *JBL* 111, no. 1 (Spring, 1992): 7.

[119] James R Edwards, "The Authority of Jesus in the Gospel of Mark," *JETS* 37, no. 2 (June 1994): 220.

[120] Leon Morris, *NICNT: The Gospel According to John* (Grand Rapids, MI: William B. Eerdmans Publishing, 1995), 331. Morris states that "'Flesh' is a strong word, bound to attract attention. Its almost crude forcefulness rivets attention on the historical fact that Jesus did give himself for others." There is simply no way of avoiding the Bible's clear, repeated, and unambiguous teaching that God was in control of Jesus' death, just as it presents him as sovereign over every other event in the entire universe. God did not merely foresee Jesus' death; much less was he a passive bystander. The fact that penal substitution affirms this constitutes an argument in *favor* of this understanding of the atonement, not an argument against it. See also Gary Burge, *NIV Application Commentary: John* (Grand Rapids, MI: Zondervan, 2000), 202.

[121] See Jeffery, Ovey, and Sach, *Pierced*, 232; cf; John M. Frame, *No Other God: A Response to Open Theism*, (Phillipsburg, NJ: P&R Publishing, 2001), 57-87.

[122] Grogan, "Atonement," 85.

[123] Richard France, *New International Greek Testament Commentary: The Gospel of Mark* (Grand Rapids, MI: William B. Eerdmans Publishing, 2002), 140.

[124] James Edwards, *The Gospel According to Mark* (Grand Rapids, MI: William B. Eerdmans Publishing, 2002), 252-53.

[125] Barrett, *St. John*, 425.

[126] France, *Mark*, 416-17.

nothing less than unique. "The experience of God as Father dominates the whole ministry of Jesus from the Baptism to the Crucifixion."[127] Edwards adds that this is "the source of Jesus' *exousia* and filial consciousness."[128]

In John 10:17-18, Jesus speaks of *his* authority that he exercises in the entire series of events regarding the death he must suffer. He declares, "For this reason the Father loves me, because I lay down my life that I may take it up again. No one takes it from me, but I lay it down of my own accord. I have authority to lay it down and I have authority to take it up again. This charge I have received from my Father."[129] Grogan rightly notes that "while he saw the participants in the crucifixion story to be fully responsible for their actions (John 19:11), there was, at the same time, a divine purpose in it (Mark 14:21)."[130]

The understanding of the Christ being one who will serve as a sacrifice for sin before God is repeated throughout the New Testament. John sees him as the Lamb of God bearing the sin of the world (John 1:29; cf. 1 John 3:5). First John primarily understands the work of the cross as a ἱλασμός, a *propitiation,* (1 John 2:2; 4:10).[131] At this point there is no need to provide a thorough lexicographical study of ἱλασμός because it will be discussed in greater detail below under Expiation and Propitiation.[132] The writer of Hebrews seeks to develop at great length the descriptions of Christ as the great sacrifice on the Day of Atonement as well as the High Priest who remains sinless in order to place humans in a righteous relationship with God once and for all.[133]

As noted above, there were more than simply sin-sacrifices offered throughout the Old Testament. Some were offered out of gratitude or thanksgiving. However, in recalling the actions of confession and banishment of the scapegoat, Marshall declares, "The confession of the sin led to the *transfer* of the sin to the goat. When we read of Christ as the Lamb of God who bears the sins of the world, it is difficult to avoid the

---

[127] T. W. Manson, *The Teachings of Jesus: Studies in its Form and Content* (Cambridge, England: Cambridge University Press, 1959),102.

[128] Edwards, "Authority of Jesus," 220.

[129] Although it is premature, it is appropriate to recall Chalke s and others' statements regarding "divine child abuse" as one reads Jesus' own words here in John's gospel.

[130] Edwards, "Authority of Jesus," 220.

[131] Kruse, John, 75-76; cf. Strecker, Johannine, 39; Leon Morris, The Apostolic Preaching of the Cross, (London, England: Tyndale, 1955), 206. David Hill, Greek Words and Hebrew Meanings: Studies in the Semantics of Soteriological Terms, Society for New Testament Studies Monograph Series (Cambridge, England: University Press, 1967), 37-38. However, Dodd views this as "expiation" exclusively, in Charles Dodd, "Hilaskesthai, its Cognates, Derivatives, and Synonyms, in the Septuagint." JTS 32, no. 128 (July 1931): 360. See also cf. Gerald Thornton, "Propitiation or Expiation? Hilasterion and Hilasmos in Romans and 1 John," Evangelical Theology, 80, (1968-9): 54-55; Raymond Brown, The Gospel According to John 1–X11, Anchor Bible Series, 29 (New York, NY: Double Day, 1982), 217-222.

[132] See Morris, *Apostolic,* 125-85; David Hill, *Greek Words and Hebrew Meanings*, 23-48; and Thornton, "Propitiation or Expiation?" 53-55.

[133] Marshall, *Aspects*, 40.

impression that the same kind of thing is happening."[134] It is exegetically sound to thus deduce a transferring of the sin of the people onto Christ, who would bear the penalty for sin against God.

The Tree: Becoming a Curse

The preachers recorded in the Acts of the Apostles are quite intentional about their word choices in describing the work of the cross. Peter and Paul reference the "tree" upon which Jesus hung (Acts 5:30; 10:39; 13:29).[135] For any devout Jew or Gentile proselyte, the words of Deuteronomy 21:23 would have struck a quite sensitive nerve amongst the hearers. Hearing of "a tree" was more than speaking of something in mere nature. This is because they would have known that "cursed is the man who is hanged on a tree."[136] The crucifixion was seen as a *curse* in the eyes of the Jews and *shameful* in the eyes of the Romans.[137]

Elsewhere, Peter and Paul both mention the "tree" (1 Pet. 2:24;[138] Gal. 3:13-14). In each of these references there is the concept of Jesus being a sin-bearer.[139] "This means they saw a divine purpose of atonement, indeed of penal substitution, in it."[140] I. H. Marshall recently states that "the death of Jesus, though brought about by evil men, is nevertheless something that was planned and purposed by God: the Messiah had to suffer, and then enter into glory."[141]

---

[134] Marshall, *Aspects* 141, italics mine.

[135] John Polhill, *The New American Commentary,* vol. 26, *Acts* (Nashville, TN: Broadman Press, 1992), 169. Polhil states that "Although Peter did not quote Deuteronomy 21:22 to develop the idea that Christ became a curse for us," the "idea seems to be present in 1 Peter 2:24 and is fully developed by Paul in Galatians 3:13." See Max Wilcox "Upon the Tree - Deut. 21.22-23 in the New Testament," *JBL* 96, no. 1 (March 1977): 85-99, www.jstor.org/stable/3265329. Cf. Paul Walaskay, *Acts* (Louisville, KY: Westminster John Knox Press, 1998), 66. Cf. John Stott, *The Message of Acts: To the Ends of the Earth,* (Leicester, England: InterVarsity Press, 1990), 116.

[136] Grogan, "Atonement," 87.

[137] Grogan, "Atonement," 87. Notice the striking balance that is achieved here that is often neglected by both advocates and opponents of PSA.

[138] J. Ramsey Michaels, *Word Biblical Commentary,* vol. 49, *1 Peter* (Waco, TX: Word Books Publisher, 1988),149. See also Karen Jobes, *BECNT, 1 Peter* (Grand Rapids, MI: Baker Academic, 2005), 195.

[139] Paul's new interpretation of Deuteronomy 21:23 comes to light here as he articulates the fact that Jesus did carry a curse on the cross and that it "was not his own, it was ours. And by willingly taking the curse of the Torah on our behalf, he redeems both Israelites and gentiles from the curse which befell us all because we did not manage to obey the Torah. Redemption is at hand!" Torleif Elgvin, "The Messiah Who Was Cursed on the Tree," *themelios,* 22, no.3 (October 1996).

[140] Grogan, "Atonement," 87. Those violently abusing and shaming Christ were venting their wrath upon him and did not view their actions as though they were being done on behalf of God outside of the condemning Jesus as a "blasphemer." Yet, the Father and Son understood their cooperative work as redemptive.

[141] Marshall, *Aspects,* 94.

Paul declares that "for our sake he made him to be sin who knew no sin, so that in him we might become the righteousness of God" (2 Cor. 5:21).[142] In commenting on this verse Kraus states that Jesus did not suffer for his own crimes but rather suffered the criminals' death.

> And inasmuch as we include all humanity in this generic reflection and dishonoring of God, we must say also "the chastisement of our sins was upon him." But this is not the substitution of a legal penalty which pays our debt to God's justice. It is rather the substitution of total identification which accepts responsibility for the group. He took our place including the consequences of this identification. Thus "he who knew no sin was made sin for us" (2 Cor. 5:21).[143]

Marshall however offers a stronger comment here. For, in order for humans to become what Christ is (righteous), somehow the sin must be removed. He argues that this section of scripture (2 Cor. 5:14-21) implies that Jesus' death "took away their sin and liability to judgment/wrath in order to become righteous. The consequences of sin, specifically death, are borne by Christ when he is made one with sinners, and, in that sense, the substitution is penal."[144]

Lastly, it serves well to briefly touch on the Apocalypse of John. Grogan states that "we might not expect the Apocalypse, with its future orientation, to touch much on the finished work of Christ, but it does."[145] Christ's finished work on the cross is now seen as redemptive (Rev. 5:9; cf. 1:5; 14:4) as well as triumphant over Satan (12:10-11). This death of Christ that purchased redemption for all who would believe is God's intention of saving human beings (17:8) from the foundation of the world (13:8).[146]

---

[142] Also commonly referred to as "the Great Exchange" coined by M. Luther.

[143] Norman Kraus, "From Biblical Intentions to Theological Conceptions: Response to Thomas N. Finger," *Conrad Grebel Review* 8 (Winter 1990): 218-19.

[144] Marshall, *Aspects,* 48. Green and Baker argue against this interpretation because they see that "such an interpretation helpfully underscores the righteousness of God but places the transformative significance in the wrong place." Rather, "what is required is not a transformation within God's heart toward sinners but a transformation of their sinful existence before God." See Green and Baker, *Scandal,* 104. See also Judith Gundry-Volf, "Expiation, Propitiation, Mercy Seat," in *DPL* (1993), 282; Dunn, "Paul's Understanding of the Death of Jesus" in *Reconciliation and Hope: New Testament Essays on Atonement and Eschatology,* Presented to L. L. Morris on his 60th birthday (Carlisle, PA: Paternoster Press, 1974), 44.

[145] Grogan, "Atonement," 94.

[146] Grogan, "Atonement," 95. See also Smalley, *Revelation,* 343. Some see this predestining act as attributed to Christ and not humans. Cf. George Beasley-Murray, *New Century Bible: The Book of Revelation* (London, England: Butler and Tanner, 1974), 214; David Aune, *Word Biblical Commentary,* vol. 52b, *Revelation 6-16* (Nashville, TN: Thomas Nelson Publishers, 1998),747; Leonard Thompson, *Abingdon New Testament Commentaries: Revelation* (Nashville, TN: Abingdon Press, 1998), 140; Robert Wall, *New International Bible Commentary (NT): Revelation* (Carlisle, PA: Paternoster Press, 1995), 170. See also Robert Mounce, *NICNT: The Book of Revelation Testament* (Grand Rapids, MI: Eerdmans Publishing, 1998), 252.

"The language of sacrifice and sin-bearing occurs frequently and the cross is presented as a place of PSA so final, so efficacious, that it did away with the Old Testament sacrificial system."[147] This study provides the grounding upon which the post-apostolic and early thinkers in the Church could construct their understandings of the cross.

PSA in Sub-Apostolic and Patristic Writings

Green and Baker support the idea that "the writers of the immediate post-apostolic period proclaimed salvation by the cross but offered little explanation on *how* the cross provided salvation."[148] Then Green and Baker proceed to give focus and much credit to the *Christus Victor* model holding that this motif of thought was the dominant way of understanding the work of Christ in the atonement. Irenaeus and others understood the cross of Christ as a *cosmic* event in which God overcame the devil, death, and hell by conquering such opposition through his crucifixion and resurrection.[149] Green and Baker assert that this understanding of the work on the cross came about because of the cultural conditions of the day.[150] They do so by appealing to the "Lordship" of Jesus over all creation and most certainly, his exaltation over Caesar is important and should not be dismissed carelessly. The declaration of Christ, not Caesar, being the true Lord is one that led to countless martyrdoms in the first few centuries of the Church.[151] Green and Baker are correct saying that "the cosmology of that era also led people to understand conflicts on earth as related to and intertwined with conflict between celestial powers."[152]

Girard agrees as he argues that it is unfortunate that soon after Christ's death, the Church fell subject to the principalities and powers and reinterpreted the death of Jesus in a mythological and sacrificial fashion, which Jesus himself never intended.[153] During

---

[147] Grogan, "Atonement," 95.

[148] Green and Baker, *Scandal,* 117, emphasis mine.

[149] Green and Baker, *Scandal,* 118.

[150] Green and Baker, *Scandal,* 118.

[151] See Everett Ferguson, *Backgrounds of Early Christianity* (Grand Rapids, MI: Eerdmans, 2003), 592-608. Also for more recent studies on Lordship in the context of the first century see, Scot McKnight and Joseph B. Modica's *Jesus is Lord, Caesar is Not: Evaluating Empire in New Testament Studies* (Downers Grove, IL: IVP, 2013).

[152] Green and Baker, *Scandal,* 118.

[153] Hans Boersma, *Violence, Hospitality, and the Cross: Appropriating the Atonement Tradition* (Grand Rapids, MI: Baker Academic, 2006), 148. Girard laments: "Thanks to the sacrificial reading it has been possible for what we call Christendom to exist for fifteen or twenty centuries; that is to say, a culture has existed that is based, like all cultures (at least up to a certain point) on the mythological forms engendered by the founding mechanism. Paradoxically, in the sacrificial reading the Christian text itself provides the basis. Mankind relies upon a misunderstanding of the text that explicitly reveals the founding mechanism to re-establish cultural forms which remain sacrificial and engender a society that, by virtue of this misunderstanding, takes its place in the sequence of all other cultures, still clinging to the sacrificial vision that the Gospel rejects." See Girard, *Things,* 181.

this time period, it was common to hail Caesar as Lord. Yet, the early Christians began to acclaim Jesus as Lord and not Caesar. Therefore, the Lordship of Christ greatly colored how the divine intentions that wrought the crucifixion were understood.[154]

Green and Baker state clearly that "Irenaeus, Origen, and Gregory of Nyssa each avoid even hinting at Christ appeasing God the Father or the Father punishing the Son."[155] Yet, in *Pierced for our Transgressions,* Jeffery, Ovey, and Sach devote 42 pages to the fact that the doctrine of PSA was clearly in circulation amongst the earliest Christian thinkers.[156]

Thiselton opens his section, "The Special Significance of the Apostolic Fathers and Early Christian Apologists," with the statement,

> Over against any tendency to play down the substitutionary nature of the death of Christ as a sacrifice "for our sins" (albeit alongside the themes of representation, identification, and participation), the sub-apostolic and early Patristic writings are striking in their repetition of this core understanding, even when the gospel has moved (with some exceptions) from Jewish to Roman soil.[157]

This is an absolutely enormous claim that, if substantiated, ought to provide enough evidence not only from sound exegesis but to anchor the understanding of PSA not in a culture such as Anselm but in Scripture and early Christian thought. This would furthermore place the burden on the modern Christian to find ways to go about articulating the doctrine amongst the other models of the atonement. Thus, it shall be demonstrated below that the substitutionary nature of Christ's death was taught amongst the earliest Christian thinkers and it was indeed *penal.*

Polycarp, Melito, Eusebius, Athanasius, Augustine, Cyril

Polycarp, the Bishop of Smyrna (c.69-155) quotes 1 Peter 2:22 and 24. Polycarp also states that "in the pledge of our righteousness ... Christ Jesus, 'who *bore our sins* in his own body on the tree,' who did not sin, neither was guile found in his mouth, endured all things for our sake that we might live in him" (Polycarp, *To the Philippians* 8.1).[158]

Melito of Sardis (c.190) states,

> The Lord clothed himself with humanity, and with *suffering on behalf of* the suffering one, and *bound on behalf of* the one constrained, and *judged on behalf of* the one convicted, and *buried on behalf of* the one entombed, rose from the dead and cried out aloud: "Who takes issue with me? Let him stand before me. I will set

---

[154] Green and Baker, *Scandal,* 118.

[155] Green and Baker, *Scandal,* 124.

[156] Jeffery, Ovey, and Sach, *Pierced,* 161-203.

[157] Thiselton, *Doctrine,* 355.

[158] Thiselton, *Doctrine,* 356, italics mine.

free the condemned. I gave life to the dead. I will raise up the entombed. Who will contradict me?[159]

Melito here is clearly emphasizing the heart of PSA, namely the notion that Jesus' actions were substitutionary (on behalf of) and *penal* by way of proclaiming that Christ was indeed *judged*. The judgment most certainly is coming from God. And yet, what must be highlighted here is that kaleidoscopic thought was clearly in play in Melito's mind. For he continues, "It is I," says the Christ, "I am he who destroys death, and triumphs over the enemy, and crushes Hades, and binds the strong man, and bears humanity off to the heavenly heights." Indeed, the *Christus Victor* motif was a part of Melito's thinking, and yet, as noted above, did not pitch this understanding *over and against* PSA but rather follows PSA.

Again, terms such as *suffering, bound, judged,* and *buried* should be understood in the *penal* sense due to the fact that they are all consequences applied to the innocent Christ "on behalf of" sinful humanity. Others, however, may not view the cross as implying a payment of penalty, but rather representation and substitution.[160]

Eusebius of Caesarea (c.275-399) was involved in the Council of Nicaea in 325 and was an advisor to the Roman Emperor Constantine. One thing he is most known for is that Constantine asked him to supervise the production of fifty copies of the Bible for use in churches throughout Constantinople, the new Roman capital.[161] Eusebius undoubtedly held to a *penal* understanding of the cross. For, he states,

> The Lamb of God ... was chastised on our behalf, and suffered a penalty he did not owe, but which we owed because of the multitude of our sins; and so He became the cause of the forgiveness of our sins, because He received death for us, and transferred to Himself the scourging, the insults, and the dishonor, which were due to us, and drew down upon Himself the appointed curse, being made a curse for us.[162]

Athanasius, (c.293) the Bishop of Alexandria also strongly proposed a penal understanding of Christ's crucifixion. Athanasius argues that the problem that was wrought by human sin was solved by God sending the divine Word into the world and

---

[159] Melito of Sardis and Alistair Stewart-Sykes, *On Pascha: With the Fragments of Melito and Other Material Related to the Quatrodecimans* (Yonkers, NY: St. Vladamir's Seminary Press, 2001), 65, italics mine.

[160] Indeed, there are early church fathers who described Christ's death as substitutionary and not in the penal sense. See Barnabas, 5.1; Ignatius, To the Trallians 2.2; cf. To the Smyrneans 6.1; Melito, Fragment 10; See also, Brad Jersak, "Nonviolent Identification and the Victory of Christ," in *Stricken by God?* edited by B. Jersak and M. Hardin, 51-52.

[161] F. F. Bruce, *The Canon of Scripture* (Downers Grove, IL: InterVarsity Press, 1988), 197-207.

[162] Eusebius, *Proof,* 195.

thus, the Son paid the debt that sinful people owed to God.[163] He states that Christ offered "the sacrifice on behalf of all, surrendering his own temple [body] to death in place of all, to settle man's account with death and free him from the primal transgression."[164] Therefore, according to Athanasius, "Christ's death was a penal satisfaction of the divine sentence of death."[165]

Augustine of Hippo (354-430) most certainly understood Christ's work on the cross in the *penal* sense as well. "Christ, though guiltless, took our punishment that He might cancel our guilt and do away with our punishment."[166] Augustine writes,

Christ endured death as man, and for man; so also, Son of God as He was, ever living in His own righteousness, but dying *for our* offenses, He submitted as man, and for man, to bear the curse which accompanies death. And as He died in the flesh which He took in *bearing our punishment,* so also, while ever blessed in His own righteousness, He was cursed *for our* offenses, in the death which He suffered in *bearing our punishment.*[167]

Cyril of Alexandria (375-444) states in his De adoratione et cultu in spiritu et veritate,

The Only-begotten was made man, bore a body by nature at enmity with death, and became flesh, so that, enduring the death which was hanging over us as the result of our sin, he might abolish sin; and further, that he might put an end to the accusations of Satan, inasmuch as we have paid in Christ himself the *penalties* for the charges of sin against us: "For he bore our sins, and was wounded" because of us, according to the voice of the prophet. Or are we not healed by his wounds?[168]

Jeffery, Ovey, and Sach point out that Cyril's explanation of the significance of Christ's death also encompasses both *participation* and *substitution*. Christ was punished in our place and also because we are "in him" through faith Cyril affirms that "*we* have paid in Christ himself the penalties for the charges of sin against us."

After noting these six early church fathers who had a clear understanding of the penal substitutionary nature of the work of the cross, Thiselton counters some of the claims that Green and Baker and others in their line of thinking have to say about the historical development of the PSA theory. Thiselton boldly states it

is utterly striking in dispelling the myth that the development of Christian doctrine almost disappeared from sight during the so-called "tunnel period," and remerged

---

163 Gordon Lewis and Bruce Demarest, Integrative Theology: Historical, Biblical, Systematic, Apologetic, Practical, vol. 2, Our Primary Need: Christ's Atoning Provisions, (Grand Rapids, MI: Zondervan Publishing House, 1990, 379.

164 Athanasius, *Incarnation,* XX.2.

165 Lewis and Demarest, *Integrative,* 379.

166 Augustine, *Against Faustus,* 208.

167 Augustine, *Against Faustus,* 208.

168 Cyril of Alexandria, *De Adoratione,* 100-102, italics mine.

as something different from the New Testament and apostolic doctrine in the Patristic period from Irenaeus (c.130-200), Clement of Alexandria (c.150-c.215), and Tertullian (c.160-c.225) onward into the third century with Hippolytus and Origen.[169]

Green and Baker lean strongly on the early Greco-Roman world in which the gospel was first proclaimed and argue that because of the given socio-political conditions of the era, the doctrine of the atonement is simply a reflection of that particular culture. These scholars direct the reader's attention to Walter Burkert's work regarding the ancient Greek gods which demonstrates that "if these powers are appeased, all kinds of blessings must return ... the traditional means to secure the one (blessing) and prevent the other (wrath and curse) are sacrifice and prayer."[170] Green and Baker then note that in both Greek and Roman mythology as well as drama were contained portraits of a hero sacrificing one's life on behalf of the city.[171] Therefore the guiding hermeneutical presupposition of the Greco-Romans was one in which God would be in great need of appeasement due to his wrathful anger and thus, blessings would follow the sacrifice.

Thiselton presents a striking blow to Green and Baker's position by stating that "it is well to heed the themes of this (subapostolic) period *before* quasisociological explanations about power play, politics, and Greco-Roman influences enter into the picture to claim reductive socio-political pressures for the shaping of this doctrine in the Patristic church."[172]

Summary

This chapter has sought to demonstrate that there is substantial biblical and historical evidence that affirm the realities of retribution, wrath, judgments, penalty for human sin within the character of God and that the theological conclusions are not wrought out of Greek mythology nor are they simply culturally conditioned conclusions. Rather, they are grounded in the Biblical text. Furthermore, because the doctrine of PSA can be found in both the Old and New Testaments it is not merely a Western approach to atonement studies. Additionally, PSA is often articulated amongst many early Christian thinkers and is not simply a later development in Christian theology

---

[169] Thiselton, *Doctrine*, 358.

[170] Green and Baker, *Scandal*, 50.

[171] Green and Baker, *Scandal*, 51.

[172] Thiselton, *Doctrine*, 359, emphasis mine.

CHAPTER 3

PRELIMINARY THEOLOGICAL UNDERSTANDING: THE "IMAGE OF GOD"

Introduction

When it pertains to studying the atonement, it is only fitting that some space be given to the ever so important and magnificent doctrine known as the *imago Dei* or as Bruggemann, creatively and effectively describes the phenomenon, "The Human Person as Yahweh's Partner."[173] The glorious doctrine of the incarnation, God clothing himself in flesh, dwelling amongst human beings in real space and real time, to live the perfect life and give his life as a ransom for many, that through his death and resurrection, all of creation, including those elected from before the foundation of the world, might be reconciled to God. Additionally, given the current cultural climate, Christians who are seeking to engage the surrounding culture with the good news of the gospel must have the ability to articulate what is meant by the *"image of God."* This is made abundantly clear due to the immense importance it carries not in marginalized theological conversations but at the forefront of the majority of world news. In the time of preparation for writing this book: Planned Parenthood has been exposed for the buying and selling of aborted fetus parts; the ongoing outrage in Ferguson, Baltimore, New York City expressed in the Black Lives Matter campaign is in the headlines daily; and the Syrian refugee crisis now on the doorstep of the West. These issues all pertain to assaults on not simply age or race, but on the image of God itself. Those who are being murdered, seeking asylum, and pleading for justice are all image bearers, human partners, of God. How Christians understand theologically *what* human beings are, plays a significant role in how we understand the gospel work of redemption as well as the urgency of mission. Equal to engaging Trinitarian thought, understanding the doctrine of the image of God has massive implications on how the relational paradigm is to be understood and applied. "In the Old Testament human personas are understood as situated in the same transactional processes with the holiness of Yahweh as is Israel, so that in a very general way the character and destiny of human persons replicates and reiterates the character and destiny of Israel. This transactional process causes a 'biblical understanding' of human persons to stand at a critical distance and as a critical protest against all modern notions of humanness that move in the direction of autonomy." [174]Rather than seeking to discuss the various theories that speak to "how" human beings were created, the following section will examine what is meant by "image" and "likeness" in the Old Testament, humankind as unique in the created order,

---

173 Walter Bruggemann, "The Human Person as Yahweh's Partner," in *Theology of the Old Testament: Testimony, Dispute, Advocacy* (Minneapolis, MN: Fortress Press, 1997), 450-491.

174 Bruggemann, "Yahweh's Partner," 451.

some implications of humankind's image-bearing state, the original "good" state in which humans were created, the marring and distortion of the image through human sin, and renewal and restoration of the *imago Dei* through Christ.

"Image" and "Likeness" in the Old Testament

"God created man in his own image, in the image of God he created him; male and female he created them" (Gen. 1:27). When seeking to understand and apply this verse and others that are directly related to this foundational principle in a proper theological position, it is crucial that one have a correct understanding of the original Hebrew terminology employed. *Tselem* ("image") is used sixteen times in the Old Testament and generally refers to a representation or a likeness. At minimum, the term means that human beings have the ability to *relate* to God in a way that is unlike the animal kingdom, botanical life, or inanimate planets.[175] There are five instances in which *tselem* refers to human beings, four as created in the *image* of God (Gen. 1:26, 27; 5:3; 9:6).[176]

Tselem appears in three other type of contexts: First, *tselem* is used twice in First Samuel in reference to the "golden copies of the mice and swellings that afflicted the Philistines" (1 Sam. 6:5, 11). This word most often is found referring to an idol.[177] The crafting of the symbols of mice and tumors served as an act of sympathetic magic in which the representation of something stands for reality itself. By means of archaeological excavation throughout the ancient Near East, archaeologists have found images of mice and other animals that are believed to have been used in magical rituals.[178]

Second, *tselem* occurs twice in the Psalms and carries a more figurative meaning as opposed to a wooden meaning. Rather than having a physical and visible representation, as in the other occurrences of *tselem*, the concepts of being transitory, unreal, or empty are emphasized.[179] In the first occurrence *tselem* is translated "phantom" and parallels *hebel* which is translated "vapor." The verses say "Man, though he stands upright is but a puff of wind, he moves like a phantom *[tselem]*; the riches he piles up are no more than a vapor" (Ps. 39:6). The second occurrence uses *tselem* to compare conscious human life to a dreamlike state. "Like a dream when one awakes, O Lord, when aroused, you will despise their form" (Ps. 73:20). Therefore, given these two translations and applications, one must have a correct understanding of the original semantics employed for developing a sound theology of the *imago Dei*.

---

[175] Paul R. House, "Creation in Old Testament Theology," *The Southern Baptist Journal of Theology: Genesis* 5, no. 3 (Fall 2001): 8. This will be developed in the chapter dedicated to the relational paradigm.

[176] R. Larrid Harris, ed., *Theological Wordbook of the Old Testament,* vol. 2 (Chicago, IL: Moody Press, 1981), 767-8.

[177] R. Larrid Harris, ed., *Theological Wordbook,* 767-8.

[178] John H. Walton, Victor H. Matthews, and Mark W. Chavalas, eds., *The IVP Bible Background Commentary: Old Testament* (Downers Grove, IL: InterVarsity Press, 2000), 288.

[179] Victor P. Hamilton, *The Book of Genesis: Chapters 1-17* (Grand Rapids, MI: Eerdmans, 1990), 134-5.

Third, the remaining occurrences of *tselem* refer to an idolatrous image (Num. 33:52; 2 Kings 11:18; 2 Chron. 23:17; Ezek. 7:20; 16:17; 23:14; Amos 5:26). In the ancient world idols were considered physical representations of spiritual powers and believed in some way to carry the essence of that which it represented.[180] In contrast to the surrounding idolatrous regions is the biblical concept of "imageless" worship.[181] The Decalogue strictly prohibited the Israelites from making any sort of images for or to worship other than what YHWH prescribes. "You shall not make for yourself an idol; you shall not worship them or serve them" (Exod. 20:4-5). Interestingly, Cornelius Tacitus, stated that

> The Egyptians worship many animals and monstrous images; the Jews conceive of one god only, and with the mind only; they regard as impious those who make from perishable materials representations of gods in man's image; that supreme and eternal being is incapable of representation and without end. Therefore, they set up not statues in their cities, still less in their temples; this flattery is not paid their kings, nor this honor given to the Caesars.[182]

The uniqueness of YHWH is incomparable to any other god. For he cannot be represented by any physical form (Isa. 40:18). However, Israel turned away from the one, true, living, and invisible God to serve and worship visible idols, *images* of pagan religious entities (Ezek. 7:20; 16:17; Amos. 5:26). The refusal of the Israelites to remove the false images from amongst them as recorded in the book of Numbers is all the more grotesque (Num. 33:52). Thus, what can be drawn from the Scriptural meaning of the *image* is that it does contain some of the essence of that which it represents. Indeed, human beings are made in the image of God and therefore the idea of "essence" though marred, flawed, incomplete, and certainly partial must be part of the thought equation.

In Genesis 1:26 and 5:1-3, *demuth*, ("likeness") is used in conjunction with *tselem* and the two form a literary relationship with one another. *Demuth* occurs 25 times in the Old Testament and all but five of the appearances are in poetical or prophetical books of the Bible.[183] The semantic range of *demuth* is full of similarities. On some occasions it refers to actual likeness and on other occasions it refers to a weakened resemblance.[184] *Demuth* can be understood as a "blueprint," "sketch," or a "plan" (2 Kings 16:10), in terms of resemblance (Ps. 58:4; Isa. 13:14), as a replica or a copy (2

---

180 John V. Walton, *The NIV Commentary: Genesis* (Grand Rapids, MI: Zondervan Publishing House, 2001), 130.

181 Bruce C. Cresson, *Holman Illustrated Bible Dictionary* (Nashville, TN: Holman Reference, 2003), 804.

182 Lewis H. Feldman and Meyer Reinhold, eds., *Jewish Life and Thought Among Greeks and Romans* (Minneapolis, MN: Augsburg Fortress Press, 1966), 111.

183 W. E. Vine, Merrill F. Unger, and William White Jr., *Vine's Complete Expository Dictionary of Old and New Testament Words,* (Nashville, TN: Thomas Nelson Publishers, 1970), 136.

184 John N. Oswalt, "1948," in *New International Dictionary of Old Testament Theology and Exegesis,* ed. Willem A. VanGemeren, vol. 1 (Grand Rapids, MI: Zondervan, 1997), 969.

Chron. 4:3; Isa. 40:10, 18), or appearance (ten times in Ezekiel 1 alone).[185] There are three popular understandings that speak to the relationship between *tselem* and *demuth*. The first suggests that *demuth* limits *tselem* and implies that mankind was made similar to yet not exactly like God. The second teaches that *demuth* in fact strengthens and clarifies *tselem*, implying extreme similarity between God and man. The third option is the result of an error in the LXX and is not presented here.[186]

Therefore, the earliest church fathers believed that "image" pertained to the natural qualities of humans while "likeness" pertained to the moral, ethical, and supernatural elements in humans that were lost in humankind's rebellion in the Fall. Thus, Genesis 1:26-27 does not provide exhaustively what it means for human beings to be made in the image and likeness of God. What can be immediately observed is that there is symmetry, a complementarity occurring in the creation of the earth and the crowing humans that inhabit it. There is land and sea, heavens and the earth, day and night, and male and female. Indeed, consider the words from N. T. Wright spoken recently regarding gay marriage, complementarity in regards to the creation account:

> With Christian or Jewish presupposition or indeed Muslim then if you believe in what it says in Genesis 1 about God making heaven and earth–and the binaries in Genesis are so important–that heaven and earth, and sea and dry land, and so on and so on, and you end up with male and female. It's all about God making complementary pairs which are meant to work together. The last scene in the Bible is the new heaven and the new earth, and the symbol for that is the marriage of Christ and his church. It's not just one or two verses here and there which say this or that. It's an entire narrative which works with this complementarity so that a male-plus-female marriage is a sign post or a signal about the goodness of the original creation and God's intention for the eventual new heavens and new earth.[187]

Tselem and *demuth* communicate the fact that humans are made unique, lifted up over all other created things in the eyes of God. One last piece of noteworthy information is recalling the ancient context of the book and writing of Genesis and the surrounding religious and political ideas that charged the word "image" and "dominion" with incredible meaning. It was a common practice for a king to erect images or statues of himself throughout land that he had dominion over — expressing his sovereignty as king. Thus, when the writing of Genesis occurs, the language of "image" and "dominion" become very important as the author is communicating the desire of God to have his

---

[185] Greg Nichols, "Doctrine of Man," Class Lectures from Trinity Ministerial Academy (Privately Printed, 1982), Lecture 6, 5.

[186] C. F. Kiel and F. Delitzch, *Commentary on the Old Testament in Ten Volumes,* vol. 1, *The Pentateuch* (Grand Rapids, MI: Eerdmans, 1978), 63.

[187] N. T. Wright, "Gay Marriage: Nature and Narrative Point to Complementarity," accessed January 18, 2015 http://www.firstthings.com/blogs/firstthoughts/2014/06/n-t-wrights-argument-against-same-sex-marriage.

own image-bearers as human beings, not inanimate objects, and that he desires these image-bearers to be "fruitful and multiply" as he delights in having fellowship with them while they cover the earth. The humans were made without sin, like God but distinct from, less than, and dependent upon him. Considering the broken heart of God revealed by Genesis 6, one can see that he feels devastation and grief at the loss and rebellion of his image-bearers.

Humankind as Unique in the Created Order

Genesis 1-2 make abundantly clear that human beings and the animal kingdom are set apart entirely, with dominion being entrusted to the humans made in the image of God. The image-bearers of God enjoy this elevated status of privilege and fellowship with God. There is a stark contrast between animal life and human beings in both distinction and class. In Genesis 1:11-12, the writer tells us that the plants and the trees were "made after their kind." Additionally, in Genesis 1:21, 24-25, animals were also made "after their kind." This wording indicates that God "bound together all creatures in a common dependence on their native elements, while giving each the distinctive character of its kind."[188] What can be learned here is that God ordained plant and animal life to both act and reproduce according to the nature that he gave each.

In Genesis 1:24-25, the formula "after their kind" in reference to animals is repeated five times. Yet, in Genesis 1:26-27, an abrupt change in the creation pattern is introduced. Human beings are made "in [God's] image according [to God's] likeness" (Gen. 1:26). Thus, creation is designed by God, though not in his image nor likeness; he would not serve as the pattern by which they would reproduce, but rather serves as the pattern-maker, the divine *demuth*. And yet, when designing and creating human beings God himself would serve as the pattern by which he would make his image-bearers. He would share some of his attributes with them while other attributes he would keep as incommunicable. Human beings would be fashioned in community, to be spiritual, and relational creatures.

Humankind can also be understood as distinctive in the created order from the differences in the manner of creation between man and other created things. In Genesis 1, human beings were *made* by the active, engaged, hands of God, while plant and animal life came forth from the earth at the command of God. "God could have called for these creatures by his mere word; instead he spoke the word that enabled them to come forth."[189]

The "hands-on" involvement in the creation of humankind is also seen in Genesis 2. In the second creation account human beings were "formed" (*"yasar"*) by God and received life through the breath of God (Gen. 2:7). The verb *yasar* describes the work of a potter with clay. However, this is not tedious, repetitive, monotonous work. Rather, *yasar* implies an artist who is creatively investing his talents in molding a masterpiece

---

[188] Derek Kidner, *An Introduction and Commentary: Genesis* (Downers Grove, IL: InterVarsity Press, 1967), 48.

[189] H. P. Leupold, *Exposition of Genesis,* vol. 1, *chapters 1-19* (Grand Rapids, MI: Baker Book House, 1942), 82.

with a plan in mind and applying a specific strategy.[190] God is personally, creatively, and lovingly involved in the creation of his image-bearers as is recalled in the poem of Job (Job 10:8-9) and celebrated in the Psalms (Ps. 139:13).

Though humankind and the animal kingdom share the dust of the earth in the substance from which they owe their origins and both were recipients of God's forming ("yasar") (Gen. 2:7, 19), only human beings were those who received the breath of God into the nostrils. This action was absolutely unique, as anthropomorphically, God has fashioned Adam with his own hands, only to bring him close, face to face, as in a kiss, and gave to him the breath of life. This was not only an act of creation but carries with it the tones of an intimate *relationship*.[191] As a result of the divine breath man became a living being ("nephesh"). Again, just as no distinction existed between mankind and the animal kingdom in their common source (dust of the earth) and means of creation (forming), no distinction exists at this point either because animals are also described as living beings ("nephesh"). Yet the means by which mankind became a living being was different. The content of the breath which man received was different. Genesis 2:7 does not use the normal Hebrew word for breath ("ruah"), which can be applied to God, man animals, and false gods. Instead, the means by which humans became living beings was by the divine *nesama* ("breath"), which is used only of God and man.[192]

Some Implications of Humankind's Image-Bearing State from Genesis 1-9

Thus far this section has demonstrated the nature of the image of God in human beings as defined by language and humankind's unique place in the created order. Now we will turn to the implications of man's image-bearing state. The implications are manifold; this section will address only a few points from Genesis 1-9. First, being created in the image of God provides a unique faculty, being that of a personal *relationship* which involves verbal and spiritual communication. Second, only human beings can receive the personal blessing of God. Third, only human beings are placed as stewards of the remainder of the created order.[193] Fourth, human beings as image bearers implies rulership. As previously demonstrated, the image of God implies that humans share some of God's communicable attributes. Karl Barth stated, "It is in consequence of their divine likeness that men are distinguished from all other creatures with autonomous life, by a superior position, by a higher dignity and might, by greater power of disposal and control."[194]

---

[190] Wenham, *Genesis*, 59.

[191] See also Kidner, *Genesis*, 60.

[192] Hamilton, *Genesis*, 159. Also, after the resurrection of Christ, the disciples are breathed upon by the resurrected Jesus. This scene, this breath, is extremely relevant to our discussion here and will be addressed below.

[193] House, "Creation," 8.

[194] Karl Barth, *Church Dogmatics*, vol. 3, bk. 1, *The Doctrine of Creation* (Edinburgh, England: InterVarsity Press, 1972), 3.

Because humans are in this unique relationship with God, human beings are told to rule and have dominion in a manner that resembles that of the sovereign creator. The relationship that humans have with God further emphasizes the fact that they are thinking, responsible, communicative persons, and it is this relationship with God that allows them to act as God's representative on earth.[195] John Murray beautifully illustrated this point: "Since God is sovereign, man's likeness to God involves the exercise of a sovereignty that is correspondent. He is God's viceregent because he is like God."[196] However, rulership is not the content of the image, instead, rulership is a consequence and function of man's image-bearing state.

Genesis 1:28 affirms that humankind's function is to rule and subdue the world. Logically, the animal kingdom falls under the greater category of the world. Furthermore, Genesis 2:19-20 restates humankind's rulership over the animal kingdom. Naming in the ancient world indicated authority. In these verses Adam engaged in this activity as God brought all the animals before him, thereby exercising dominion over them.

Fifth, the fact that humankind was created in the image of God insinuates that nothing else in the created order could serve as a counterpart for man except another being which also bore the divine image. Genesis 2:18-20 clearly states that although Adam gave names to all animals, he could not find among their ranks one that shared his nature or one that corresponded to him. The activity of naming, in addition to implying authority, was also Adam's observance of the traits, character, and nature of the beasts. Therefore, Genesis 2:18-20 portrays Adam's search for a counterpart which does not result in the desired outcome. God's observation in Genesis 2:18 is that Adam needed a counterpart, one with a corresponding nature. Correspondence, in this context, indicated a focus on the equality of man and his helpmate in terms of their essential constitution.[197] Adam was uniquely formed by God and bore God's image, therefore, only one who was also uniquely formed and who bore the image would be a suitable helpmate.

Sixth, the image of God in humankind implies humankind's sonship and daughterhood under God. "Man is the son of the Great King... [And he] is made for filial fellowship with the divine and intended to express the family-likeness in righteousness, holiness, and integrity."[198] This is affirmed by Luke 3:38, in which the Evangelist used the genealogy in Genesis 5 to trace Jesus's descent all the way back to God. In order to demonstrate the continuity of the human race, Luke had to identify Adam as the son of God.

---

[195] House, "Creation," 8.

[196] John Murray quoted in Jeong Koo Jeon, Covenant Theology: John Murray's and Meredith G. Kline's Response to the Historical Development of Federal Theology in Reformed Thought, rev. ed., pbk ver. (Lanham, MD: UPA, 2004), 111.

[197] Kenneth A. Matthews, The New American Commentary, vol. 1a, Genesis 1-11:26 (Nashville, TN: Broadman & Holman Publishers, 1996), 213.

[198] Sinclair B. Ferguson, "Image of God," in New Dictionary of Theology, ed. Sinclair B. Ferguson and David F. Wright (Downers Grove, IL: InterVarsity Press, 1988), 329.

Seventh, Genesis 5:1-3 and 9:6 indicate that the image of God was not lost because of sin's inception into humankind. This point will be elaborated below.

Eighth, Genesis 5:1-3 maintains that the image of God is transmitted to the descendants of Adam. The text states that Adam "had a son in his own likeness, in his own image" (Gen. 5:3). Because Seth inherited the image of God from Adam, then the entirety of humankind must also possess the divine image. However, this text can also be the source of speculation regarding the source of the soul and the image of God. Two main theories exist: Traducionism and Creationism. Traducionism holds that because God created humankind in his image, human beings share God's ability to create the soul as well as the physical body. However, Creationism maintains that God creates a new soul for each person and connects it to the physical body sometime between conception and birth.[199] Both views have strong biblical arguments.

Ninth, Genesis 9:1-6 mandates that death is required for the one who kills the bearer of the divine image, yet God allows man to kill animals who do not bear the image of God. Furthermore, to murder one who possesses the divine image is an attack on God himself. "Because man is God's representative, his life is sacred: every assault on man is an affront to the Creator and merits the ultimate penalty."[200]

Human Being's Original Upright Status

Several observations can be made to vouch for humankind's original upright status. First, God deemed all of creation good: "God saw all he had made, and behold, it was very good" (Gen. 1:31). Obviously, Adam belonged to the created order, therefore Adam was declared to be good by God. Second, the fact that humans were patterned after God indicated the original upright state in which humans were created. To be made like God is to be made good, sinless, and upright because these attributes mark God's character and nature. Third, the promised restoration of the image in mankind through Jesus Christ indicates that what was marred will be returned to its original state. If the restored state is good, then the original state is as well. Finally, Solomon also affirms humankind's original upright state: "Behold, I have found only this, that God made men upright, but they have sought out many devices" (Eccles. 7:29).

The Image: Marred and Distorted by Sin

Karl Barth maintains that man is basically good, since his created being comes from God. Barth describes sin as an "ontological impossibility." Barth holds this position because he believes that it is not presupposed in man's original freedom. It happens as something irrational and inexplicable and thereby distorts man's nature and humanity.[201] Genesis 5:1-3 and 9:6 fully affirm that man did not lose the divine image at

---

[199] Wayne Grudem, Systematic Theology: An Introduction to Biblical Doctrine (Grand Rapids, IL: Zondervan, 1994), 484.

[200] Wenham, Genesis, 32.

[201] Karl Barth, Church Dogmatics, Vol. 4, bk. 2, The Doctrine of Reconciliation (Edinburgh, England: T.&T. Clark, 1958), 441.

sin's inception into the world. Emil Brunner reflects the position of the Reformed tradition as he says, "By sin the nature of man, not merely something in his nature, is changed and perverted."[202]

Yet some do not believe that the former verses imply such a position. Their argument holds that after Adam sinned, he inherited a new nature which had no connection whatsoever to God, which was in turn transmitted to Seth. However, this interpretation is more the result of eisegesis than exegesis. Furthermore, those who hold this view on the image of God have a problem in Genesis 9:6, which does not allow for an alternate reading. Man and animals are prohibited from killing an image-bearer because human beings still bear the divine image.

If sin did not destroy the divine image in humanity, then how did it affect God's image? First, death entered into the human race (Gen. 3:19) and second, humans became a wholly inaccurate representation of God.[203] In the pre-fall existence, Adam and Eve had full access to the tree of life (Gen. 2:9, 16). After sin's introduction into the world humankind was cursed by God and thus would return to the dust from which humans were created. Not only did sin affect humankind's physical life, but sin also affected humanity's spiritual identity and moral fiber. Humankind ceased to perfectly represent God's holiness. Furthermore, by retaining the divine image in a sinful state the intensity of sin was greatly amplified. "The higher is our conception of man in his intrinsic essence, the greater must be the gravity of his offence in rebellion and enmity against God."[204] Because humankind represents God and yet also retains a fallen sinful nature, God's name is infinitely disgraced. Such is the grievance that couches the theology of the wrath of God that provides the context for developing a theology of penal substitution. One can conclude that the divine image in man was not lost. Instead, the divine image was marred and distorted by sin.

Renewal and Restoration of the Image Through Christ

Adam failed to uphold the divine image and finite members of Adam's line are totally unable to satisfy the infinite debt of sin. Therefore, a new Adam, Jesus Christ, was required to renew and restore the divine image in humankind. Only by the grace and mercy of God was this accomplished. Through Christ, the believer will be transformed and will begin to bear Christ's image (2 Cor. 3:18) who is the image of God (Col. 1:15a cf. 3:10). Following redemption in Christ, the believer will experience a progressive change in relationship with God (vertical) that will also affect relationships with others (horizontal). Gradually the Christian will be "renewed in knowledge according to the image of its creator" (Col. 3:10). In this life the believer will grow, manifesting a greater likeness to Christ, and therefore also to God himself. However, the full measure of the believer's creation in the image of God is not seen in the life of Adam who sinned, nor is it fully seen in the believer's current life, for each awaits the

---

[202] Emil Brunner, *Man in Revolt* (New York, NY: Scribner's Press, 1939), 137.

[203] Nichols, "Doctrine of Man," Lecture 7, 13.

[204] John Murray, *Systematic Theology*, vol. 2, *Collected Writings of John Murray* (repr., London, England: Banner of Truth, 1991), 38.

redemption that is still to come. Instead, a future promise of total and complete restoration awaits the believer so that he will be like Christ (cf. Rom. 8:29; 1 Cor. 15:49; 1 John 3:2) and fully bear the image of God.

At the risk of sounding premature, there are a couple of remarks that also must be interjected here regarding the relational implications of the cross of Jesus, his glorious resurrection, and the ever so curious "Johannine Pentecost." For, the nature of justification lies at heart of the doctrine of penal substitution: human beings, image-bearers of God, the partners of YHWH, turned enemies, are now family again as the wrath of God is averted and love of God is fully extended. The work of Good Friday and Easter Sunday are what provide the context for which we can construct a relational paradigm that functions both vertically and horizontally. This opens the door and beckons us to consider the Person and Work of the Holy Spirit because he not only *informs* the horizontal relationships, but is himself the grounding, the energy, the active agent who applies the work of Christ–extending his peace in the ministry of reconciliation (2 Cor. 5:17-21). The reason why this is relevant to this discussion on the image of God is because a crucial key to understanding the work of the Holy Spirit in the wake of Easter Sunday is found in John 20:22. With the creation narrative in mind, consider as John writes, "And when he [Jesus] had said this, he breathed on them and said to them, "Receive the Holy Spirit." Though there have been numerous attempts at developing two different Pentecost accounts, sound exegesis coupled with reading the Bible in light of the larger metanarrative (creation, fall, redemption, and restoration), guards against such erroneous understandings of the "giving" of the Holy Spirit in this Easter breakfast passage. In the earthly incarnate ministry of Jesus, prior to Calvary, the life and activity of the Holy Spirit could not have been understood or experienced apart from the physical body of the Lord Jesus. Thus, the Holy Spirit upon Jesus had a profound impact only on those with whom he came in contact (physical proximity) as they experienced the Divine life of God in the flesh.[205]

Cornelius Bennema comments:

> Although Genesis 2:7 mention's God's "breath of life" as the human life-principle, elsewhere Spirit is synonymous with breath in this sense of "life" (cf. Gen. 7:15 and 7:22; see also Job 27:3, 33:4; Isa. 42:5; Wis. 2:2-3). Thus, the insufflation of divine Spirit in [John] 20:22 evokes the creation story in Genesis 2:7 (cf. Wis. 15:11) and the recreation envisaged in Ezekiel 37:9. These verbal allusions virtually assure that 20:22 depicts Jesus re-creating the disciples by imparting the life-giving Spirit. This interpretation fits in well with John's presentation of the Spirit in relation to life thus far (3:34; 4:10-14; 6:63; 7:38-39).[206]

Don Carson agrees with this interpretation as he says,

> [O]ne of the reasons why [John] 20:22-23, difficult as they are, are best *not* taken as the Johannine Pentecost, *for nothing dramatically changes in their wake* – not in the

---

[205] Cornelis Bennema, 'The Giving of the Spirit in John 19-20: Another Round," in *The Spirit and Christ,* ed. I. H. Marshall, V. Rabens, and C. Bennema, 97.
[206] Bennema, "Spirit." 95.

remaining verses of chapter 20, and certainly not in chapter 21. It seems much wiser to take 20:22-23 as a symbol-laden anticipation of what is still to come in the gift of the Spirit, rather than as the actual outpouring of the Spirit.[207]

The glorious, loving, Triune, interperichoretic, communal, relational God made human beings in his sacred image. He graciously imparts communicable attributes to those graced with life elevated above and beyond those belonging to realms of plant or animal. God is depicted as a master craftsman who carefully handcrafts the human pair, engages with the intimacy of a kiss by breathing into the nostrils the breath of life, causing Adam (and all to follow) to become "a living being" (Gen. 2:7). This closeness, familiarity, loving-*shalom* experienced between the Creator and the couple reflect the nature and character of the Godhead. In John 20, what we find is Jesus reenacting the creation account, having destroyed the work of the serpent through his death and resurrection, he breathes on the disciples, creating living beings, new creations, in harmony with God and one another through the person and work of the Holy Spirit.

---

[207] Don Carson, 'Is Faith in Christ Without Evidence Superior Faith?" in *The Spirit and Christ,* ed. I. H. Marshall, V. Rabens, and C. Bennema, 112-13.

CHAPTER 4

THEOLOGICAL FOUNDATION FOR PSA

Introduction

After examining some of the Biblical and historical support for PSA, it is now appropriate to direct attention towards the *theological* implications of this doctrine. This chapter addresses some of the Biblical terminology employed as the writers seek to communicate the penal understanding of Christ's death. In particular, attention will be given to the notions of *expiation* and *propitiation,* despite the fact that other *forensic* terms employed by the NT writers equally deserve special attention.

The doctrine of God and the cross event are inextricably related. What one says about the cross indicates what one believes about the very character of God. In recent days it has become increasingly popular to question the character of God in light of the penal view of the death of Jesus. As has been demonstrated, both Old and New Testaments declare God to be one who administers grace,[208] justice,[209] and righteousness.[210] How these terms are interpreted, however, lead to various conclusions.

Gunton/Schleiermacher and Dodd/Morris

Schleiermacher sought to employ a Kantian method towards interpreting the meaning of the cross, seeking to construct a more rationalistic articulation of the doctrine of PSA. This was achieved primarily in terms of *experience* as opposed to a more objective interpretation of the cross, i.e., through a "forensic" lens. Schleiermacher held to a more exemplarist[211] interpretation of the suffering of Jesus. He argues that Jesus did not necessarily alter mankind's position before God forensically but rather humankind identifies with "the climax of his suffering ... sympathy with misery."[212] In summarizing Schleiermacher's position, Gunton says that "it is taken to mean not that

---

[208] Goldingay, *BCOTWP,* vol. 2, *Psalms 42-89,* ed. T. Longman III, 622-23. Goldingay suggests that YHWH does not merely forgive at whim, rather, he forgives due to his nature. See also, Thomas Abbott, *The Epistles to the Ephesians and to the Colossians: A Critical and Exegetical Commentary* (Edinburgh, England: T&T Clark, 1979), 50-51. Cf. Harold Hoehner, *Ephesians: An Exegetical Commentary* (Grand Rapids, MI: Baker Academic, 2002), 340-41.

[209] Tigay, Deuteronomy, 108. Hoehner, *Ephesians,* 337, Moo, *Romans,* 241.

[210] Sara Japhet, *I & II Chronicles: A Commentary* (London, England: SCM Press, 1993), 680. Cf. Charles Kingsley Barrett, *Black's New Testament Commentary: A Commentary on the Epistle to the Romans* (1957; repr., New York, NY: Harper, 1991), 159.

[211] See also Socinius' attack upon PSA in Faustus Socinus, *De Iesu Christo Servatore,* in *Opera Omnia,* vols. 1-2 *Bibliotheca Fratrum Polonorum Quos Unitarios Vocant* (Irenopoli: post, 1656), 2.115-246 as referenced in Jeffery, Ovey, and Sach, *Pierced,* fn. 3.

[212] Friedrich Schleiermacher, *The Christian Faith* trans. H. Mackintosh and J. Stewart (Edinburgh, England: T&T Clark, 1976), 436 (cf. Moral Influence Theory).

God is to be conceived as judge of human sin, but that outside the person-forming influence of the redeemer we experience sin as punishment."[213] Following this, Gunton rightly asks,

> Does the language of law, punishment, and penalty provide a suitable vocabulary in which to speak of the relationship between God and his people? To abandon it would be to lose not only a central theme of Biblical witness – beginning with Paul's great treatise in Romans – but also much of what the Christian tradition has made of it.[214]

Dodd interprets the wrath of God as being one in which humankind is allowed to go its chosen path into sinful lifestyles that end in destruction. Essentially, it is a cause and effect.[215] Thus, when looking particularly at Jesus' teaching "anger as an attitude of God to men disappears, and His love and mercy become all-embracing."[216] Morris responds to Dodd's claims by citing over twenty references in the gospels alone that express God's divine hostility to all evil.[217] Morris argues, "In the face of all this it is difficult to maintain that Jesus had discarded the conception of the wrath of God. For Him the divine reaction in the face of evil was a solemn and terrible reality."[218] Therefore, with these concepts in mind, it is now appropriate to examine some of the theological implications of PSA. First, we must turn our attention to the terms "expiation" and "propitiation."

Expiation and Propitiation

Hill has demonstrated that "the terms 'propitiation' and 'expiation' are so closely related that they are often regarded as *interchangeable* in religious contexts."[219] He

---

[213] Colin E. Gunton, *Actuality of Atonement: A Study of Metaphor, Rationality, and the Christian Tradition* (London, England: Bloomsbury Academic, 2003), 14. Schleiermacher's position raises questions because his approach is simply reductionistic as he changes key concepts into something else. Gunton notes that "this approach is a refusal to accept concepts, particularly those adjudged 'anthropomorphic,' for what they say and attempt to change them into something else. That is not to claim that some original meaning can be found and kept totally sacrosanct, immune from change. Language is not like that. But it is also true that there comes a time when the meaning is changed so much that a word is made to say something entirely different, so that the tradition is not interpreted but broken," 15.

[214] Gunton, *Actuality,* 15.

[215] Dodd, *Romans,* 23. See also Green and Baker, *Scandal,* 54.

[216] Dodd, *Romans,* 23.

[217] Morris, *Apostolic,* 181. Morris cites the following for support: Mark 3:5; Luke 21:23; Matt. 3:7; Luke 3:7; John 3:36; Matt. 5:22; 18:8; Mark 9:48; Luke 12:5; Matt. 11:20, 24; Matt. 23; Luke 13:3, 5; Mark 3:29; 14:21; Matt. 25:41, 46; Matt. 13:42, 50; 18:34; 21:44; 22:7, 13; Matt. 8:12; 24:51; 25:30; Luke 13:28.

[218] Morris, *Apostolic,* 181.

[219] David Hill, *Greek Words,* 23, italics mine.

adds his belief that "this is due also to the fact that there is no difference in the actions performed to bring about expiation or propitiation."[220]

Historically, controversy has continued about the meaning of the root *kipper*. The main division has been between those who advocate that it means "to cover" (Arab. *kaphara*) and those who claim that the original significance is "to wipe away" (Babyl. *kuppuru*).[221] Thus, when examining the lexical implications of *kipper*, one is at a loss when seeking to make a conclusion about the original meaning of the word. Therefore, the context in which the word is used ought to serve as the next key for unlocking the meaning of the word.[222]

The meaning "to cover" could refer to the covering of the face of the angry or wronged person (i.e., propitiation), and it could also suggest the covering of the sin, in the sense of making it without any additional consequences on the person who committed the fault or on the wronged party (i.e., expiation). However, if "to wipe away" is the original significance, this could refer to the removal of wrath (propitiation) or of the cause of wrath, the sin (expiation).[223]

For Dodd, the concept of Christ functioning as a penalty-bearer did not suit well.[224] Passages that specifically address the subject of propitiation are Romans 3:21-26,

---

[220] David Hill, *Greek Words*, 23. Also, in speaking of the close relationship between propitiation and expiation McIntyre states "the difference that I have in mind between 'expiation' and 'propitiation' can best be brought in the two verb forms, which show that we speak of 'propitiating God,' but of 'expiating our sins and their guilt.' These cases, in both of which we are speaking of the action of Christ on the cross, both therefore carry the connotation of great pain and suffering, and in that respect there is no distinction to be drawn between them. Perhaps, then, the outcome is to affirm the *necessity* [italics mine] of both 'propitiation' and 'expiation' in the shaping up of our soteriology, on the grounds that the two models are saying things that are different, and without either of which our doctrine would be less than complete." See John McIntyre, *The Shape of Soteriology: Studies in the Doctrine of the Death of Christ* (Edinburgh, England: T&T Clark, 1992), 39.

[221] David Hill, *Greek Words*, 23.

[222] James Barr, "Etymologies and Related Arguments," in *The Semantics of Biblical Language*, (London, England: Oxford University Press, 1961), 107-160. More discussed in regard to *hilasterion*.

[223] David Hill, *Greek Words*, 31.

[224] See also, Travis' statement: "Rather than saying that in his death Christ experienced retributive punishment on behalf of humanity, Paul says that he entered into and bore on our behalf the destructive consequences of sin. Standing where we stand, he bore the consequence of our alienation from God. In so doing he absorbed and exhausted them, so that they should not fall on us. ... He experienced divine judgment on sin in the sense that he endured the God-ordained consequences of human sinfulness. But this is not the same as to say that he bore our punishment." Travis, "Christ," 37. Yet, the question remains how can this statement be interpreted as anything other than a penalty bearing sacrifice? Furthermore, terms such as "absorbed" and "exhausted" are not found in biblical terminology in reference to Christ's death. See Henri Blocher, "Biblical Metaphors and the Doctrine of the Atonement," *JETS* 47, no. 4 (December 2004): 643. Elsewhere, Smail manipulates McIntyre's words in order to make him appear as though he is not in favor of PSA. He does this by only including part of what McIntyre says. It is true that McIntyre initially finds difficulty with the vicarious nature of the atonement.

Hebrews 2:17, 1 John 2:2, and 4:10. Dodd opted to translate ἱλαστήριον as meaning "purge," "forgive," or "expiate" in both Jewish Greek writings as well as the Septuagint. Therefore, according to Dodd, ἱλαστήριον should hold alternative meanings other than the idea of a wrath-bearing propitiatory sacrifice. Dodd believes that these alternative etymological understandings serve the word usage in Paul, Hebrews, and John in a more appropriate manner.[225] He wrote, "In accordance with biblical usage, therefore, the substantive (*hilasterion*) would mean not propitiation, but a 'means by which guilt is annulled'... Propitiation is misleading."[226] Furthermore, Dodd states that the "wrath" in Romans refers not to "a certain feeling or attitude of God towards us, but some process or effect in the realm of objective facts."[227]

However, Jeffery, Ovey, Sach, and Morris have offered sufficient evidence that counters both the Jewish Greek and the LXX arguments thoroughly[228] citing eleven passages that speak directly to the fact that the Jewish Greek historians as well as the LXX refer to ἱλαστήριον as primarily averting the wrath of God through a penalty being exacted as that which is plainly described in the context.[229] Propitiation is the gracious provision made by God himself, whereby the effects of his righteous anger against sin may be averted and the sinner may receive the blessings of his paternal love without infringement of his holiness and moral government.[230]

There is no reason to restrict the meaning of ἱλαστήριον to meaning *propitiation* exclusively.[231] Dodd was incorrect in his definition because he excluded propitiation, yet, he was correct in that *hilasterion* also carries with it the meaning of *expiation*. Buschel wrote that "*hilasmos* ... is the action in which God is propitiated and sin

---

For he says that "the biblical status of the idea of punishment is not immediately self-evident. For example, I cannot find New Testament statements which outrightly affirm that the death of Christ was a punishment visited upon Jesus rather than upon the mass of sinful mankind." This is where Smail stops quoting. See Smail, *Once*, 93. If one reads on, he or she will discover that McIntyre says, "However, it is not difficult to see how, if several texts are taken together, the death of Christ may be so described. For example, we have all along made the claim that Isaiah 52:13-53:12 has a central place in the understanding of the death of Christ, not least because it seems to have been very influential in Jesus' self-understanding; e.g., 53:5. 'He was wounded for our transgressions, he was bruised for our iniquities' could scarcely be more explicit on the punitive nature of the death of the Suffering Servant." See McIntyre, *Shape of Soteriology*, 45.

[225] Dodd, "Hilaskesthai," 352-360. See also Dodd, *Romans*, 54-55; C. H. Dodd, *The Moffatt New Testament Commentary*, vol. 16, *The Johannine Epistles* (London, England: Hodder & Stoughton, 1946), 25-26.

[226] Dodd, *Romans*, 55. See also Barrett, *Romans*, 77.

[227] Dodd, *Romans*, 22.

[228] See Jeffery, Ovey and Sach, *Pierced*, 82-3. Morris, *Apostolic*, 155-174; Leon Morris, "The use of *Hilaskethai* etc. in Biblical Greek," *Expository Times* 62, no. 8 (May 1951): 233; Roger Nicole, "C. H. Dodd and the Doctrine of Propitiation," *WTJ* 17, no. 2 (May 1955): 117-57.

[229] B.J. 5.385, Ant. 6.124; 8.112; 10.59; 1 Clem. 7:7; Herm. 2:1; Ex. 32.:4; cf. vv.11-12; Num. 16:46; cf. v. 47; 25:13; cf. v. 11; Lam. 3:42; cf. v. 43; 2 Kgs. 24:4; cf. 23:26; 22:20; Ps. 78:38; cf. v. 31 in Jeffrey, Ovey, and Sach, *Pierced*, as well as Morris, *Apostolic*, 157-158; Roger Nicole, "Dodd", 359.

[230] Roger Nicole, "Propitiation," *Christianity Today,* April 15, 1957, 8.

[231] Thomas Schreiner, *BECNT: Romans* (Grand Rapids, MI: Baker Books, 1998), 192.

expiated."[232] Smail favors the term "reconciliation" over terms like propitiation and expiation. The reason that he is unsatisfied with a term like expiation is that he understands it as being much more disconnected and "impersonal" – sacrificial language.[233] However, expiation itself is a legal term nevertheless it is *bound up with personal and relational implications.* Thus, in speaking of humankind's relation to God, Lincoln used the phrase "from wrath to justification" in order to describe the first section of Romans.[234]

Yet, the question remains, "How does an unjust person become justified?" Paul answers this question using PSA as part of his foundation. Mody states that "this is a justification that is dependent on *penal* substitution, the solution that deals with the problem of wrath."[235] In the case of Romans 3:21-26, one must look to the context, lending special attention to the previous sections that specifically address the fallen condition of humankind, and the wrath of God. For in Romans 1-3, Paul demonstrates the impending *wrath* of God and this is what forms the backdrop as he prepares to explain the *penalty bearing* work of the cross that brings about justification.[236] Carson states that "the flow of argument that takes us from Romans 1:18-32 to Romans 3:9-20 leaves us no escape: individually and collectively, Jew and Gentile alike, we stand under the just wrath of God, because of our sin."[237]

Furthermore, Paul states that this ἱλαστήριον comes through the "blood" of Jesus. Although the death of Christ encompasses a number of metaphors and accomplishes many things, it is impossible to separate it from also averting the wrath of God. For, Romans 5:9 states clearly "Since, therefore, we now have been justified by his blood, much more shall we be saved by him from the wrath of God."[238] After noting the use of

---

[232] Fredrick Buschel, *"Hilaskomai,"* in *Theological Dictionary of the New Testament,* vol. 3, (Grand Rapids, MI: Eerdmans, 1965), 317.

[233] Smail, *Once,* 90.

[234] A. T. Lincoln, "From Wrath to Justification," in *Pauline Theology,* vol. 3, *Romans,* ed. David Hay and Elizabeth Johnson (Minneapolis, MN: Fortress, 1995), 130-59.

[235] Rohintan Mody, "Penal Substitutionary Atonement in Paul: An Exegetical Study of Romans 3:25-26," in *The Atonement Debate,* ed. D. Tidball, D. Hilborn, and J. Thacker, 115-135, emphasis mine.

[236] Don Carson, "Atonement in Romans 3:21-26: God Presented Him as a Propitiation," in *The Glory of the Atonement,* ed. C. Hill and F. James III, 120. Moo states that wrath and anger "remind us that the judgment [of God] is the reaction of a personal God to the violation of his just order." See Moo, *Romans,* 137.

[237] Carson, "Atonement," 120.

[238] Forsyth states that "God's feeling toward us never needed to be changed. But God's treatment of us, God's practical relation to us – that had to change." See P. T Forsyth, *The Work of Christ* (London, England: Hodder & Stoughton, 1910), 105. Following this statement, Stott says that "It is God himself who in holy wrath needs to be propitiated, God himself who in holy love undertook to do the propitiating, and God himself who in the person of his Son died for the propitiation of our sins. Thus God took his own loving initiative to appease his own righteous anger by bearing it his own self in his own Son when he took our place and died for us." See John Stott, *The Cross of Christ,* (Leicester, England: IVP, 1989), 175. Cranfield agrees and says that "God purposed Christ as a propitiatory victim [which] means that God, because in His mercy He willed to forgive sinful

hilasterion in both secular and Biblical Greek as well as amongst apocryphal and intertestamental literature it is appropriate to be reminded of N. T. Wright's statement, "Paul's context here demands that the word *hilasterion* not only retains its sacrificial overtones (the place and means of atonement), but that it carries with it the note of propitiation of divine wrath – with of course, the corollary that sins are expiated."[239]

Forensics

One focus of this work beckons the question, "what does PSA say about God?" Many Evangelical scholars state that having a God who gets angry simply is incompatible with Scripture.[240] Throughout the past 100 years numerous objections have been raised regarding the retributive nature of God. For example, in 1910, Forsyth stated that the concept of God punishing Jesus is completely unacceptable. He says, "Well, it cannot be true in the sense that God punished Christ. That is absolutely an unthinkable thing. How could God punish Him in whom He was always well pleased? The two things are a contradiction in terms."[241]

More recent scholars such as Northey, Smail, and N. T. Wright strongly object to the courtroom-like treatment of the atonement. Northey rejects the idea of God being a Judge stating that "just desserts and punishments became the primary thrust of law in the course of Christian thinking *rather than* an understanding of a call to forgiveness and repentance."[242] Furthermore, he states that in his own lectures he asks his classes "How many times did Jesus call God 'Judge' in the Gospels? The answer is *never*."[243] Yet, Northey pays no attention to John 8:15-16, 50, 12:48 in which Jesus refers to God as *Judge*. Smail responds to the penal nature of the atonement by asking the question, "By what right or justice can punishment be imposed on anybody except the person who has committed the offense? Is the bearing of punishment *not* one of those things that cannot be done by one person for another...?"[244]

---

man, and being truly merciful, willed to forgive them righteously, that is, without in any way condoning their sin, purposed to direct against His own very self in the person of His Son the full weight of that righteous wrath which that deserved." See C. E. Cranfield, *A Critical and Exegetical Commentary,* 2 vols., *The Epistle to the Romans,* International Critical Commentary Series (Edinburgh, England: T&T Clark, 1979), 1:217.

[239] N. T. Wright, The New Interpreter's Bible, vol. 10, The Letter to the Romans: Introduction, Commentary, and Reflections (Nashville, TN: Abingdon, 2002), 476.

[240] Green and Baker, *Scandal,* 32; Brown and Bohn, "For God So Loved the World," 1-30; Smail, "One Man," 73-93; Colin Greene, "Is the Message of the Cross Good News for the Twentieth Century?" in *Atonement Today,* ed. J. Goldingay, 222-39; Chalke and Mann, *Lost,* 182; Forsyth, *Work,* 146.

[241] Forsyth, *Work,* 146.

[242] Wayne Northey, "The Cross: God's Peace Work Towards A Restorative Peace Making Understanding of the Atonement," in *Stricken by God?* ed. B. Jersak and M. Hardin, 357, italics mine.

[243] Northey, 358.

[244] Smail, "One Man," 85, italics mine.

Following this, Smail argues that even though one may be guilty of a crime and another is willing to suffer in another's place, it is simply incoherent for a judge to consent, arguing that "it would be an unjust judge that would permit let alone organize such an illegitimate transfer."[245] Smail does not account for the fact that the doctrine of penal substitution does not propose a transfer of guilt between *unrelated* persons. Rather it asserts that guilt is transferred to Christ from those who are united to him.[246]

Wright also objects to the forensic conclusions reached by penal advocates. By using the Hebrew law court as the rubric under which one must interpret the term "forensic" Wright states that in such a court of law,

> The judge does not give, bestow, impute, or impart his own "righteousness" to the defendant. That would imply that the defendant was deemed to have conducted the case impartially, in accordance with the law, to have punished sin and upheld the defenseless innocent ones. "Justification," of course, means nothing like that. "Righteousness" is not a quality or substance that can thus be passed or transferred from the judge to the defendant.[247]

Yet, Carson keenly presents some convincing rebuttals to these objections,[248] demonstrating that trying to force God into a contemporary or Hebrew court scenario is going to lead to misconstrued conclusions. An earthly judge and God the Judge are two completely different entities. The earthly judge functions simply as an administrator of the law, upholding justice according to the laws of the land. This earthly judge is bound by the state to act in such a manner. Yet, when God is the Judge, one must keep in mind Psalm 51:4, the fact that God is not merely a person abiding by a law, rather, it is God, who has been sinned against. The law processed from his own being. "Righteous Judge he doubtless is, but never distanced or dispassionate judge serving a system greater than he is."[249]

---

[245] Smail, "One Man," 85.

[246] Jeffery, Ovey, and Sach, *Pierced,* 243.

[247] N. T. Wright, "Romans and the Theology of Paul," in *Pauline Theology,* vol. 3, *Romans,* ed. David M. Hay and E. Elizabeth Johnson (Minneapolis, MN: Fortress Press, 1995), 39.

[248] Carson, "Atonement," 132-35.

[249] Carson, "Atonement," 133. Jesus' incarnation "is associated with sin (Rom. 8:3; 2 Cor. 5:21; Col. 1:14; 1 Tim. 1:15; Titus 2:14) ... apart from sin and its consequences, Paul sees no place for the person and activity of the incarnate Christ whom, uniquely, 'all the fullness of the Deity lives in bodily form' (Col. 2:9 cf. Rom. 9:5)." See Richard B. Gaffin Jr., "Atonement in the Pauline Corpus: 'The Scandal of the Cross,'" in *The Glory of the Atonement,* ed. C. E. Hill and F. A. James III (Downers Grove, IL: IVP; Leicester, England: Apollos, 2004), 145. Moltmann states that "A God who cannot suffer is poorer than any human. For a God who is incapable of suffering is a being who cannot be involved. Suffering and injustice do not affect him. And because he is so completely insensitive, he cannot be affected or shaken by anything. He cannot weep, for he has no tears. But the one who cannot suffer cannot love either. So he is also a loveless being." See Jürgen Moltmann, *The Crucified God: The Cross of Christ as the Foundation and Criticism of Christian Theology,* trans. John Bowden and R. A. Wilson (Minneapolis, MN: Augsburg Fortress Publishing, 1993), 222.

Indeed Romans 2:5-10; 3:19; 5:9 testifies of a wrathful judgment, that brings about penalties to be borne by sinful people who do not repent. This wrath is the just retribution for sin. Carson says that because he is love, God provides a redemption that simultaneously wipes out the sin of those who offend and keeps his own "justice" intact.[250] Peterson says, "A properly formulated view of penal substitution will speak of retribution being experienced by Christ because that is our due. Moreover, the penalty inflicted by God's justice and holiness is also a penalty inflicted by God's love and mercy, for salvation and new life.[251]

The NT continually references the death of Jesus as being "for us" (Rom. 5:8; Gal. 3:13; Eph. 5:2; 1 Thess. 5:10; Titus 2:14; 1 John 3:16).[252] This means that the death of Jesus is in the place of us. If God were to merely acquit sinners and neglect his justice altogether, he himself would be a liar for he promised to punish sin (Gen. 2:17). Penal advocates continually make the connection between the Suffering Servant of Isaiah 53 and passages like Romans 5:21 and 2 Corinthians 5:21. For, "God made [Christ] who had no sin to be sin for us" (2 Cor. 5:21).[253] Humankind can be saved and reconciled to God not because God refuses to address sin. Rather, humankind can be redeemed because the penalty has been paid, the *just* suffered *for* the *unjust.*[254] Therefore, it is God himself, who is the Judge, who has been sinned against, who sends his Son who bears the penalty (as sinless) in order that God may be both just and the justifier (Rom. 3:26).

Recalling Stott's statement noted above regarding "God taking his own loving initiative to appease his own righteous anger by bearing it in his own self in his own Son when he took our place and died for us,"[255] Smail argues that this is "contradictory." That is, the wrath of God and the love of God are a "juxtaposition." He holds that "it seems to suggest that the atonement is concerned with a manipulation of conflicting internal attributes of the divine nature in order to enable him to forgive and accept us."[256] Also, it is worth noting Green and Baker's statement, "Old Testament scholars today continue to debate in what sense it is appropriate to attribute anger to God in any other way than metaphorical ... perhaps we attribute 'anger' to God only because we have no language other than human language with which to comprehend God."[257]

---

[250] Carson, "Atonement," 133.

[251] David Peterson, "Atonement in the New Testament," in *Where Wrath and Mercy Meet: Proclaiming the Atonement Today* (Carlisle, PA: Paternoster, 2001), 38. Peterson states, "If our guilt was not transferred to him and he did not bear our penalty, we are destined to endless alienation from God and enslavement to our own fallen natures." See also Lewis and Demarest, *Integrative*, 404.

[252] Verses such as these emphasize the *substitutionary* nature of the atonement. However, some could object by noting that *substitution* and *penalty* are not the same thing.

[253] Carson notes that "even if one decides to render this 'sin' by the paraphrastic 'sin offering,' the ideal of penal substitution remains inescapable," Carson, "Atonement," 134. Also see R. Gaffin, "Scandal," 140-163.

[254] Carson, "Atonement," 134.

[255] Stott, *Cross*, 175.

[256] Smail, *Once*, 87.

[257] Green and Baker, *Scandal*, 53-54.

Returning to Smail's objection, Smail seems to think that having *both* divine love and divine wrath within the same being is nothing short of schizophrenia.[258] This is a grave distortion. For "God's attributes cannot be pitted against one another."[259] One must be reminded that although Smail may see a "contradiction" in terminology, these *are* the terms in which God is revealed in Scripture and the Scriptures testify that God desires mankind to understand him (2 Tim. 3:16; 1 Pet. 1:20-21).[260]

In seeking to articulate a penal understanding of the atonement, one must not be so naive as to pick and choose what one will believe about God from the Bible. Smail is offering a pre-selected view of the God of the Bible. Alongside Chalke and Mann, Smail is wearing the suggested "lenses" of God's love as he interprets the atonement, therefore he is guilty of choosing to interpret God as *exclusively* a God of love and not a God who is wrathful and exercises his right to punish as well. The theological implications of this hermeneutical method lead to a distorted view of God.

It must be recognized that God is undoubtedly recorded as loving.[261] Yet, the penal understanding of the cross offers a God who is not only benevolent, he is also a God who honors his word by maintaining justice.[262] Furthermore, God's character would be compromised were he to resign from being just. For, "his character ... might have been viewed with suspicion had sinners ... been permitted to slip by without facing the full

---

[258] Smail, *Once,* 87.

[259] Jeffery, Ovey, and Sach, *Pierced,* 293. McCurdy insists that "we must be careful not to draw easy parallels between human and divine personalities." See Leslie McCurdy *Attributes and Atonement: The Holy Love of God in the Theology of P. T. Forsyth* (Carlisle, PA: Paternoster, 1999),116. Furthermore, Forsyth states that "In all of us the personality is incomplete; and it misleads us in the most grave way when we use it as an analogy for the ever complete and holy personality of God." See Forsyth, *Positive Preaching and the Modern Mind* (London, England: Hodder & Stoughton, 1909), 262. The kaleidoscopic model will seek to provide some clarity here.

[260] Jeffery, Ovey, and Sach, *Pierced,* 290.

[261] "God demonstrates his own love for us in this: While we were still sinners, Christ died for us" (Rom. 5.8); "This is love: not that we loved God, but that he loved us and sent his Son as an atoning sacrifice for our sins" (1 John 4:10).

[262] Jeffery, Ovey, and Sach, *Pierced,* 293. "Because God takes Himself, His love infinitely seriously, and in so doing also takes man infinitely seriously, He cannot do otherwise than be angry although 'really' He is only Love. His wrath is simply the result of the infinitely serious love of God." See Emil Brunner, *The Mediator,* 170. Luther claims that God's wrath is his *opus alienum* ("strange work"). Luther calls God's wrath "strange" "because it does not spring from the essential will of God, but because it is forced upon Him by the sinful resistance of man." See Luther, *W.A.,* 42:356, found in Emil Brunner, *Dogmatics I: The Christian Name of God,* trans. Olive Wyon (Cambridge, England: James Clarke Company Limited n.d.). Cf. Green and Baker, *Scandal,* 54, where they state, "perhaps we attribute 'anger' to God only because we have no language other than human language with which to comprehend God." See also Gary Heiron, "Wrath of God (OT)," in *Anchor Bible Dictionary,* vol. 6, edited by David Noel Freedman (New York, NY: Doubleday, 1992), 989-996.

severity of condemnation for sin."[263] This information thus far all testifies to a consistent and holistic view of God, namely that God is demonstrating both grace and justice in PSA and thus His character is consistent.

Child Abuse

A key spokesperson on child abuse, Alice Miller, states that victims of child abuse experience feelings of "anger, helplessness, despair, longing, anxiety, and pain."[264] Furthermore, they find themselves giving expression to the feelings "in destructive acts against others (criminal behavior, mass murder) or against themselves (drug addiction, alcoholism, prostitution, psychic disorders, suicide)."[265] These are the natural repercussions for child abuse. If one removes the *cooperation* within the Trinity, the *necessity* that sin must be punished, and Jesus' *own will* transpiring in being the penal substitute (John 19, etc.) and so forth, then Jesus *really is* a victim, of cosmic child abuse. And because of his humanity, it would be (theo)logically consistent for the reader to expect this type of behavior (or at least tendencies) in his life. However, this is not remotely close to the Biblical account.

One more instance of the questioning of the character of God will be addressed here. In recent years, the term "cosmic child abuse" has become quite popular amongst feminists, activists, and scholars alike. Pattison suggests that some theologians would encourage victims of child abuse to look to Jesus, the passive, suffering Son for encouragement and strength and to forgo their own personal suffering.[266]

Chalke and Mann's recent publication of *The Lost Message of Jesus* captures the essence of the issue at hand. They state, "How ... have we come to believe that at the cross this God of love suddenly decides to vent his anger and wrath on his own Son? The fact is that the cross isn't a form of cosmic child abuse – a vengeful Father, punishing his Son for an offense he has not even committed."[267]

Author and activist Brian McLaren writes of a fictional character named Kerry who also states regarding the punishment of one innocent person in order to bring about peace that it "sounds like one more injustice in the cosmic equation. It sounds like divine child abuse."[268] Compounding this thought is Brown and Parker's statement mentioned in the introduction,

---

263 Carson, "Atonement," 138. Carson also states, "for Paul, justification is bound up not only with the vindication of sinners, but even more profoundly with the vindication of God." "Atonement," 138. Also See Seifrid, *Christ,* 64. See also, Moo, *Romans,* 240.

264 Alice Miller, *The Untouched Key: Tracing Childhood Trauma in Creativity and Destructiveness,* trans. Hildegarde and Hunter Hannum (London, England: Virago Press, 1990), 165.

265 Miller, *Untouched,* 165.

266 Stephen Pattison, "'Suffer the Little Children': The Challenge of Child Abuse and Neglect to Theology," *TCJCSTS (Theology and Sexuality)* 4, no. 9 (September 1998), 58.

267 Chalke and Mann, *Lost,* 182. Jeffery, Ovey, and Sach also point out that "Joel Green and Mark Baker also claim that penal substitution 'has been construed' in this way." See Green and Baker, *Scandal,* 32, Jeffery, Ovey, and Sach, *Pierced,* 229.

268 Brian McLaren, *The Story We Find Ourselves in: Further Adventures of a New Kind of Christian* (San Francisco, CA: Jossey-Bass, 2003),102. Carson responds that "the objections are never

Is it any wonder that there is so much abuse in the modern society when the predominant image of the culture is of "divine child abuse" – God the Father demanding and carrying out the suffering death of his own son? If Christianity is to be liberating for the oppressed, it must itself be liberated from this theology. We must do away with the atonement, this idea of a blood sin upon the whole human race which can be washed away only by the blood of the lamb.[269]

Dale reminds us that Jesus is not merely a man suffering an unjust punishment. Rather, "Dale stresses that the divinity of Christ is at the heart of the matter."[270]

In recalling the theology of R. W. Dale, Gunton is impressed with his careful attention to a detail that is often overlooked, namely, Christ as Judge.[271] Gunton summarizes Dale's position by stating that "it is the divine judge who undergoes judgment, not a human substitute who bears a penalty equivalent to that which others have merited"[272] This paved the path for Barth's declaration that "The Judge Judged in our place."[273]

Lastly, it is worth noting Greene's statement regarding the *penal* understanding of the cross. He says that it depicts Christ as "the whipping-boy who appeases the wrath of God."[274]

These representations, however, do not present a holistic understanding of the vicarious work of the cross and there are many who have risen to address the fallacies of this language. Chalke and Mann depict God as *"suddenly"* choosing "to vent his anger." This accusation raises two issues: First, it presents God as though he had never been angry before and that his anger is exactly like human anger. Secondly, this accusation presents us with a God who is acting impulsively in a fit of explosive, uncontrolled rage, something that even fallen humans will not excuse amongst themselves, let alone God. Yet, as has been demonstrated throughout the Scripture, God does get angry towards

---

answered and are elsewhere voiced by McLaren himself, who makes no attempt either to show how those who support substitutionary atonement would answer such objections or to examine the extent to which substitutionary atonement is taught in Scripture." See Don Carson, *Becoming Conversant with the Emerging Church: Understanding a Movement and Its Implications* (Grand Rapids, MI: Zondervan, 2005), 166.

[269] Brown and Parker, quoted from the "Introduction" of McLaren, *The Story*, 26.

[270] Cited by Colin Gunton, *Theology Through the Theologians: Selected Essays 1972-1995.* London, England: Bloomsbury Academic, 2003), 177.

[271] Gunton, *Theology*, 177. Dale recalls Matt. 25:34, 41; John 5:22; Acts 10:42, 17:31; 2 Cor. 5:10 to support this position. He declares, *"the penalties of sin are to be inflicted by Christ."* R. W. Dale, *The Atonement* (London, England: Congregational Union of England and Wales, 1896), 362.

[272] Gunton, *Theology*, 179.

[273] Karl Barth, *Church Dogmatics: The Doctrine of Reconciliation,* vol. 4, trans. G. W. Bromiley (Peabody, MA: Hendrickson Publishers, 2010), vol. 4 bk. 1: 59.2.

[274] Colin Greene, "Message of the Cross,'" in *Atonement Today* ed. J. Goldingay, 232.

sin according to his justice.[275] "God's wrath is an integral constituent of his love. The wrath of God is the active manifestation of God's essential incapacity to be morally indifferent and let sin alone. It denotes the attitude of God in his love toward willful sin."[276]

Jeffery, Ovey, and Sach have reminded us that Jesus suffered this death willingly, that he was in control of it (John10:17-18), that "Jesus died to bring glory to himself (John17:1; Phil. 2:8-9; Heb. 2:9; Rev. 5:12) and to save his people (Rom. 5:8; 1 Cor. 15:3; 1 Tim. 2:6; 1 Pet. 3:18), as well as to glorify his Father. By contrast, child abuse is carried out solely for the gratification of the abuser.[277]

Williams has shown that there is a problem with the child abuse criticism in that although Jesus was a son, he was not a *minor*. Rather, "as an adult, Jesus had a mature will and could choose whether to cooperate with his Father."[278]

In addition, Thiselton points to the "integrity" of the work of the Father and Son in the crucifixion.[279] For, Jesus himself says in the Synoptic gospels that "The Son of Man *must* (δεῖ) suffer much" (Mark 8:31; Luke 9:22); "It was necessary (δεῖ) for Christ to suffer" (Acts 17:3). However, Thiselton rightly notes that it is not as though God *has* to do anything, i.e., respond to external compulsion. Rather, the statement,

> "God must ..." or "Jesus must ..." is always to be explained in terms of a conditional clause: "If God wills to be true to his promise and has committed himself already to follow this course of action." If Jesus wills to live out the role assigned to him by his Father and to embody the suffering-vindication pattern of the Scriptures, his only course is to go all the way to the cross.[280]

Furthermore, Thiselton writes this with Anselm's statement regarding the internal logic of God in mind. Anselm says, "We shall attribute to God nothing that is at all

---

[275] Also, Jeffery, Ovey, and Sach state that "it is useful to highlight the instances where Jesus or the apostles explicitly refer to a specific Old Testament text in relations to Jesus' death. This list would include Matt. 27:46, Mark 15:34 (Ps. 22.1); John 13:18 (Ps. 41:9, 55:12-15); John 19:28-29 (Pss. 22:15, 69:21); John 19.32-37 (Exod. 12:46, Ps. 22:16, Zech. 12:10); Acts 1:16-20 (Pss. 69.25, 109:8-15); 1 Pet. 2:22-25 (Isa. 53:3-9); Heb. 2:14, 1 John 3:8 (Gen. 3:15). See Jeffery, Ovey, and Sach, *Pierced*, 232.

[276] R. Culpepper, *Interpreting the Atonement* (Grand Rapids, MI: Eerdmans, 1966),133. "God's wrath is God's grace. It is his grace smitten with dreadful sorrow. It is his love in agony." See James Stewart, *A Man in Christ: The Vital Elements of St. Paul's Religion* (New York, NY: Harper & Row, 1938), 22.

[277] Jeffery, Ovey, and Sach, *Pierced*, 230.

[278] Gary Williams, "Penal Substitution: A Response to Recent Criticisms," in *The Atonement Debate*, ed. D. Tidball, D. Hilborn, and J. Thacker, 185.

[279] Thiselton, *Doctrine*, 346.

[280] Thiselton, *Doctrine*, 346-47, contra Luther. See P. Stuhlmacher, *Gerechtigkeit Gottes bei Paulus* (Gottingen, Germany: Vandenhoeck und Ruprecht, 1965), 19-23, and Gordon Rupp, *The Righteousness of God: Luther Studies* (London, England: Hodder & Stoughton, 1953), 225, 255.

unfitting ... nothing that is in the least degree unseemly can be acknowledged in God."[281] Because of God's nature and divine government, the necessity of punishment abounds and therefore God *must* be faithful to himself.[282] Tidball offers a summation of Anselm's *Cur Deus Homo* by way of saying, "Only if God takes the initiative and fundamentally changes the basis for our relating to him can we be secure."[283]

Marshall agrees with Jeffery, Ovey and Sach that the label "child abuse" "is misleading, disturbing – even blasphemous – and should be abandoned."[284] Indeed one must recall that the work of the cross-event is a communal, Trinitarian action.[285] Williams agrees stating that "the Father wills to send the Son, and the Son wills to go. There is no injustice here, because the purpose is good and both parties are willing."[286] Furthermore, "it was God who initiated the cross, it was God himself who suffered on the cross and bore the sin of the world."[287] Describing PSA as child abuse is simply unwarranted.

Rather than finding ground for condemning the character of God due to the nature of PSA, Marshall finds this ground to praise God's action in Christ. He declares, "A parent who puts herself into the breach and dies to save her child from a burning house is considered praiseworthy. The God who suffers and dies in the person of Jesus for human sin belongs in the same category."[288]

Marshall does not seek to present this as something that is simple to be grasped. Rather, he states clearly that "it is true that the concept of God the Son suffering and dying is paradoxical and incomprehensible, and we have to recognize that fact, but it is what Scripture says. It is part of the mystery of the incarnation."[289] The only way for these criticisms to stand is to "remove the necessity"[290] of God's response to sin. If God is not faithful to himself (integrity) then "the suffering of the Son is unjustifiable."[291] If God is without anger, we would be indifferent towards his love; without his wrath

---

281 Thiselton, *Doctrine,* 361-62. Citing Anselm, *Cur Deus Homo: Why God Became Man* (Pickerington, OH: Beloved Publishing, 2014), I, 10, 118.

282 Williams, "Penal," 187. Contra Green and Baker: "Within a penal substitution model, God's ability to love and relate to humans is circumscribed by something outside of God – that is, an abstract concept of justice instructs God as to how God must behave." See Green and Baker, *Scandal,* 147.

283 Derek Tidball, "Penal Substitution: A Pastoral Apologetic," in *The Atonement Debate,* ed. D. Tidball, D. Hilborn, and J. Thacker, 333-34.

284 Jeffery, Ovey, and Sach, *Pierced,* 230.

285 Marshall, *Aspects,* 62; Stott, *Cross,* 175; Thiselton, *Doctrine,* 345.

286 Williams, "Penal," 187. Contra Smail who declares this to be "unjust." See Smail, "One Man," 85.

287 Marshall, *Aspects,* 62. Stott has also stated that "We must never make Christ the object of God's punishment or God the object of Christ's persuasion, for both God and Christ were subjects not objects, taking the initiative together to save sinners." See Stott, *Cross,* 151.

288 Marshall, *Aspects,* 62.

289 Marshall, *Aspects,* 62.

290 Williams, "Penal," 187.

291 Williams, "Penal," 187.

humanity is bound to trivialize forgiveness.[292] Thus, the character of God is fully vindicated as he is both just and the justifier in the penal view.

Summary

This chapter has sought to demonstrate some of the theological implications of PSA through thoughtful engagement of key words and sources contributing to the arguments both for and against the subject at hand. Though PSA is not the only model of the atonement, it most certainly stands as one that is thoroughly Biblical and is theologically sound.

---

[292] Tidball, "Penal," 356-57.

CHAPTER 5

THE THEORECTICAL INTEGRATION OF PSA AND RELATIONAL PARADIGM

Introduction

The very core of the Christian faith is summed up in the word, *"gospel."* The gospel is the announcement that Israel's King, Jesus Christ, reigns over all of creation. And this word, *gospel,* is an extremely *relational* term, meaning "good *news."* Immediately, this communicative word brings the reader into the world pertaining to *relational* dynamics. A message must have an origin, an actual *meaning,* a messenger, and recipient(s). Who is the originator of the news? What is the content of the news? With whom is the news to be shared? What is to be done (if anything) in light of receiving the news? These are all *relational* categories of thought. *"The God of the Christian gospel is the Father, Son, and Spirit working in perfect communion for an even greater communion."*[293] This "communion" points directly toward the doctrine of reconciliation as will be addressed below. However, the gospel itself simply cannot be understood apart from thinking first and foremost of the Trinity. The reason for this is that the gospel can be defined as what God was doing *"in Christ"* to reconcile the world to himself and the gospel is applied by the ongoing work of the Holy Spirit in bringing people *to Christ* for salvation. Understanding the inter-relational dynamics of the Trinity is therefore essential for a more robust understanding of the gospel.

As John Calvin articulated the doctrine of PSA, he did so in terms of vertical and horizontal relationally-bound language as he speaks of God and man in terms of "propitiation" (vertical), "redemption" (horizontal), and "reconciliation" (vertical and horizontal).[294] Regarding propitiation, Calvin states "God, to whom we were hateful because of sin, was appeased by the death of his Son to become favorable to us."[295] This is incredibly relational as words such as "hateful" and "favorable" are used in describing a broken and restored relationship. And this has both vertical (with God) and horizontal (with other human beings) implications. London School of Theology lecturer Graham McFarlane writes about a *"Theology of Togetherness"* (horizontal) saying,

> The imperative towards togetherness rests on both the presupposition of the cross and the empowering of the Spirit. The heart of the matter is that we cannot separate atonement from ecclesiology and pneumatology without rendering the narrative of the gospel devoid of any real help. The work of Christ, who reveals the togetherness of Father, Son, and Spirit in the redemptive action towards a messed-

---

[293] Kevin Vanhoozer, *Remythologizing Theology: Divine Action, Passion, and Authorship* (Cambridge, England: Cambridge University Press, 2010), 259, italics in original.

[294] Bruce A. Demarest and Gordon R. Lewis, Integrative Theology: Historical, Biblical, Systematic, Apologetic, Practical: Three Volumes in One, vol. 2 (Grand Rapids, MI: Zondervan, 1996), 379.

[295] John Calvin, *Institutes*, 2.17.3.

up humanity is endorsed by the Father by raising the dead body of Jesus through the agency of the Holy Spirit.[296]

Thus, atonement theology has an immediate bearing on both one's understanding of the work of the Holy Spirit as well as the Church. Essentially, when speaking of the Trinity, to speak of One is to speak of the Other. How we think about, speak of, and value God (vertical) will be manifest most clearly in how we think, speak of, and engage one another as image-bearers. In order to even speak properly of any of these, it is imperative to begin with the Trinity. Hartford professor, Najib Awad reminds us,

> [W]ith the escalating emphasis in our so-called "postmodern" or "late-modern" intellectual context, on notions such as "personhood," "relationship," "participation," "event," "movement," "narrative," and so on, today's theologians are also reevaluating, and rapidly revising, Christian theology's previous understanding of "personhood" and "relationality" within the framework of the doctrine of God and theological anthropology.[297]

More of this line of thinking will follow in the next chapter, focusing specifically on the horizontal implications of PSA. As is explored in this book, the atoning work of Christ involves actions done by, to, and for human beings. Additionally, through the atoning work of his death and resurrection, Jesus purchased a people from every tribe and tongue for himself (Rev. 5:9). Christians not only are to understand their identity as individuals grounded in their justification by Christ but are to also understand their *relationships* to the community as a whole as one defined by the cross of Christ. (John 13:34-35; Eph. 5:25). The metaphor of a kaleidoscope is helpful to illustrate this reality.

The Kaleidoscope

Joel Green coined his model of the atonement as the "Kaleidoscopic" approach.[298] In this, he argues that the New Testament provides many models for describing the work of Christ in the atonement and that one model should not be privileged over another. Yet, as noted in the dissertation of Alex Early, Green does not allow for PSA to enter the kaleidoscope at all. However, as has been demonstrated earlier in this book, PSA *does* in fact, find great emphases throughout the totality of Scripture. The present writer (Early) is in agreement with Schreiner in that PSA can and should serve as the "anchoring color" of the kaleidoscope.[299] Furthermore, I follow in the line of theologians

---

[296] Graham McFarlane, "Towards a Theology of Togetherness," in *The Spirit and Christ,* edited by I. H. Marshall, V. Rabens, and C. Bennema, 327.

[297] Najib Awad, *Persons in Relation: An Essay on the Trinity and Ontology* (Minneapolis, MN, Fortress Press, 2014), 3.

[298] Joel Green, "Kaleidoscopic View," in *The Nature of the Atonement: Four Views* (Downers Grove, IL: Intervarsity Press, 2006),157-185.

[299] Schreiner's comment is "I would maintain ... that the root problem in the human condition is sin, and penal substitution grounds our redemption, illumination, freedom, forgiveness, victory over demonic powers, moral life, and so forth. In other words, the kaleidoscope has an anchoring

such as Bloesch who refers to PSA as the "heart" of the atonement,[300] Jeffery, Ovey, and Sach who speak of PSA as "absolutely central,"[301] and Packer who speaks of the "essence" of the atonement.[302] The aim thus far of the book has been to demonstrate that PSA is indeed central to understanding what is accomplished in the cross of Christ. At the risk of sounding reductionistic, having *Christus Victor* as the primary model would not constitute as good news for those who have followed in the rebellion of Satan. To be morally influenced by the death of Christ, (though certainly praiseworthy and virtuous), does nothing to address one's own sinful state before a holy God. PSA is the model that does accomplish humankind's greatest need and "root problem"[303] as it pertains to reconciliation with God.

Throughout the book, I have made the case for PSA. At this point, I will borrow the kaleidoscopic metaphor from Green and use it in a different manner. Rather than juxtaposing atonement theories, my aim with the kaleidoscope is to provide a helpful metaphor that demonstrates the *relational* interactions between various doctrines that occur as PSA fits within the kaleidoscope. That is to say, all too often when the doctrine of PSA is affirmed; the tenderness of *Abba*, the sympathy of the Brother, and the Comfort of the Holy Spirit fade out of the picture altogether. Instead, holiness, wrath, and sin tend to be the predominant points emphasized. My desire is to show that the attributes of God such as his wrath and love are not opposed to one another, that the atonement is Trinitarian in nature, and that humankind, though made in the image of God through sin became his enemies, are now reconciled to God through the cross (PSA), thus bringing about new *relational* dynamics, understood primarily as *family* members. "To know God is to worship him ... to know God is to be known by him, a two-way relationship of acknowledgement and obligation (Gal. 4:9)."[304]

Following are a set of diagrams used to illustrate the importance of placing PSA at the center of the kaleidoscope, then to observe the relational dynamics (vertical) that result. In each diagram there are seven triangles that represent the members of the Trinity, human image bearers, as well as PSA. Due to space limitations, I have selected three relational aspects between God and humans that change as a result of the doctrine of PSA being accomplished.

---

color (penal substitution) that brings coherence to all the dimensions of the atonement." Thomas Schreiner, "Penal Substitution Response," in *The Nature of the Atonement* (Downers Grove, IL: IVP, 2006), 193.

[300] Donald Bloesch, *Jesus Christ: Savior and Lord* (Downers Grove, IL: IVP, 1997), 158.

[301] Jeffery, Ovey, and Sach, *Pierced,* 211.

[302] J. I. Packer, In My Place Condemned He Stood: Celebrating the Glory of the Atonement (Wheaton, IL: Crossway, 2007), 25.

[303] Schreiner, "Response," 193.

[304] James Dunn, "The Body of Christ in Paul," in *Worship, Theology, and Ministry in the Early Church,* ed. M. J. Wilkins and T. Paige (Sheffield, England: Sheffield Academic Press, 1992), 47.

Description of the seven triangles:
1. **Judge**: Each member of the Trinity is referenced numerous times throughout Scripture performing the role of *judging* sinners.

2. **Imago *Dei***: Human beings are created in the image of God and are understood as vapors (temporary), are to have dominion over the earth, and are uniquely relational between each other and God.

3. **PSA**: Penal Substitutionary Atonement follows due to the fact that sin enters the kaleidoscope and PSA places both the wrath and love of God on display.

4. **Family**: This results in the wrath of God being averted and the love of God displayed, accomplished, and relayed in atonement and adoption. The enemies of God now become part of the family of God. Thus, the Judge(s) relationship(s) toward the child of God now undergoes such changes in which the child now relates to the Father as *Abba*, the Son as "Brother," and the Holy Spirit as "Comforter."

5. **Abba**: With an intimate relationship with the Father, the child of God is admonished to (amongst many other things): 1) come before the throne of grace, 2) ask for wisdom, and 3) expect tenderness.

6. **Brother**: The relationship with God the Son is now one of brotherhood. In this relationship with wrath removed and righteousness imputed, the sibling of Christ finds him to be one who expresses: 1) immeasurable love, 2) serves as the Advocate of the sibling, and 3) is able to sympathize with those he saves.

7. **Comforter**: The Holy Spirit, though occasionally judges severely in the lives of the family of God, is the one who comforts the child of God by remaining present, guiding in the truth, and empowering the believer in the ongoing process of transformation.

Figure 4 – PSA kaleidoscope components and relational dynamics (vertical)

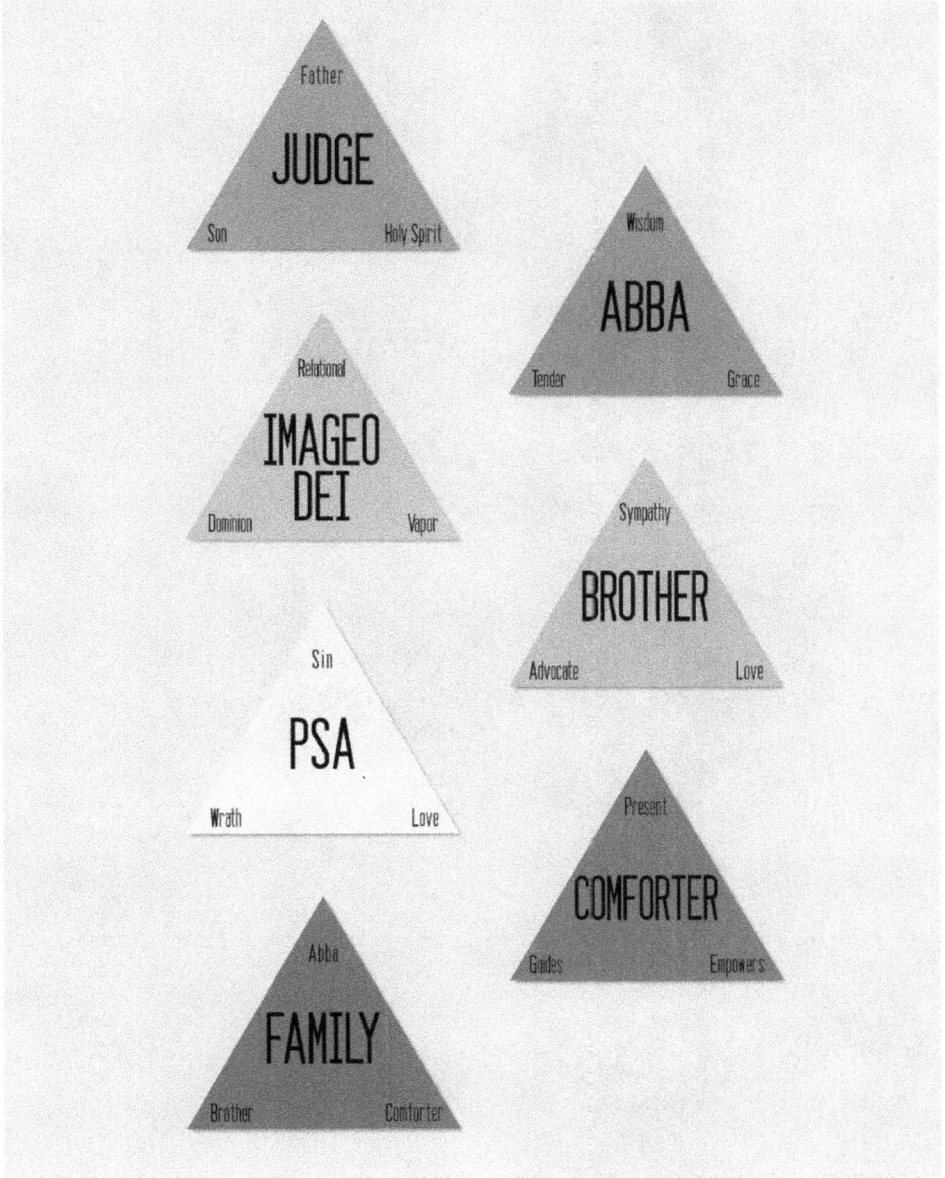

Figure 5 – PSA kaleidoscope and relational dynamics (vertical)

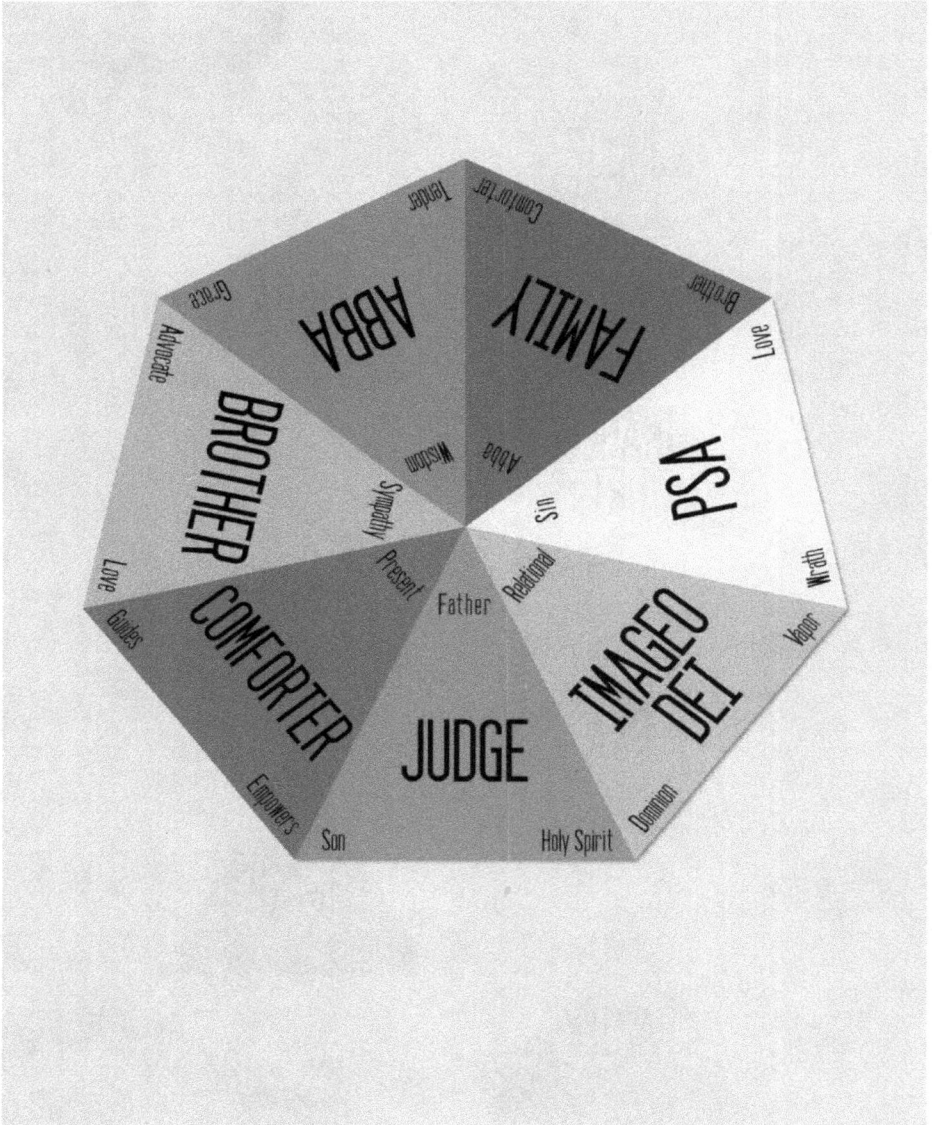

The purpose of placing each of the triangles in this shape provides the reader the ability to see them all together at once and not as disconnected doctrines, thus emphasis is given to the interrelatedness of PSA and these examples.

Figure 6 – Kaleidoscope and functionality of PSA (vertical relational)

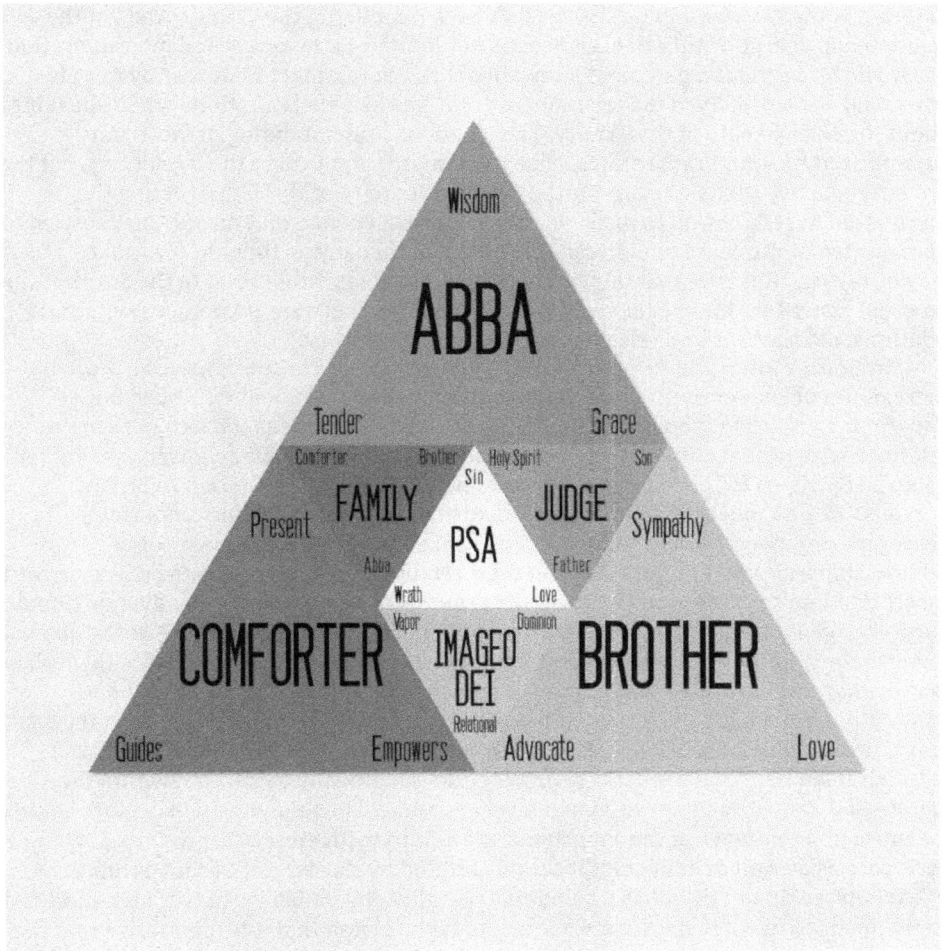

This diagram now places PSA in the center of the kaleidoscope with the intention of visually demonstrating the functionality of PSA in regard to the vertical relational paradigm that it establishes and ensures.

Theologian, Kevin Vanhoozer, rightly states that "we should begin our thinking about meaning and interpretation as Christians with the paradigm of the triune God in communicative action."[305] Indeed, God has revealed himself as Triune, a community of

---

[305] Kevin Vanhoozer, Is There A Meaning in this Text?: The Bible, the Reader, and the Morality of Literary Knowledge (Grand Rapids, MI: Zondervan, 1998), 6.

one and three, and therefore is in a constant state of perfect *relationship* within the Godhead. Christian theological conceptualizations of God are *measured* or *understood*, in terms of the *relationship* he shares with each member of the Trinity. And yet the relationship shared within the Godhead is not limited to the transcendent, rather, God has made himself immanent, and knowable, through relating to humans by both his Spirit and his Word. Even the term "measured" has its own limitations when speaking about the relationality of the Trinity. The orthodox understanding of the Trinity summarized by John Frame states, "The persons are identical to their relations, but they are not *reducible to* their relations; they are not mere relations."[306] Avoiding the temptation to reduce God to *mere* relations is one challenge that must be acknowledged here. Jürgen Moltmann popularized this model of theological thought ("sociality") by way of saying, "It is true that the Father is defined by his fatherhood to the Son, but this does not constitute his existence; it presupposes it ... there are no persons without relations, but there are no relations without persons either.[307]

Vanhoozer interjects by pointing out that even more questions arise as the "egregious consequences of equating personhood *with* relationality"[308] become apparent. Trinitarian theologian, Collin Gunton, defines *personhood* as a network of relations with others and "just as God is who he is in inextricable fellowship of Father, Son, and Spirit, so for us to be *personal* is to be what we are in *relation* to other persons."[309] One must consider Harris' rhetorical question: "will this undermine the personhood of people who cannot *form* relationships, cannot *sustain* healthy relationships, or who are not valued *in* their relationships?"[310] Certainly, it is an error to assert that one's *personhood* is lost on the grounds of being relationally dysfunctional. For it too would be an error for one to insist on being perfect in one's relationships. Nevertheless, for our purposes here, it must be stated that the Bible repeatedly declares that the harmonious relationship human beings once enjoyed with God and one another has been marred by *sin* and the remedy is in fact as multifaceted as is the cause. In order to be able to speak of relational implications of the atoning work of Christ within human beings, we must first explore the relationship that exists within the Triune God, in whose image human beings are made. The following will explore some of the more popular ways of thinking about the Trinity with emphasis given to perichoresis as well as some modifications offered by more recent scholarship.

When seeking to establish a relational paradigm by which we may understand and apply the doctrine of penal substitution, it must be stated that it is imperative that the focus be limited only to texts that deal with the atoning work of the cross and the implications both vertically and horizontally. The material addressing the biblical-

---

[306] John M. Frame, *Doctrine of God: A Theology of Lordship* (Grand Rapids, MI: Zondervan, 2002), 703, emphasis mine.

[307] Jürgen Moltmann, *Trinity and the Kingdom* (Minneapolis, MN: Fortress Press, 1993),172.

[308] Vanhoozer, *Remythologizing*, 142, emphasis mine.

[309] Collin Gunton, *The Triune Creator: A Historical and Systematic Study* (Grand Rapids, MI: Eerdmans, 1997), 197, emphasis mine.

[310] H. A. Harris, "Should We Say that Personhood is Relational?" *Scottish Journal of Theology* 51, no. 2 (May 1998): 215, emphasis mine.

historical foundations, theological implications, and hermeneutical challenges of PSA all serve to establish *that* PSA is essential to the gospel message being rightly interpreted. But what are, if any, the *relational* implications between an individual and God? What does it mean for believers *now,* knowing that the wrath of God was averted due to the sacrifice of the Son of God at Calvary? How does *this* affect one's view, relational grounding, and experience of God the Father, Son, and Holy Spirit? Furthermore, it is recognized that in relational theology, Karl Barth established the seven spheres of being-in-relation: 1) Intra-Trinitarian, 2) Jesus to the Father in the Spirit, 3) Humankind to God through Jesus, 4) Jesus to other humans, 5) Humankind: one to another, 6) Body to Soul, and 7) Eternity to Time.[311] Due to space restrictions, this book is going to be limited in providing examples of how an individual now relates to God (vertical) because of PSA and then to one another (horizontal).

Some, such as Steve Chalke, as stated earlier, would argue that with PSA in the picture, one is left to conclude that God himself is an abusive father,[312] one with whom one would hardly want a relationship. Chalke and those who would agree with him would argue that the love of God simply fades into the background of a bloodthirsty, out of control, abuser. Having already exposed that erroneous theology, what I seek to establish in this chapter is that the love of God is not only put on display in the death of Jesus but that it is in fact, extended to those who would become children of God, as God is not only to be understood as Creator or Judge (Rom. 14:10), but now as *"Abba,* Father" (Rom. 8:15; Gal. 4:6). As is consistent with sound Christian doctrine, Jesus is the second person of the Godhead, and is also involved in the creation of all things (John 1:1-3; Phil. 2:6; Col. 1:16-17; Heb. 1:1-3). In several places in Scripture Jesus is referred to not only as the Creator or the unique Son of God (Matt. 3:17; 17:5; 1 John 4:10, for example) but also, as part of his responsibilities, functions as "Judge" (Acts 10:42; 2 Cor. 5:10). However, because of the penal substitutionary atonement that he paid, those who the Father has given to him now relate to him as "Brother" (Heb. 2:11-15). This too, will be examined in this chapter.

Lastly, the Holy Spirit was present and active in the creation of the world as well as human beings and is himself also One who carries out judgment on those who would rebel against God, even post-Pentecost (Acts 5:1-10). Thus, all three members of the Holy Trinity are God, and function as Creator, and Judge. After Jesus averts the wrath of God, is resurrected, and ascended to the Father, the Holy Spirit is sent to believers-in-Jesus and as the Spirit carries out many roles, one major *relational* role he plays is that of "Comforter" (John 14:16). In this chapter I want to demonstrate how the Father, Son, and Holy Spirit *still* function as *Judge* in the life of the Christian yet those roles of judgment are not the same as upon those who do not belong to the family of God. Additionally, I want to highlight the implications of relating to God as *"Abba,"* Jesus as "Brother," and the Holy Spirit as "Comforter" in the relational paradigm.

---

[311] Gary Deddo, Karl Barth's Theology of Relations: Trinitarian, Christological, and Human: Towards an Ethic of the Family (Eugene, OR: Wipf & Stock, 2015), 41.
[312] Chalke and Mann, *Lost,* 182.

Throughout this book I have sought to articulate a sound understanding of the doctrine of PSA from a biblical-historical grounding, drawing theological implications, and engaging in the hermeneutical challenges that arise from this ever so important doctrine of the Christian faith. I have demonstrated that there is no conflict within the Trinity, no abuse, no random act of sudden violence, but rather a cooperative action between the Father and the Son, accomplishing redemption for those whom God would adopt into his family. One's beliefs about God's holiness, personhood, character, wrath, judgment, and love are all held together in this doctrine. Due to space restrictions, I have limited the research on the relational paradigm demonstrating how the three Persons of the Trinity are: A) God, B) Function as "Judge," C) Have various relationships with the redeemed, and D) Some implications of those relationships.

Triune God	Identity	Vertical Relationship
Father	Father as God Judge *Abba*	• Giver of wisdom (James 1:5, 17-18) • Approachable throne of grace (Heb. 4:16) • Tender Father (Jer. 31:3, Hosea 11:1-3, Gal. 4:6, Rom. 8:15)
Son	Son as God Judge Brother	• Immeasurable love (Eph. 3:18-19) • Advocate (1 John 2:1) • Sympathizer (Heb. 4:15)
Holy Spirit	Spirit as God Judge Comforter	• Present (John 14:16) • Guides (John 16:13) • Empowers (Gal. 5:16-26)

Figure 7 – PSA, Trinity, and vertical relationships

God as Judge

The Hebrew Scriptures are abundantly clear as they repeatedly declare the existence, sovereignty, and eternality of *YHWH*. The ongoing theme of the wrath of God is one that simply cannot be ignored and there are most certainly those who take up great offense at the idea of a holy and just God who meets out judgment to those who transgress his commands. For example, in his now famous, *God Delusion,* Richard Dawkins opens the second chapter by writing:

> The God of the Old Testament is arguably the most unpleasant character in all of fiction: jealous and proud of it; a petty, unjust, unforgiving control-freak; a vindictive, bloodthirsty ethnic cleanser; a misogynistic, homophobic, racist,

infanticidal, genocidal, filicidal, pestilential, megalomaniacal, sadomasochistic, capriciously malevolent bully.[313]

God's wrath is inextricably related to the judgment in which his holiness provides context for him to carry out.[314] Paul wrote to the Romans saying that "the wages of sin is death" (Rom. 6:23). This death is not only physical, it also has spiritual ramifications.[315] Consider that John Lennox has responded to Dawkins and those in this line of thinking by way of stating, "In spite of the hopelessness of their position, many prominent atheists content themselves with crude, dismissive, and puerile caricatures of the very message that, for centuries, has brought hope, forgiveness, peace of mind and heart, and power for living to multitudes of ordinary men and women."[316]

When thinking biblically about the three cultures by which we understand personal beings (Theo-culture, Angel culture, and human culture)[317] we observe that both the angels who rebelled against God and all humans have sinned against God and are therefore subject to his judgment (1 Cor. 6:3; Rom. 2:6).

Throughout the entire Old Testament, God judges both the pagan nations for their wickedness in rebellion and the nation of Israel when they chose to break covenant. It is important to note that the nature of judgment executed in these situations is different because of the intended outcomes determined by God.[318] The pagan nations such as Egypt, for example, in the story of the Passover, suffer plague after plague with no healing or restoration extended by God. God's judgment in each of these occasions is fair, just, and warranted.[319] And yet, the nature of judgment changes when God deals with his own covenantal people, Israel. That is, "with Israel in the time of Moses, grace reached out to redeem and restore (Exod. 6:4) and looked for responsive, loving obedience (20:1ff.)."[320] Within the covenant, God promised both blessings to follow

---

[313] Richard Dawkins, *The God Delusion* (New York, NY: Houghton Mifflin, 2006), 51.

[314] "God's condemnation is based on his justice, and such condemnation is deserved (1 Kings 8:32; Rom. 3:8)," Ronald Youngblood, "Judgment," in *Evangelical Dictionary of Theology,* 2nd ed. (Grand Rapids, MI: Baker Book House, 1984), 639.

[315] Moo, *Romans,* 408, Dunn, *Romans,* 356. Origen states, "The death being referred to here is not the death which separates the body from the soul but the death by which because of sin the soul is separated from God," in *Commentary on the Epistle to the Romans,* CER 3:226, 230.

[316] John Lennox, Gunning for God: Why the New Atheists Are Missing the Target (Oxford, England: Lion Hudson, 2011), 145.

[317] Enoch Wan, *Christian Witness in Pluralistic Contexts in the 21st Century,* vol. 11, EMS Series (Pasadena, CA: William Carrey Library Publishers, 2004), 190.

[318] "Among the more important judgments of God prior to the Exodus are those on Adam, Eve, and the serpent after the Fall (Gen. 3), the Flood (6:5), Sodom and Gomorrah (18:20), and the confusion of tongues (11:1-9). God brings judgment to his creatures when they rebel against his will," Steven Barabas, "Judgment," in *New International Bible Dictionary* (Grand Rapids, MI: Zondervan, 1999), 558.

[319] Those who would condemn God for being cruel here should simply consider that each plague was preceded by a warning given to Pharaoh through the mouth of Moses.

[320] Barabas, "Judgment," 558.

obedient living and punishing curses to follow disobedience (e.g., Deut. 27:1-26; 28:1-68; cf. Lev. 26:3-13ff).[321] And yet, his discipline as seen repeatedly is not carried out without restoration as the intended purpose. "The purpose of the judgment of God's people is not their total destruction but their purification."[322] God punishes his covenantal people, his children, as "a father disciplines his children" (Heb. 12:7), out of great love to see them walking in health, holiness, and fidelity. His patience abounds all through the Old Testament.[323]

Though there are numerous examples throughout the Old Testament where we see the judgment of God being executed upon his own people, the most famous is undoubtedly when the people of Judah are carried off into Babylonian exile. We read,

Nebuchadnezzar king of Babylon came up, and Jehoiakim became his servant for three years ... the LORD sent ... Chaldeans ... Syrians ... Moabites ...Ammonites, ... against Judah to destroy it, according to the word of the LORD that He spoke by His servants the prophets. ... Surely this came upon Judah ... to remove them out of His sight .... Jehoiachin his son reigned in his place ... And he did what was evil in the sight of the Lord .... Nebuchadnezzar king of Babylon came to [Jerusalem] while his servants were besieging it, and Jehoiachin gave himself up ... the king of Babylon took him prisoner ... and carried off all the treasures of the house of the LORD and the treasures of the King's house .... He carried away all Jerusalem ... except the poorest people of the land ...

Zedekiah ... became king, and he ... did what was evil in the sight of the LORD ... because of the anger of the LORD it came to the point in Jerusalem and Judah that He cast them out from His presence. ... Nebuchadnezzar king of Babylon came with all his army against Jerusalem and laid siege to it ...they captured [King Zedekiah] and ...passed sentence on him ... bound him in chains and took him to Babylon. ... So Judah was taken into exile out of its land (2 Kings 24-25).

The loss of the Promised Land, home, places of work, and worship, being forced to live among those whom they despised, the Israelites were disciplined. And yet, God in his sovereign grace, through the ministries of Ezra and Nehemiah, then liberated those who would return to Israel. As seen in these two examples, God's judgment is very different. To those outside the covenant, his judgment stands alone. To those who are inside the covenant his judgment is always performed with the aim of seeking

---

[321] Barabas, "Judgment," 558.

[322] Barabas, "Judgment," 558.

[323] "To explain what he is constantly 'forgiving,' or 'bearing with,' Yahweh mentions three specific words that help define sin in the Old Testament. This triad appears thirteen times in the Old Testament, so placing them together is a fairly common way of expressing sin's totality. First, Yahweh forgives 'iniquity' (*awon*). This word basically expresses the conscious twisting of a personality, idea, or a thing. Second, he forgives 'transgression' (*pesa*), a word that describes rebelling against Yahweh that 'breaks with him, takes away what is his, robs, embezzles, misappropriates it.' Third, Yahweh bears with 'sin,' a word that means 'missing a goal.' So, Yahweh's compassionate and merciful nature bears with and forgives people's twisting his words and will. It endures breaches of trust by persons with whom he has a *relationship* and suffers the missing of the goals he sets for his people." Paul R. House, "Sin in the Law" in *Fallen: A Theology of Sin,* ed. C. W. Morgan and R. A. Peterson (Wheaton, IL: Crossway, 2013), 43, (emphasis mine).

repentance by extending grace and thus relationships being reconciled. In moving from relating to *YHWH* primarily as "Judge" to a warm, intimate, close, caring, involved Father, his justice towards sin, must be averted and that is accomplished in PSA. This does not imply that his wrath and his love are in any way conflicted within himself. "God who only loves but does not pass judgment would be a forgiveness dispenser who could be manipulated at will. A God who only passes judgment but does not love, first and foremost, would be a monster."[324]

Robert S. Paul states, "Real forgiveness is not in foregoing the satisfaction due by law (though it may include it), but in the restoration of a *relation* of trust between two persons and this brings us near to the heart of the real meaning of atonement."[325]

Reconciliation is Accomplished and Relationship is Established

The literal meaning of the term "to reconcile" speaks of bringing estranged parties "back into council again, and this calls for restoring broken relationships."[326] It is a term that is used in five key New Testament passages and is used of both individual relationships with God as well as relationships with one another.[327] In the New Testament the verb *to reconcile* is used eight times and the noun form only once (Acts 3:21).[328] H. G. Link, in the *New International Dictionary of New Testament Theology* defines reconciliation as, "the restoration of a good relationship between enemies. In order to achieve this good relationship in the confrontation of God and man, it is necessary that the factors which produced the enmity be removed. This is achieved by atonement."[329]

What is interesting to note is that Scripture does not speak of God being reconciled to humans or the world but rather, he reconciles humans and the world to himself. Paul writes, "For if while we were *enemies* we were *reconciled* to *God by* the *death* of his Son,

[324] Ulrich Luz, *The Theology of the Gospel of Matthew* (Cambridge, England: Cambridge University Press, 1995),132. Though God is under no obligation to extend grace to anyone. His judgment would not make him a "monster." Human sin is monstrous.

[325] Robert Paul, The Atonement and the Sacraments: The Relation of the Atonement to the Sacraments of Baptism and the Lord's Supper (Eugene, OR: Wipf & Stock, 1992), 66, (emphasis mine).

[326] John Driver, Understanding the Atonement for the Mission of the Church (Eugene, OR: Wipf & Stock, 2005), 177.

[327] "*Katallasso* appears (twice) in Romans 5:10 and in 2 Corinthians 5:18-20. *Katallage* appears in Romans 5:11; 11:15; 2 Corinthians 5:18-19. *Apokatallasso* occurs in Ephesians 2:16 and Colossians 1:20, 22. The reference to the restoration of relationships among humans is explicit in Romans 11:15; 2 Corinthians 5:16-21; Colossians 1:19-22 (cf. Col. 3:10-22; Eph. 2:11-22). It is implicit in Romans 5:10-11, which is set in a context which deals with the incorporation of both Jews and Gentiles into Jesus Christ (Rom. 1:5-6, 16-17; 3:21-30; 4:16, 18; 5:1-2). That 'we have peace with God' (Rom. 5:1) and 'access to this grace' (5:2) 'through our Lord Jesus Christ' (5:1) is a spiritual reality which is both personal and social. This is clear in Ephesians 2:17-19 where the same terminology is in an explicitly social context." Driver, *Understanding*, 258.

[328] H. G. Link, "Reconciliation, Restoration, Propitiation, Atonement" in *New International Dictionary of New Testament Theology*, vol. 3 (Grand Rapids, MI: Zondervan, 1986), 147.

[329] Link, "Reconciliation, Restoration, Propitiation, Atonement," 145.

much more, now that we are reconciled, shall we be saved by his life. More than that, we also rejoice in God through our Lord Jesus Christ, through whom we have now received reconciliation (Rom. 5:10-11)."[330] Thus, God creates the repentant, trusting, reconciling heart in those who were once his enemies, and now adopts them into his family, forever relating to them, and them to him as "Father," and them as his "sons" and "children."

Due to the breadth of names, metaphors, and ways in which God relates to his people, I will look at one aspect found in two places in the New Testament, namely, how PSA establishes the reality for one to relate to God no longer as enemy (Rom. 5:10) but now as "*Abba*, Father." The two Scriptures are Galatians 4:6 and Romans 8:15. As discussed earlier under the section, "The Tree: Becoming a Curse," we examined the penal substitutionary aspects in Galatians 3:13. In his epistle to the Galatians, Paul works out his covenantal theology, not avoiding the cross, but *through* the penal sacrifice of Christ (Gal. 3:13) thus providing background, foundation, and doorway into relating to God now as "*Abba*, Father" (4:6). One's understanding of the doctrine of God is ever so important as it is often quite reductionist to pit the holiness, justice, judgment, and wrath of God against his love. There is no conflict in God. It is in the cross of Christ that God's perfect judgment toward sin is rendered and his unfathomable love is put on display (Rom. 5:8). Yet, one cannot relate to the Father outside of his judgment that is due the sinner (slave!) apart from the penal substitution of Christ. The vertical relationship with the Father is established and secured entirely through the work of Christ alone and the once enemy, now son of God never need fear anything ever separating him/her from the great love of God (Rom. 8:37-39). Even Paul's word choice in both Galatians 3:13-14 and 4:5-6 are nearly repetitive, as he demonstrates this reality. James Dunn helpfully provides the following diagram.

Figure 8– James Dunn's analysis of Apostle Paul's word choice

Galatians iii.13-14	Galatians iv.4-6
Having become a curse for us, Christ redeemed us from The curse of the law	Born under the law, In order that he might redeem Those under the law
....	....
In order that we might receive The promise of the Spirit	In order that we might receive the (Spirit of) adoption[331]

Dunn continues,

> The parallel indicates that the redemption was achieved not by incarnation, but by death[332] (cf. Rom. 8:3), and strengthens the recognition that Paul saw Jesus' ministry in almost exclusively soteriological terms: the purpose of his coming, not

---

[330] Link, "Reconciliation, Restoration, Propitiation, Atonement," 178.

[331] Dunn, *Galatians*, 216.

[332] Consider McKnight's comments below.

as a teacher with the human condition (here, of Jews), his death might be the price necessary to free them from the slavery endemic to that human condition – a good example of what has appropriately been called "interchange in Christ," (Hooker, *Adam*, 59-60).[333]

Including the entire text here would be helpful:

> I mean that the heir, as long as he is a child, is no different from a slave, though he is the owner of everything, but he is under guardians and managers until the date set by his father. In the same way we also, when we were children, were enslaved to the elementary principles of the world. But when the fullness of time had come, God sent forth his Son, born of woman, born under the law, to redeem those who were under the law, so that we might receive adoption as sons. And because you are sons, God has sent the Spirit of his Son into our hearts, crying, *"Abba!* Father!" So you are no longer a slave, but a son, and if a son, then an heir through God (Gal. 4:1-7).

The movement from "slave" to "son" is accomplished through the penal sacrifice of Christ and the *adopting* action of the Father. Paul is unique among the writers of the New Testament in his description of salvation, opting for more legal images (i.e. "justification" and "adoption") whereas John and Peter tend to speak of "regeneration."[334] In both Greek and Roman contexts adoption was a fairly routine practice. Under the Roman law the free citizen would be adopted and become a slave under the adopting father. "Adoption conferred rights, but it came with a list of duties as well."[335] And yet, as Christians, "the reason for adoption is given in Ephesians 1:4-5: God's love."[336] Furthermore, one's eschatology and soteriology overlap in this adoption by the Father and filling of the Holy Spirit *experientially* as past, present, and future event(s). That is to say that justification has occurred (past), there is the "crying out"

---

[333] Dunn, *Galatians*, 216-7.; see also Morna D. Hooker, *From Adam to Christ: Essays on St. Paul* (Cambridge, England: Cambridge University Press, 1990), 59-60.

[334] P. H. Davids, "Adoption," in *Evangelical Dictionary of Theology*, ed. Walter A. Elwell. (Grand Rapids, MI: Baker Book House, 2004), 25.

[335] Davids, "Adoption," 25. "His thought may have included the legal possibility of a father's releasing his son from his *potestas* by formally selling him (*emancipatio*). According to early Roman law, if this was done three times the son was finally free of his father's *potestas*. After the first two sales, however, the son could be manumitted (like a slave) back to his father, who would receive him back by a fresh act of *adoptio*. This helps explain how Paul's thought could move so easily from the thought of redemption (from slavery) to that of adoption to sonship. Presumably also included in Paul's use of the analogy was the fact that the adopted person was for all legal purposes in the same position as the natural son, with the same rights of succession – so that 'adoption' is fully equivalent to 'sonship'... it is worth noting that whereas John's Gospel distinguishes Christ as 'Son' (*huios*) from Christians as 'children' (*tekna*), Paul does not hesitate to use the same term (*huios*) for both." Dunn, *Galatians*, 217-8.

[336] Davids, "Adoption," 25.

(present), and "redemption of our bodies that is to come" (Rom. 8:23, *future*).[337] On the sending of the Spirit of the Son into the hearts of the adopted, "The twin effects of the two missions: both with a view to effecting sonship – that is, not only in (legal) fact (iv.4-5), but also in reality of subjective experience."[338] This is profoundly *relational*. Before moving towards speaking of reconciliation between God and man accomplished through the work of the Trinity, it would be helpful to briefly look at the relationality of the Trinity.

Perichoresis and the Relationality of the Trinity

Speaking about the Trinity is as old as theological thinking is in and of itself. Indeed, "the Trinity was the first doctrine explored in church history. It replaces the view of gods as individual beings with the biblical view of God as a plurality."[339] God has always existed in and of himself in perfect, personal, relational, unity within the Godhead. This, in turn, has affected literally everything and everyone as St. Paul reminds us that "From him, through him, and to him are all things. To him be the glory forever. Amen" (Rom. 11:36). Fordham scholar, W. Norris Clarke, suggests:

> [I]t would be a waste of time for God to create a material universe with no rational beings to appreciate it, beings capable of recognizing it as a person-to-person gift and responding appropriately with gratitude and love to the Giver. It follows that the intelligibility of being – all being – is inseparable from the context of persons: it is rooted *in* personal being, flows out *from* it, *to* other persons, who complete the circle by returning it back again to its personal source. In a word, the ultimate meaning of being is: Person-to-Person Gift![340]

Christian theologians would do well to recognize the limits of the concept of *perichoresis*, not least because, in a strict sense, *perichoresis* cannot be true of nor experienced by human beings. Volf substantiates this: "Another human self cannot be internal to my own self as subject of action. Human persons are always external to one another *as subjects.*"[341] Throughout Church history various theologians have opted for the language of speaking of the Trinity as "modes of being."[342] Others have employed

---

[337] Davids, "Adoption," 25-6.

[338] Dunn, *Galatians*, 219.

[339] Norman Gulley, *Systematic Theology: God As Trinity* (Berrien Springs, MI: Andrews University Press, 2003), 3.

[340] W. Norris Clarke, SJ, *The One and the Many: A Contemporary Thomistic Metaphysics* (Notre Dame, IN: University of Notre Dame Press, 2001), 309.

[341] Mirslov Volf, After Our Likeness: The Church as the Image of the Trinity (Grand Rapids, MI: Eerdmans, 1998), 210-11.

[342] Examples include Basil, Gregory of Nyssa, Amphilochius, and Barth. McGrath notes Gregory of Nyssa and Basil as examples in Alister McGrath, *Christian Theology: An Introduction*, 3rd ed. (Oxford, England: Blackwell Publishers, 2001), 330-31. See Karl Barth, *Church Dogmatics: The Doctrine of the Word of God*, vol.1, bk. 1, trans. G. T. Thomson (New York, NY: T&T Clark, 2004), 407, especially several sections summarized in McGrath, *Christian Theology*, 334. See also T. F.

the language of *perichoresis* meaning an "intimate mutual union" in which there are relations of paternity, filiation, and spiration. The Father, Son, and Spirit are "distinguished from each other" by these relations.[343] Twenty-five years ago, Moltmann stated some things in the preface to his monumental work, *The Trinity and the Kingdom*, that carry as much authority today (possibly more!) as when they were originally penned:

> I turned my attention to a theological problem that has remained open since the era of the patristic church: What is the relation of the Trinitarian history of God, the Father, the Son, and the Spirit, which the New Testament relates, to God's sovereignty? My own teachers, Karl Barth and Karl Rahner, decided the question to be in favour of the sovereignty of the One God and were then able to talk about the Trinity only as the "three modes of being" or the "three modes of subsistence" of that One God. I myself have proposed instead that the question be decided in favour of the Trinity, and here I have developed a *social doctrine of the Trinity*, according to which God as a community of Father, Son, and Spirit, whose unity is constituted by mutual indwelling and reciprocal interpenetration. If this is correct, then we find the earthly reflection of this divine sociality, not in the autocracy of a single rule but in the democratic community of free people, not in the lordship of the man over the woman but in their equal mutuality, not in an ecclesiastical hierarchy but in a fellowship church.[344]

Before proceeding, Scot McKnight helpfully reminds readers to heavily consider the relational dynamics within the Trinity before delving into atonement studies. McKnight offers a critique of thinking *only* of the cross and not the entire life, death, resurrection, and ascending work of Jesus in order to accomplish salvation. Thus,

> A *crux sola* theory of atonement is inadequate, but not because there is something insufficient in the cross. The atonement begins in the *perichoresis* of God, that eternal communion of interpersonal love, and that *perichoresis* becomes incarnate in the Son of God, the *Logos*, Christ Jesus, who assumes – hence the cross – what we are (cracked *Eikons*) in order to draw us into the *perichoresis*. And it is the entire life of Jesus (not to mention yet Pentecost) that creates atonement. A genuinely biblical atonement is incarnational as it sets the stage now for what happens on the cross.[345]

The Bible records each member of the Trinity honoring one another as Divine Being – Jesus refers to the Father as "God" (John 6:27b; 8:42), the Father refers to Jesus

---

Torrance, *The Trinitarian Faith: The Evangelical Theology of the Ancient Catholic Faith* (New York, NY: T&T Clark, 1997), 327.

[343] Francis Turretin, *Institutes of Elenctic Theology*, vol. 3, *Eighteenth Through Twentieth Topics*, trans. J. T. Dennison and G. M. Giger (Phillipsburg, NJ: P&R Publishing, 1997), 257, 280.

[344] Moltmann, *Trinity*, viii, italics in original.

[345] Scot McKnight, *A Community Called Atonement* (Nashville, TN: Abingdon Press, 2007), 60.

as "God" (Matt. 3:17; Heb. 1:8),[346] and Jesus refers to the Spirit as "God" (John 14:16, 18). It is with this now in mind that we turn our attention to the *attributes of love* shared within the Trinity.

The Loving-Relationality of the Triune God

"The uniqueness in the Old Testament is the One God distinguished from multiple gods, the uniqueness in the New Testament is the Trinity distinguished from any other god."[347] The nature of this section is limited to exploring how Scripture communicates the *loving relational* dynamics between the members of the Trinity rather than discussions pertaining to "substances," "essences," and clauses that are exhaustively covered elsewhere.[348] Augustine stated that "The Father and the Son reciprocally love one another."[349] When speaking of the Trinity, it is not uncommon to hear metaphors applied that in the end prove to be unhelpful, insufficient, or even heretical. Mindful of this, thoughtful theologians remind us of and warn us to avoid the pitfalls of *reductionism* when discussing the ontology of God. For example, David Tracy writes:

> All methods of reductionism, whether by believers or nonbelievers, are grounded in an unacknowledged confession of their own: the belief that so secure is their present knowledge of truth and possibility that the religious classics can at best be peculiar expressions of more of the same. Anything different, other, alien must clearly be untrue and impossible – that "goes without saying."[350]

Thus, reductionism not only proves to be erroneous logic, it is also immoral on the grounds of arrogance. When speaking of the attributes of God, it must be acknowledged that *all* theological language itself is also conditioned as it reflects the time, place, political, sociological, and moralistic institutions and frameworks of a given context. This profoundly impacts the ways in which thought of God is conceived and then communicated. Pastor A. W. Tozer writes, "What comes into our minds when we think about God is the most important thing about us."[351] Thinking historically, at one time

---

[346] "In these instances 'Son' is in the context of his full deity and does not imply that he is in any way less than God," Gulley, *God As Trinity*, 12.

[347] Gulley, God As Trinity, 29.

[348] Benjamin Schneider, "A Certain Kind of Trinity: Dependence, Substance, and Explanation," *Philosophical Studies* 129, no. 2 (May 2006): 393.

[349] Augustine, *On the Holy Trinity; Doctrinal Treatises; Moral Treatises*, ed. Anthony Uyl (Woodstock, Ontario: Devoted Publishing, 2017), 230. Augustine also states that the "Holy Spirit should be specially called Love," Augustine, *Holy Trinity*, 232.

[350] David Tracy, *Plurality and Ambiguity: Hermeneutics, Religion, Hope* (Chicago, IL: University of Chicago Press, 1994), 100. Following this, Tracy writes, "conflicting reductionist procedures are temptations that in a hundred forms beset every interpreter of religion. Hiding within all of them are some secret presuppositions. In some methods and hermeneutics of suspicion there lives the belief that we moderns and post-moderns, as the vanguard of social evolution, have finally discovered that one argument, the one method, the one critical theory that explains all – and explains it usually as more of what we already knew." Tracy, *Plurality and Ambiguity*, 101.

[351] A. W. Tozer, *Knowledge of the Holy* (Glendale, CA: Bibliotech Press, 2016), 4.

(medieval period, for example), it was more commonplace in the West to speak of God's being as *holy* or *transcendent* with less attention given to his love and immanence. More common today, in both secular and sacred thought, God is popularly defined almost exclusively as "love" and only *love*. But this love constitutes a very much self-centered means of using God in a pragmatic or selfish way for one's own self-determined "good." The person defines love *for* God and *as* God. Further, it is increasingly popular that this may be the only *acceptable* way to speak of God at all.[352] Christians keeping the whole council of the Word of God before themselves understand God to be perfect in each of his attributes at all times and ways.[353] And neither God's holiness nor his love need be posed against one another but are in complete harmony within himself. McKnight is correct in saying, "The *perichoresis,* or God's essential mutual interiority, defines both love (the interpenetration) and holiness (the sacredness and purity of its interpenetration)."[354] Vanhoozer explains, "Augustine's solution to the paradox of God's love is to posit a properly divine kind of love, a gift-love: *agape.*"[355]

Regarding the relational dynamic between the Father and the Son, the two are "one" John 10:30) and are in constant loving communication (Mark 1:35; Matt. 11:25-26; 14:23; Luke 6:12; 22:32; 23:34; John 11:41-42; 12:27-28; 17:1-26; Heb. 5:7). Regarding the oneness they share, "God is not a substance underlying the communication; he is the substance of communication."[356] God is repeatedly shown to be a relational Trinity and this profoundly impacts the ontology, the horizontal implications, that we as his redeemed image bearers live in light of, are empowered by,

---

[352] As Carson notes, "If people believe in God at all today, the overwhelming majority hold that this God – whoever he, she, or it may be understood – is a loving being. That is what makes the task of the Christian witness so daunting. For this widely disseminated belief in the love of God is set with increasing frequency in some matrix other than biblical theology. The result is that when informed Christians talk about the love of God, they mean something very different from what is meant in the surrounding culture. Worse, neither side may perceive that is the case." Don Carson, *The Difficult Doctrine of the Love of God,* (Wheaton, IL: Crossway, 1999), 9-10.

[353] Michael Horton more recently writes, "As human beings, we are complex and compound creatures. That is, we are made up of various parts. However, God is simple and spiritual. On the one hand, this means that God is not the sum total of his attributes but is simultaneously everything that all of the attributes revealed. On the other hand, each of these attributes identifies a different aspect of God's existence and character that cannot be reduced to the others. This latter point is especially important, given the tendency of recent critiques to identify this doctrine with an extreme view that denies any real difference between attributes. One implication is that we cannot rank God's attributes or make one more essential to God than another. God is love even when he judges; he is holy and righteous even in saving sinners; he is eternal even when he acts in time." Michael Horton, *The Christian Faith: A Systematic Theology for Pilgrims on the Way,* (Grand Rapids, MI: Zondervan, 2011), 228.

[354] McKnight, Community Called Atonement, 16.

[355] Kevin Vanhoozer, *First Theology: God, Scripture, and Hermeneutics* (Downers Grove, IL: IVP, 2002), 74.

[356] Stephen Daniel, "Postmodern Concepts of God and Edwards' Trinitarian Ontology," in *Edwards in Our Time: Jonathan Edwards and the Shaping of American Religion,* ed. Hyun Lee Sang and Allen C. Guelzo (Grand Rapids, MI: Eerdmans, 1999), 55.

and strengthened through. "The three Persons of the Godhead experience an eternal, divine, reciprocal *love* among themselves, which necessitates a temporal experience in the give-and-take exchange in their nature as a God of *love*."[357] Christology speaks directly to the Person and Work of Jesus. "The Person of Jesus and his mission are together grounded in and flow from his unique relation to God: God and I, I and God, the incarnate I AM of the one Lord God of heaven and earth. That is who Jesus is, as the Son of Man, the Son of God become human, the very Light, Life, and Love of God Almighty."[358]

The following is an exegesis of selected texts from the gospels that demonstrate the ἀγαπάω love shared within the Trinity. Certainly, there are other attributes of God that can be discussed such as light, life, and holiness. However, for the purposes here, the study is limited to the *love* shared within the Trinity. The passages describing Jesus' baptism and transfiguration provide excellent source material enlightening how one may go about viewing the loving relationality of the Godhead. The nature of the section at hand here is going to be limited to exploring how Scripture speaks of the *relational* aspects between the Father and Son rather than discussions pertaining to "substances," "essences," etc. though the content of *what* the Father says strongly affirms the deity of the Son. The focus here will be on the two occasions in which God the Father (audibly) speaks to God the Son during his incarnate ministry, namely at his baptism and his transfiguration. The focus below is not only *that* the Father is speaking, but *what* is actually being said. "The social or conversational analogy of the Trinity suggests that the three persons relate in dialogical fashion: The Divine personas are not only in dialogue, they *are* dialogue."[359]

Jesus' Baptism and Transfiguration

The Father speaks to the Son clearly, boldly, authoritatively, and definitively. The purpose is not only for the benefit of the Son, but to witness to his unique personhood and role in the world for those around. At Jesus' baptism and again at his transfiguration, the Father speaks words over Jesus that set him apart from every other person who had or would ever live. Due to the immense nature of what transpires in

---

[357] Gulley, *God As Trinity*, 3, emphasis mine.

[358] Thomas Torrance, "The Christ Who Loves Us," in *A Passion for Christ: The Vision that Ignites Ministry*, ed. Gerrit Dawson and Jock Stein (Eugene, OR: Wipf & Stock, 2010), 10.

[359] Walter Kasper, *The God of Jesus Christ* (Spring Valley, CA: Crossroad Publishing, 1986), 290. "...the exercise proceeds on the presumption of Trinitarian orthodoxy, namely, that because of the oneness of being between the Father and his incarnate Son, God is antecedently in his eternal being what he is consequently to us in the Son. *We therefore come closest to understanding God's inner life by attending to the intra-Trinitarian communicative action in the economy, particularly the dialogical integration between the Father and Son that is on conspicuous display in the fourth Gospel.* There are three main topics in these Father-Son dialogues: mutual glorification; the giving of life; the sharing of love. God's being-in-communicative-act is thus a way of describing God's inner being as light, life, and love on the basis of his historical/relation/revelation to the world in these terms.... God's doing that which nothing greater can be conceived corresponds to the perfect life that God is in himself as Father, Son, and Spirit," Vanhoozer, *Remythologizing*, 243-4.

each of these events both biblically and theologically, the following will be limited merely to highlighting the loving relationship experienced and expressed between the Father and the Son. The "[Intra-Trinitarian dialogues] come at crucial moments in the narrative of the unfolding drama of the Trinity, and they mark the nodal points of the inner relations of the Trinity, worked out in time and space."[360]

Only the synoptic gospels record the events of the baptism and transfiguration of Jesus though some would argue that John 1:14 is a reference to the transfiguration. Also, John's gospel does not contain an exact account of the baptism but rather references the Holy Spirit descending and remaining upon Jesus (1:29-34). In each of the synoptic accounts of the baptism (Matt. 3:13-17; Mark 1:9-11; Luke 3:21-23) and transfiguration (Matt. 17:1-9; Mark 9:2-8; Luke 9:28-36) the Evangelists record that all three members of the Trinity are present and active, and that very specific words are spoken by the Father *to/about* the Son (Matt. 3:16-17; Mark 1:11; Luke 3:22).[361]

The Father's Love for the Son

In all three baptism accounts the Father refers to Jesus as his "beloved" (Matt. 3:16; Mark 1:11; Luke 3:22). Matthew writes, "this is my beloved" οὗτός ἐστιν ὁ υἱός μου ὁ ἀγαπητός "this is my one dear Son"[362] and not "*you* are my beloved" as is found in the other synoptic accounts. The majority of scholars understand the statement by the Father to/over Jesus as one that carries tones from a number of Old Testament texts (Gen. 22:2; Exod. 4:22-23; *especially* Ps. 2:7; Isa. 42:1). Specifically, it is worth noting the Septuagintal rendering of Genesis 22:2, "your son, your only son, whom you love" as the Abrahamic story of sacrifice serves as a well-suited backdrop for the gospel account told in John 3:16 as God gave "his *only* son." The reason for Matthew's choice of wording this in the third person is that it objectifies the experience and enables it to function as "more suitable [as] catechetical material for the church."[363] Schnakenberg emphasizes that the words of the Father spoken to/about Jesus offers the hearers then and the readers now a "dense, pregnant statement about him, and reveals the Christological

---

360 Oliver Davies, *A Theology of Compassion* (Norwich, England: Hymns Ancient and Modern Ltd, 2001),199-200.

361 Augustine states that "here then we have the Trinity presented in a clear way: the Father in the voice, the Son in the man, the Holy Spirit in the dove... a Trinity – inseparably one God, not three gods. But yet one God in such a way that the Son is not the Father, and the Father is not the Son, and the Holy Spirit is neither the Father nor the Son but the Spirit of the Father and of the Son. This ineffable Divinity, abiding ever in itself, making all things new, creating, creating anew, sending, recalling, judging, delivering, this Trinity, I say, we know to be at once indescribable and inseparable" Augustine, Sermon 2.1-2, PL 38:355; NPNF 1 6:259, cited in Manlio Simonetti, *Ancient Christian Commentary*: New Testament 1a: *Matthew 1-13,* 54 (Downers Grove, IL: IVP Academic, 2001), 54.

362 J. P. Louw and Eugene Nida, *Greek-English Lexicon of the New Testament: Based on Semantic Domains,* 2nd ed., vol. 1 (New York, NY: United Bible Societies, 1996), 590, Logos Bible Software, for Mac.

363 Donald Hagner, *Word Biblical Commentary: Matthew 1-13,* (Grand Rapids, MI: Zondervan), 58.

understanding of the primitive church."[364] It is imperative to note that "following Jesus' acceptance of John's baptism as the will of God for him, it declares both God's pleasure in that obedience and also, more fundamentally, his own unique *relationship* with God."[365] Condemned early in church history alongside Arianism was the doctrine of adoptionism espoused by the Ebionites as the heresy denied the divinity of Jesus. Indeed, in light of Mark 1:1 and Luke 1:32-35, 2:49, the doctrine of adoptionism finds no grounding being that Mark opens his gospel with affirming the identity of Jesus, the Son of God. Thus, in the Father's declaration the relationship between the two is not established, rather is simply a continuation of what already existed.[366]

Additionally, scholarship is divided over whether the "voice" that is heard is the *bath qol* ("daughter of the voice") or the *actual* voice of God, though most recent scholars dismiss the idea of the *bath qol*, affirming that God is indeed breaking the silence and speaking to Jesus, the true Israel.[367] What are readers to make of the *love*, the utter delighting in professed by the Father for, over, and in the Son? Certainly, this love is not a trivial or nonsensical romantic sort of love, this love, rather, pertains "to one who is the only one of his or her class, but at the same time is particularly loved and cherished—'only, only dear.'"[368] It is not uncommon to observe scholars breaking apart the etymology of the Greek words for *love* in the New Testament. C.S. Lewis is probably the most often cited in this discussion due to the popularity of his book, *The Four Loves*. In this work he "cites four distinct terms: *storge* (affection, especially within families),

---

[364] Robert Schnakenberg, *Matthew* (Grand Rapids, MI: Eerdmans, 2002), 35.

[365] France, *Matthew*, 122-123, emphasis mine.

[366] James Edwards, *Pillar New Testament Commentary: Mark* (Grand Rapids, MI: Eerdmans, 2002), 38. Additionally, Hofius writes, "The New Testament authors desire to make clear: The one who is promised in the Scriptures as the Son of God is *in truth* according to his beginning and being, and therefore from his very inception, the *divine* Son who belongs at the side of God. Accordingly, *nowhere* in the New Testament is there talk of the man Jesus of Nazareth being adopted as Messiah." Otfried Hofius, "Ist Jesus der Messias? Thesen," in *Der Messias*, JBTh 8, ed I. Baldermann (Neukirchen, Germany: Neukirchener Verlag, 1993), 125, italics in original (cited in Edwards, *Commentary: Mark*).

[367] The *bath qol* is the idea that refers to how God communicated during the intertestamental period in which no prophecy was uttered, hence "echo" or "daughter of the voice." See also L. Sabourin, *L'Evangile selon saint Matthieu et ses principaux paralleles* (Rome, Italy: Biblical Institute Press, 1978), 39. France comments, "There is no reason to believe that Matthew intends us to understand anything less than a direct declaration by God himself about his Son," France, *Matthew*, 122. For references to the *bath qol*, see Midrash Rab. Eccles. 12.7, B. Berakoth 3a.

[368] Louw and Nida, *Greek-English Lexicon*, 590. Don Carson suggests that the term here may not only be a term of affection but also may be pointing towards *election*, being that it is "reinforced by the aorist tense that follows (lit., "with him I was well pleased"), suggesting a pretemporal election of the Messiah (cf. John 1:34)," D. A. Carson, *Expositor's Bible Commentary*, vol. 8, *Matthew, Mark, and Luke* ed. F. E. Gaebelein (Grand Rapids, MI: Zondervan, 1984-99), 109.

philia (friendship), *eros* (love between the sexes or being in love), and, of course, *agape* (charity or self-giving love)."[369]

Though the baptism account most certainly is not intended to be a lengthy excursus on the relationality between the Father and Son, it is worth noting at this point that a survey of several contemporary commentaries speak more to the *bath qol* and semantics over *that* God spoke rather than examining the relational nature of *what* was spoken; some of which say absolutely nothing about the Father's *love* for the Son.[370] For our purposes here, it will serve well to examine the ἀγαπητός mentioned by the synoptic evangelists. Hendriksen states, "No higher love is possible than the love which the Father cherishes toward his Son. According to the verbal adjective (beloved) here used, this love is deep-seated, thorough-going, as great as is the heart of God himself. It is also as intelligent and purposeful as is the mind of God. It is tender, vast, infinite!"[371]

Going beyond Carson's suggestions about the uniqueness and "election," of Jesus, Guelich does well to emphasize the second phrase of the divine pronouncement, ἐν σοὶ εὐδόκησα. Guelich states,

> The voice consistently addresses Jesus both in terms of his role (Ps 2:7, "son" = the anointed king; Isa 42:1, "my chosen" = the servant] *and* his relationship to the Father ("my son, the only/beloved one," cf. Gen. 22:2; "very pleased," εὐδόκησα instead of the more explicit ἐκλεκτός of Isa. 42:1) .. The "filial" relationhip ("beloved son," cf. Gen. 22:2; and "very pleased," Isa 42:1) remains unspecified. Yet it is preciesly this enigma in Jesus' role and relationship with the Father that marks his earthly minsitry as depicted in the Gospels.[372]

The Father loves and thoroughly delights in his only Son. "Within the inner history of the Trinity is an eternal, divine community of love in which reciprocal love for one another needs no process, no fuller development through a sort of evolution. This love of God is as unchangeable as God Himself (Mal. 3:6). This God is a relational God, the God of covenantal love, the God whose love for humans overflows from the inner-Trinitarian history into human history, into minds and hearts to bring redemption and

---

[369] Stanley Grenz, *The Social God and the Relational Self: A Trinitarian Theology of the Imago Dei* (Louisville, KY: Westminster John Knox Press, 2001), 313. See also C. S. Lewis, *The Four Loves* (New York, NY: Mariner Books, 1971).

[370] Edwards, *Commentary: Mark*, 36-37 as noted above, cites Hofius, but only mentions Jesus as the one who is "anointed," "equipped," "and "servant." See also Craig Blomberg, *Matthew* (Nashville, TN: Broadman Press, 1992),81-82, France, *Matthew*, 122-124, Carson, *Matthew*, 109, Morna Hooker, *The Gospel According to St. Mark* (Grand Rapids, MI: Baker Academic, 1991), 47. Ben Witherington III, *A Socio-Rhetorical Commentary: The Gospel of Mark* (Grand Rapids, MI: Eerdmans, 2001], 75. Joel Green, *NICNT: The Gospel of Luke* (Grand Rapids, MI: Eerdmans, 1997),185-187; John Nolland, *Word Biblical Commentary*, vol. 35a, *Luke 1:1-9:20* (Nashville, TN: Thomas Nelson, 1989), 167-175.

[371] William Hendriksen, *New Testament Commentary: Exposition of the Gospel of Luke* (Grand Rapids, MI: Baker Academic, 1980), 218-219.

[372] Robert Guelich, *Word Biblical Commentary*, vol. 34a, *Mark 1-8:26* (Nashville, TN: Thomas Nelson, 1989), 34.

restoration to all who are willing to receive."[373] "The experience of God as Father dominates the whole ministry of Jesus from the Baptism to the Crucifixion."[374] This is the Father who so loved not only his Son, but so loved the world that he gave his only Son that whoever would believe in him would not perish, but have everlasting life (John 3:16). This saving delivers the believers from "wrath that abides" upon the sinner (3:36). As Calvin so aptly states just one pastoral and relational implication of PSA, "We must specially remember this substitution in order that we may not be all our lives in trepidation and anxiety, as if the just vengeance, which the Son of God transferred to himself, were still impending over us."[375]

In so doing, the believer who was once an enemy of God (Rom. 5:10) now stands justified and blameless before God forensically but also has the privilege of enjoying a close, intimate relationship with God *personally*, exactly as Jesus himself. It is with this in mind that we turn our attention to the experience of "*Abba*, Father."

Abba, Father

In the Gospel of Matthew, the term "Father" is used forty-four times in total, all of which are spoken by Jesus himself. Jesus taught the disciples to pray "our Father" and yet, when *he* prayed, he prayed "*my* Father."[376] "Everything that is distinctively Christian as opposed to merely Jewish, is summed up in the knowledge of the fatherhood of God, 'Father' is the Christian name of God."[377] In his profound and sometimes controversial work, Joachim Jeremias brings much to bear on the unique vertical relationship now given to the adopted children of God, namely, a close, intimate, relationship with a tender Father. "*Abba* as a form of address to one's father was no longer restricted to children, but also used by adult sons and daughters. The childish character of the word ('daddy') thus receded, and *abba* acquired the warm, familiar ring which we may feel in such an expression as "dear father."[378]

---

[373] Gulley, God as Trinity, 270.

[374] T. W. Manson, *The Teachings of Jesus: Studies in its Form and Content* (Cambridge, England: Cambridge University Press, 1959), 102. And this is highlighted explicitly in the temple account as a young boy (Luke 2:41-52).

[375] Calvin, *Institutes* 2.16.5, quoted in Martin Davie, "Dead to Sin and Alive to God," *SBET* 19, no. 2 (Autumn 2001): 162.

[376] Damon W. K. So, *Jesus' Revelation of His Father: A Narrative-Conceptual Study of the Trinity with Special Reference to Karl Barth,* (Carlisle, PA: Paternoster Press, 2006), 84. See Matthew 7:21; 10:32, 33; 11:27; 12:50; 15:13; 16:17; 18:10, 19, 35; 20:23; 25:34; 26:39, 42, 53.

[377] J. I. Packer, *Knowing God* (Downers Grove, IL: IVP, 1993), 182-3.

[378] Otfried Hofius, "*Abba*," in *New International Dictionary of New Testament Theology,* ed. Colon Brown, vol. 1 (Grand Rapids, MI: Zondervan, 1986), 614. Hofius, however went on to make an error in stating "Nowhere in the entire wealth of devotional literature produced by ancient Judaism do we find *abba* being used as a way of addressing God. The pious Jew knew too much of the great gap between God and man (Eccl. 5:1) to be free to address God with the familiar word used in everyday family life." For there is one reference (Ben Sira) in Eccl. 51:10 in which the term is used. See So, *Jesus' Revelation,* 84.

We turn our attention now to the tenderness extended and expressed by God as *Abba*, Father.

Abba, Father: Tenderness

It must be emphasized that "Jesus' use of this unusual and rather intimate form for addressing God in prayer suggests strongly that Jesus' religious life was characterized by relating to God in a very intense and personalized way that is not fully paralleled even in other examples of very devout spirituality in the ancient Jewish setting."[379] Jesus seems to have thought of himself as God's son in a *distinctive* sense.[380]

> This special sense of sonship to God likely provided the experiential impetus of Jesus' mission ... And the mission to which God called Jesus apparently included *extending an unusually intimate relationship to God as "Father" among those who accepted Jesus' proclamation of God's kingdom* ... there is no parallel for Jesus' sense that God called him to become the pioneer and catalyst for a special filial relationship to God to be enjoyed by his disciples.[381]

Furthermore, the only time that the gospel writers actually retain the Aramaic "*Abba*" is in Jesus' prayer in the garden of Gethsemane. "And he said, '*Abba*, Father, all things are possible for you. Remove this cup from me. Yet not what I will, but what you will'" (Mark 14:36). Even here, as referenced earlier, the cup speaks of the wrath of God. In this moment, Jesus is not using sloppy sentimentalism, rather, he reveals that his heart is completely bound to the will of God, no matter the cost. Trumper states, "the trauma of Gethsemane reminds us powerfully that the appropriating language of *Abba* bespeaks not dripping sentimentality – as if daddy were a big softy to be manipulated at will – but the *seriousness of filial love, devotion, and obedience.*"[382] The Apostle Paul's repeated emphasis on believers now being identified as sons (Gal. 3:26) and co-heirs (Rom. 8:17) with Christ implies that the adopted saint now made holy by the Person and the Work of Jesus and the indwelling, out-crying Holy Spirit, can enjoy, be sustained by, and rest in the *same* intimate relationship that Jesus had while in his incarnate, earthly ministry. The Father clearly speaks over Jesus, "this is my beloved Son" (Matt. 3:17). And now that sin is atoned for (Rom. 3:21-26), righteousness is imputed (2 Cor. 5:21), and adoption accomplished (Rom. 8:15; Gal. 4:5-6), the Father delights in the believer (Zeph. 3:17), the son (Rom. 8:14), the child (John 1:12) in the same way. Indeed, "By encouraging his disciples to pray to God as *Abba*, Jesus is teaching them that God is not a transcendent God who is remote from his people, but a God who desires to

---

[379] Joel Green, Scot McKnight, and Howard Marshall, eds., "God," in *Dictionary of Jesus and the Gospels* (Downers Grove, IL: IVP Academic, 1992), 275.

[380] James Dunn, Jesus and the Spirit: A Study of the Religious and Charismatic Experience of Jesus and the First Christians as Reflected in the New Testament (London, England: SCM Press, 1975), 38.

[381] Green, McKnight, and Marshall, "God," 275, emphasis mine.

[382] Tim J. R. Trumper, "A Fresh Exposition of Adoption: I. An Outline," *SBET* 23, no. 1 (Spring 2005): 74.

draw his people close to himself in a highly personal and intimate matter."[383] David DeSilva reinforces this by referring to Paul's early paternal citations saying, "Paul uses references to God as the Father of believers at the start of many of his letters, showing the prominence and almost "givenness" of this new household and its *paterfamilias* within Christian culture."[384]

Without belaboring the point, it is also important to note that the intimate, longing heart of God brought to bear so clearly in the New Testament is hardly a *new* idea introduced in Scripture. For in Jeremiah 31:20, the LORD speaks, "Is Ephraim my dear son? Is he my *darling* child? For as often as I speak against him, I do remember him still. Therefore my heart yearns for him. I will surely have mercy on him, declares the LORD." The term "darling" connotes pleasantness and utter delight. In Hosea, the tender heart of God is laid bare:

> When Israel was a child, I loved him and out of Egypt I called my son. The more they were called, the more they went away; they kept sacrificing to the Baals and burning offerings to idols. Yet it was I who taught Ephraim to walk; I took them up by their arms, but they did not know that I healed them. I led them with cords of kindness, with the bands of love and I became to them as one who eases the yoke on their jaws, and I bent down to them and fed them (Hosea 11:1-4).

Not only do the children of God now have an intimate relationship with God as *Abba*, Father, they can go before his throne of grace, continually, boldly, and confidently. Ferguson exhorts believers to think deeply upon this reality of speaking to and approaching God as *Abba* by saying, "Think of the privilege of calling the Creator of the ends of the earth "*Abba*, Father." It defies comprehension and calculation."[385] And yet, for all whom God has adopted as sons and daughters into his family it is true!

Abba, Father: Throne of Grace

Another vertical relational implication of PSA is access to the throne of God. Though the Father is the judge ruling over all creation, the child of God need not be afraid to *approach the throne.* These revelations of God as judge and Father abound throughout the letter to the Hebrews and are intended to point the original recipients and readers today in the direction of perseverance.[386] And while the throne is the most

---

[383] So, Jesus' Revelation, 85.

[384] David DeSilva, Honor, Patronage, Kinship, and Purity: Unlocking New Testament Culture (Downers Grove, IL: IVP, 2000), 207.

[385] Sinclair B. Ferguson, *The Christian Life: A Doctrinal Introduction,* (Edinburgh, England: Banner of Truth, 2013), 86.

[386] Hebrews 2:10; 4:1-11, 13; 5:8; 9:14; 10:19-22; 12:4-11, 23, 29. When commenting on the nature of the Epistle to the Hebrews David DeSilva writes, "It resembles the sort of speech one would hear on the eve of a great battle, in the midst or at the end of a long campaign. Some of the hearers are ready for the fight, and so the speech reinforces the commitment with which they come to the field. Some have lost their initial vision and zeal for the fight and need encouragement to reinvest themselves in the endeavor. Some need to be kept from running off the field during the night." David DeSilva, *Perseverance in Gratitude: A Socio-Rhetorical*

lofty place in all of the universe, it is declared to be a "throne of grace" to those who belong to Jesus. The writer of Hebrews admonishes the children of God saying, "For we do not have a high priest who is unable to sympathize with our weaknesses, but one who in every respect has been tempted as we are, yet without sin. Let us then with confidence draw near to the throne of grace (χάριτος), that we may receive mercy and find grace (χάριν) to help in time of need" (Heb. 4:15-16).

Verse 15 will be addressed below, speaking of Jesus, our Brother, the divine sympathizer. In order to better understand and appreciate the access granted to the throne of God's grace, one must recall that this is an entirely new idea to the Hebrew audience who now professes faith in Christ as the messiah of God, to whom this letter was addressed. Throughout the Old Testament the ark of the covenant represented the throne of God, his presence (e.g., 1 Sam. 6:2; Ps. 80:1; 99:1; Isa. 37:16; cf. Ps. 22:3). The sacredness of Yom Kippur has been discussed in the section on "Sacrifice"; the Hebrews, acknowledge that their sin has offended God and has resulted in a broken relationship and that only the appointed high priest can go before God once a year, offering sacrifices, and thus making atonement for the sins of the people.[387] Yet, because of the penal sacrifice of Christ (Rom. 3:21), the mediator (1 Tim. 2:5), the lamb of God who takes away the sins of the world (John 1:29), the writer of the letter admonishes the reconciled people of God to come *boldly* before not a throne of judgment but a throne of grace!

The admonition for believers to "approach" or draw near to God is a recurrent theme in Hebrews. The origin of such language is certainly cultic.[388] O'Brien and Peterson helpfully note that ability to now draw near to God (cf. Heb. 7:25) implies that "the sense of a new *relationship* with God through the mediation of Christ is primarily in

---

Commentary on the Epistle "to the Hebrews" (Grand Rapids, MI: Eerdmans, 2000), 57. See also Howard Marshall, *New Testament Theology: Many Witnesses, One Gospel* (Downers Grove, IL: IVP, 2014), 620-1.

[387] Or as Hughes states, "In the Levitical system that had prevailed up till the time of Christ's advent only the high priest was permitted to approach into the sanctuary of God's presence, and then only once a year, on the Day of Atonement, when he passed from sight into the holy of holies. The people, however, were *excluded* from the divine presence because of their sinfulness and *prohibited* from drawing near. But the atonement effected by Christ's sacrifice of himself on the cross opened the way that had hitherto been closed. This was dramatically symbolized by the rending of the temple curtain from top to bottom at the time of the crucifixion, indicating that through an act of divine grace access into the holiest place was now available to all the people of God." Phillip Hughes, *Hebrews* (Grand Rapids, MI: Eerdmans, 1987), 173, emphasis mine.

[388] "Sometimes προσερχώμεθα ('approach, draw near') in the LXX describes the action of all the Israelites, coming before the Lord in solemn assembly (Exod. 16:9; 34:32). The congregation could draw near to the tent of meeting to stand before the Lord (Lev. 9:5), but only the priests might draw near to the altar to make offerings (Lev. 9:7, 8; 21:17, 21, 23; 22:3)," Peter O'Brien, *Pillar New Testament Commentary: The Letter to the Hebrews* (Grand Rapids, MI: Eerdmans, 2010), 185 n. 178.

focus (see 7:19)."[389] Believers now are no longer to "keep their distance in fear and trembling, but on the contrary are now invited to *draw near*"[390] to God in prayer and to do so with "confidence." This *confidence* can be understood as a state of boldness and confidence, sometimes implying intimidating circumstances—"boldness, courage."[391] No Jew would ever think with the simple boldness and confidence of a child to approach God because of the understanding of God's holiness and their sinfulness. Yet because of PSA, this access is granted.[392]

Not only is the vertical relationship with the Father established and prayer directly to God made available, but the throne of God itself is "a throne characterized by grace."[393] DeSilva states that "the throne of God has become a source of 'favors' (i.e., the resources that will provide 'timely help') due to the 'favorable disposition' toward the addressees of the One who sits upon it."[394] And yet, this is not negating the honor, reverence, and worship due the Father. For the "boldness … here in view is clearly not a public 'freedom of speech,' but a confident self-expression before God, above all in prayer."[395] In step with the favorable disposition and gracious throne from which resources are extended to the children of God, one further piece will strengthen our understanding of the vertical relationship established between *Abba* and the redeemed, namely, *Abba* as the giver of wisdom.

Abba: The Origin and Giver of Wisdom

One massive theme that runs throughout Scripture is humankind's need for wisdom and God's ability and willingness to provide such.The Scripture speaks of all three members of the Trinity playing a vital role in the extending of wisdom. Jesus is said to be the wisdom of God (1 Cor. 1:24) and the Holy Spirit is said to give wisdom to the children of God (Col. 1:9). The focus here will be limited to the Father's role in extending wisdom to his children with whom he is now completely reconciled. Solomon writes that "The fear of the LORD is the beginning of knowledge and fools despise wisdom and instruction" (Prov. 1:7) and that "The beginning of wisdom is this: Get wisdom, and whatever you get, get insight" (4:7).[396] The fear of the LORD and wisdom are commonly mentioned together in wisdom literature of the Old Testament. And yet, fearing the LORD is not the same as being terrified of him, though both are present in

---

[389] David Peterson, *Hebrews and Perfection: An Examination of the Concept of Perfection in the Epistle to the Hebrews* (Cambridge, England: Cambridge University Press, 1995), 79, emphasis mine. See also O'Brien, *Hebrews*, 185.

[390] Hughes, *Hebrews*, 173.

[391] Louw and Nida, *Greek-English Lexicon*, 306.

[392] O'Brien states regarding the "boldness" referenced here, it often describes a subjective confidence that is objectively grounded: "the listeners are to approach God in prayer freely and openly on the basis of Jesus' high-priestly work for them," O'Brien, *Hebrews*, 185.

[393] O'Brien, *Hebrews*, 185.

[394] DeSilva, *Hebrews*, 182.

[395] Harold Attridge, Hermeneia, A Critical and Historical Commentary on the Bible: Hebrews: A Commentary on the Epistle to the Hebrews (Minneapolis, MN: Fortress Press, 1989), 142.

[396] See also Psalm 111:10; Proverbs 9:10, 15:33.

Scripture. The fear of the LORD is "building on attitudes of awe and reverence; it is the proper and elemental response of a person to God."[397] Furthermore, "It is not too much to say that fearing God is virtually synonymous with having saving faith in him."[398] Again, "wisdom in Scripture is inseparable from allegiance to God and moral living."[399] And yet, in light of the above statements about coming boldly before God's throne of grace in which his children may receive the resources necessary to living the life that he would have (Heb 4:16), it would be helpful to look in one place in the New Testament where the character of God is revealed as a giver of wisdom to his children. Much like the writer of the epistle to the Hebrews, addressing an audience who is in danger of neglecting their salvation and falling away from their relationship with God, so too, the Apostle James opens his letter to the persecuted diaspora with a strong admonition to endure joyfully under the providence of God, seeking him and his wisdom diligently. James writes,

> Count it all joy, my brothers, when you meet trials of various kinds, for you know that the testing of your faith produces steadfastness. And let steadfastness have its full effect, that you may be perfect and complete, lacking in nothing. If any of you lacks wisdom, let him ask God, who gives generously to all without reproach, and it will be given him (James 1:2-5).

The vertical relationship is not merely experienced once but intended to be something that is ongoing. James echoes the Old Testament and Jewish belief that "The LORD gives wisdom" (Prov. 2:6). "In all Christian temptation wisdom is to be had 'just for the asking,' a gift here described by James with an adverb etymologically meaning 'simply,' a word often used in Greek in contrast to another Greek word connoting complex variety, in nature or art, from a patchwork quilt to an elaborate financial fraud."[400]

The *simplicity* here must not be overlooked, for it is profoundly *relational*, calling to mind a particular kind of closeness, approachability, and intimacy. The posture of the Father's heart toward the one going before him in prayer asking for his wisdom is one that is *"generous."* Generously can also be translated "kind" or "whole-hearted."[401] The best word translated here is probably "freely" according to Adamson.[402] However, Moo reveals that etymologically speaking, James uses a word that is a *hapax logomeneon* and the root of God's giving means "single," "simple," "an idea retained in Paul's use of a word cognate to this one in Ephesians 6:5 (cf. Col. 3:22): "Slaves, obey your earthly

---

[397] Ryken, Wilhoit, and Longman III, eds., "Fear of God," in *Dictionary of Biblical Imagery*, 277.

[398] Ryken, Wilhoit, and Longman III, eds., "Fear of God," in *Dictionary of Biblical Imagery*, 277.

[399] Craig Blomberg, Mariam Kamell, and Clinton Arnold, eds., *Zondervan Exegetical Commentary on the New Testament: James* (Grand Rapids, MI: Zondervan, 2008), 61.

[400] James Adamson, *NICNT: The Epistle of James* (Grand Rapids, MI: Eerdmans, 1976), 56.

[401] Otto Bauernfeind, "ἁπλῶς," in *Theological Dictionary of the New Testament*, ed. Gerhard Kittle, trans. Geoffrey W. Bromiley, vol. 1 (Grand Rapids, MI: Eerdmans, 1965), 386. Hort argues that the word *graciously* here is perhaps the best word because it recalls the Old Testament concept of *hesed.*

[402] Adamson, *James*, 56.

masters ... with *sincerity* of heart."[403] The semantic range of this word is also important to this understanding of singleness or simplicity of God's provision of wisdom. For, when considering the twelve times the word surfaces in the LXX, only once is it used implying "generosity." The remaining eleven times denote "integrity" or "blamelessness." Thinking through wisdom texts such as Proverbs 10:9, "The man of integrity walks securely, but he who takes crooked paths will be found out" or Christ's own statement, "The light of the body is the eye: therefore when the eye is single, the whole body is also full of light" (Luke 11:34), Moo comments, "Taken together, then, the evidence suggests that James is not so much highlighting God's generosity in giving as his single, undivided intent to give us those gifts we need to please him."[404]

Not only is the Father's heart one that is good, freely providing all good gifts for his children (1:17), but James introduces the concept of the Father's deliberate decisive will to not bring *reproach* into the wisdom exchange experience. The word *reproach* (ὀνειδίζω) here can be understood as "to rail at, revile, assail with abusive words,"[405] or a term used "with the implication of that individual being evidently to blame—'to reprimand.'"[406] Adamson helpfully notes that "God gives his wisdom to man not only just for asking but also without chiding a man for his previous sins, many of which the man may not even know he has committed."[407] For the Father to give graciously and freely, and purposefully not bring reproach is an intentional, loving decision to keep the *relationship* grounded not in accounting, legal terms but in grace. Furthermore, the Father need not give begrudgingly due to sin, for sin has been defeated in Christ's penal sacrifice. Thus, in the experience of prayer and requesting for wisdom, "God is, then, one who gives sincerely, without hesitation or mental reservation. He does not grumble or criticize. His commitment to his people is total and unreserved: they can expect to receive."[408] Though certainly not exhaustive, these examples of the tenderness, approachability, and giving nature of *Abba* towards his children demonstrate that the vertical relationship with the Father is established and thus the relationship is one defined by love, intimacy, holy reverence, and communion with him. Cranfield states, "Christians are men [and women] who have great expectations, that their expectations are based upon their being sons [and daughters] of God, that these expectations are of sharing not just in various blessings God is able to bestow but in that which is peculiarly His own, the perfect and imperishable glory *of his own life.*[409]

---

[403] Douglas Moo, *Pillar New Testament Commentary: The Letter of James* (Grand Rapids, MI: Eerdmans, 2000), 58.

[404] Moo, *James,* 59. Calvin writes, "Since we see that the Lord does not so require from us what is above our strength, but that he is ready to help us, provided we ask (relational!), let us, therefore, learn whenever he commands anything, to ask of him the power to perform it." John Calvin, *James* (Grand Rapids, MI: Baker Books, 1974), 282.

[405] Spiros Zodhiates, "reproach=ὀνειδίζω," *The Complete Word Study Dictionary: New Testament,* Logos Bible Software, for Mac (Chattanooga, TN: AMG Publishers, 2000).

[406] Louw and Nida, *Greek-English Lexicon,* 436.

[407] Adamson, *James,* 56.

[408] Davids, "Adoption," 73.

[409] Cranfield, *Romans,* 419, emphasis mine.

How profound is the relationship established! "*Abba's* sons are also *Abba's* heirs, the inheritance believers can look forward to is God himself."[410] This is all accomplished through the Person and the Work of the Son, Jesus Christ, with whom the believer also has a relationship by the indwelling Holy Spirit.

The Son as God

Theologian Kevin Vanhoozer rightly states that "we should begin our thinking about meaning and interpretation as Christians with the paradigm of the triune God in communicative action."[411] This is important since we have not only a relationship, but also *relationships* with the members of the Trinity. It must be briefly repeated that it is the Christian Scriptures and orthodox Christianity that have been unmistakably clear in identifying, confessing, and following Jesus as the unique Son of God, holding that he is both co-equal and consubstantial with the Father. Jesus repeatedly declares that he is "one with the Father" (John 10:30) and that if one has seen Jesus, then that person has seen the Father as well (14:9). As in line with what is said above under the section pertaining to the baptism and transfiguration of Jesus, the New Testament leaves no room for any understanding of Jesus to be less than God, rather, rightfully belonging to the Holy Trinity as the second member (John 1:1-4; Phil. 2:5-11; Col.1:15-20; Heb. 1:1-3, etc.).

How profound is the relationship established! "*Abba's* sons are also *Abba's* heirs, the inheritance believers can look forward to is God himself."[412] This is all accomplished through the Person and the Work of the Son, Jesus Christ, with whom the believer also has a relationship by the indwelling Holy Spirit.

the inheritance believers can look forward to is God himself."[413] This is all accomplished through the Person and the Work of the Son, Jesus Christ, with whom the believer also has a relationship by the indwelling Holy Spirit.

Trinitarian theologian Colin Gunton states, "If we fail to identify three distinct agents, we are not being true to the biblical witness."[414] Early Church Father, Gregory of Nyssa declares, "Every operation which extends from God to the creation ... has its origin from the Father, proceeds through the Son, and is perfected in the Holy Spirit."[415] Again this, too, must be kept in mind when thinking in terms of PSA and the vertical relationship being established and accomplished. Aquinas is careful to note the

---

[410] Trevor Burke, *Adopted into God's Family: Exploring a Pauline Metaphor* (Downers Grove, IL: IVP Academic, 2006), 99.

[411] Vanhoozer, *Remythologizing*, 6.

[412] Trevor Burke, *Adopted into God's Family: Exploring a Pauline Metaphor* (Downers Grove, IL: IVP Academic, 2006), 99.

[413] Trevor Burke, *Adopted into God's Family: Exploring a Pauline Metaphor* (Downers Grove, IL: IVP Academic, 2006), 99.

[414] Colin Gunton, Act and Being: Towards A Theology of the Divine Attributes (Grand Rapids, MI: Eerdmans, 2003], 143.

[415] Gregory of Nyssa, *To Abalabius, on "Not Three Gods,"* Nicene and Post-Nicene Fathers, 2nd term, 5:334.

uniqueness in each of the persons communicating. "It is not true that the Father, Son, and Holy Spirit are one speaker."[416] The "oneness" and "three-ness" must continually be placed within the PSA conversation. Indeed, Norman Gulley notes that the Son "receives equal honor and worship as the Father, and .... They are both on the throne, and they receive joint worship and praise."

Figure 9 – The "Oneness" and "Three-ness" of the Trinity re: the PSA

Father	Son	Father and Son
"You are worthy, our Lord and God, to receive glory and honor and power, for you created all things, and by your will they were created and have their being."	"Worthy is the Lamb, who was slain, to receive power and wealth and wisdom and strength and honor and glory and praise."	"To him who sits on the throne and to the Lamb be praise and honor, and glory and power, forever and ever!"
Revelation 4:11	Revelation 5:12	Revelation 5:13b[417]

And as the second member of the Trinity, Jesus too, exercises final judgment of the world he created.

Jesus as Judge

The Scriptures are abundantly clear that all three members of the Trinity are involved in the judgment of humankind though with less emphasis given to the role of the Holy Spirit as will be discussed below. The role of the Son in the judgment of humankind is emphasized in a few places within the New Testament outside of the gospels. For example,

> And he commanded us to preach to the people and to testify that he is the one appointed by God to be *judge* of the living and the dead (Acts 10:42). On that day when, according to my gospel, God *judges* the secrets of men by Christ Jesus (Rom. 2:16). I charge you in the presence of God and of Christ Jesus, who is to *judge* the living and the dead, and by his appearing and his kingdom (2 Tim. 4:1).

On some occasions the Son is said to function as a witness to the Father's judgment (Matt. 10:32-33). Yet, in other cases, final judgment is said to be carried out explicitly by the Son. As Jesus speaks of the coming judgment, he follows along the lines of Jewish thought, placing emphasis on good and evil works (Matt. 7:21-23; 12:36-37; 25:31-46).

And yet, Jesus is very clear that one's works are not all that are going to be taken into account by him at judgment. Jesus repeatedly reminds us that human beings are judged by him based on a *relationship* to him (Matt. 7:24-27; 25:31-46). The vertical relationship must be established for one to experience salvation.

---

[416] Thomas Aquinas, *Summa Theologica,* trans. Fathers of the English Dominican Province (New York, NY: Christian Classics, 1981), I.34:1a.

[417] Gulley, *God As Trinity*, 15.

Not everyone who says to me, "Lord, Lord," will enter the kingdom of heaven, but the one who does the will of my Father who is in heaven. On that day many will say to me, "Lord, Lord, did we not prophesy in your name, and cast out demons in your name, and do many mighty works in your name?" And then will I declare to them, "I never knew you; depart from me, you workers of lawlessness" (Matt. 7:21-23).

And again, Jesus says, "For the Son of Man is going to come with his angels in the glory of his Father, and then he will repay each person according to what he has done" (Matt. 16:27).

In the Apocalypse, John writes of the judgment by Jesus, "he also will drink the wine of God's wrath, poured full strength into the cup of his anger, and he will be tormented with fire and sulfur in the presence of the holy angels and in the presence of the Lamb" (Rev. 14:10). Beale states, "The point is that those who have denied the Lamb will be forced to acknowledge him as they are being punished 'before' him (as in 6:16). A similar purpose is achieved where Jewish writings depict the wicked seeing the reward of the righteous."[418]

However, what of penal substitutionary atonement, the Lamb mentioned above, and the judgment by Jesus, as it pertains to the believer today? Need the believer fear *this aspect* of Jesus? Karl Barth, as noted earlier, reminds us that the "Judge [has been] judged in our place."[419] Those who are *in Christ* need not fear final judgment as it pertains to salvation (Rom. 8:1). The wrath of God was averted through Christ and does not threaten those who would become part of the family of God. The judgment that the believers will face as mentioned by Paul as he speaks of the *judgment seat of Christ* is different. Immediately before addressing the ministry of reconciliation, and what Luther famously coined as "the Great Exchange," the Apostle Paul writes,

> Yes, we are of good courage, and we would rather be away from the body and at home with the Lord. So whether we are at home or away, we make it our aim to please him. For we must all appear before the judgment seat of Christ, so that each one may receive what is due for what he has done in the body, whether good or evil (2 Cor. 5:8-10).

At the beginning of this passage, the believer who is reconciled with God and experiences the established vertical relationship is assured that he or she will be "at home with the Lord" providing the reason *why* "we make it our aim to please him." And yet, this confidence in one's justification is not to be taken lightly, rather stewarded as faithful sons and daughters – Christ's disciples. Paul warns that all must appear before the judgment seat of Christ." Here too, Jesus is judge.[420]

---

[418] G. K. Beale, *NIGTC: The Book of Revelation* (Grand Rapids, MI: Eerdmans, 1999), 760.

[419] Barth, *Dogmatics: Reconciliation,* vol. 4, bk. 1: 59.2.

[420] Clearly, the two positions – God-given salvation (see, e.g., Rom. 3:21-31; 5:1-11; Gal. 5:4-5) and the judgment of each according to his works (see, e.g., Rom. 2:6-11; 14:10; 1 Cor. 14:13; Eph. 6:8; Col. 3:25; cf. Matt. 16:27; 1 Pet. 1:17; Rev. 2:23; 20:12; 22:12] – were reconcilable to Paul." Paul Barnett, *NICNT: 2 Corinthians* (Grand Rapids, MI: Eerdmans, 1997), 276.

This judgment is a judgment based on one's works *in Christ* and the motives of which are evaluated finally. Even in this text, Paul emphasizes the fact that one's salvation is not in jeopardy! The reason is that salvation is *accomplished* in Christ. C. K. Garland comments,

> The teaching about the judgment seat before which all believers must come reminds us that we have been saved, not for a life of aimlessness or indifference, but to live as to the Lord (2 Cor. 5:15). This doctrine of the universality of the judgment of believers preserves the moral seriousness of God. ... The sure prospect of the judgment seat reminds the Corinthians—and all believers—that while they are righteous in Christ by faith alone, the faith that justifies is to be expressed by love and obedience (Gal. 5:6; Rom. 1:5), and by pleasing the Lord (2 Cor. 5:9).[421]

Barnett articulates this as "Those 'outside Christ' face the sinner's judgment; on the other hand, those 'in Christ' face his judgment bench as saints."[422] The believer's salvation is secure; wrath no longer awaits the child of God. The judgment seat of Christ is there to evaluate the motives and the works done "in Christ." The relationship with Christ must therefore be one that is ongoing through the Holy Spirit who reveals Christ and empowers the believer to carry out works that are pleasing to him (Eph. 2:10) as will be discussed below. For our purposes here regarding the relational paradigm, Christ is not only future judge, but is also our present and future "Brother." Peering through and turning the kaleidoscope, the brotherhood of Jesus now comes into focus.

Jesus as Older Brother

All three synoptic accounts record an occasion in which Jesus *distances* himself from his own biological family and establishes and expands the family of God being one not born of flesh but of the Spirit and is evidenced by obedience to the Father. These are whom Jesus refers to as "brother," "sister," and "mother" (Matt. 12:46-50; Mark 3:35; Luke 8:19-21).

> While he was still speaking to the people, behold, his mother and his brothers stood outside, asking to speak to him. But he replied to the man who told him, "Who is my mother, and who are my brothers?" And stretching out his hand toward his disciples, he said, "Here are my mother and my brothers! For whoever does the will of my Father in heaven is my brother and sister and mother" (Matt. 12:46-50).

In this passage, Jesus' *brotherhood* is first explicitly stated in the gospel of Matthew. The teaching of the disciples to pray "Our Father" (6:9) is the first implicit reference to a newfound family that is coming into existence. "The implied repudiation of Jesus' own family is a matter of priority rather than an absolute dissociation. But the focus here is not on their rebuff but on the positive assertion that Jesus' disciples are his true

---

[421] David Garland, *The New American Commentary,* vol. 29, *2 Corinthians* (Nashville, TN: Broadman & Holman Publishers, 1999), 266–267.
[422] Barnett, *2 Corinthians,* 277.

family."[423] Breaking with one's traditional family in an Eastern first century family was "radical in a traditional patriarchal culture where blood is seen as thicker than water or any other substance."[424] The epistle to the Hebrews where Jesus' brotherhood to the saints is emphasized in the context of atonement. The writer says,

> For it was fitting that he, for whom and by whom all things exist, in bringing many *sons* to glory, should make the founder of their salvation perfect through suffering. For he who sanctifies and those who are sanctified all have one source. That is why he is not ashamed to call them *brothers*, saying, "I will tell of your name to *my brothers*; in the midst of the congregation I will sing your praise." And again, "I will put my trust in him." And again, "Behold, I and the *children* God has given me." Since therefore the *children* share in flesh and blood, he himself likewise partook of the same things, that through death he might destroy the one who has the power of death, that is, the devil, and deliver all those who through fear of death were subject to lifelong slavery. For surely it is not angels that he helps, but he helps the offspring of Abraham. Therefore he had to be made like his *brothers* in every respect, so that he might become a merciful and faithful high priest in the service of God, to make *propitiation* for the sins of the people. For because he himself has suffered when tempted, he is able to help those who are being tempted (Heb. 2:10-18).

Couched within this passage of Scripture the language of family ("sons," "brothers," and "children") and atonement are found in complete harmony. In fact, the family is the result of the *propitiatory* sacrifice of Christ. Jesus, who is the judge of all humankind, is uniquely related to those whom he provided atonement for; namely the relationship is understood now in terms of "brotherhood."

Again, in the vertical paradigm, one can begin to understand that the Creator/creation, Judge/offending party relationship undergoes a change, speaking and relating now in familial terms without compromising the transcendence and holiness of God. Before proceeding to speaking of the brotherhood of Jesus, we must initially acknowledge the references to atonement here in this passage. First, the writer speaks of the destruction of "the one who has the power of death, the devil" (Heb. 2:14, cf. 1 John 3:8). As has been repeated, the atonement is surely multidimensional and cannot nor should not be reduced to a singular model (i.e., here in this context one thinks of Aulen's *Christus Victor* model). However, the writer of Hebrews specifically uses the phrase "to make *propitiation* for the sins of the people' when speaking about the work of Christ. The semantic range of *hilaskesthai* as discussed earlier in the book is quite large, sometimes meaning *expiation* and other times translated *propitiation*. Morris has probably the most popular and accessible section in print on the subject.[425] O'Brien writes that "the notion of atonement has to do with the restoration of a relationship marred by sin, and this encompasses both expiation, the removal of sin, and

---

[423] France, *Matthew,* 497.

[424] Witherington, *Mark,* 159.

[425] Morris, *Apostolic,* 125-160.

propitiation, the averting of divine wrath. Our author assumes that divine wrath threatened his listeners, just as it threatened Moses' generation (Heb. 3:7-4:13; 10:26-31; 12:29)."[426]

Followers of Jesus are frequently referred to as "brothers" throughout the New Testament (Matt. 12:46-50; Mark 3:35; Luke 8:21; Heb. 2:11). However, the reference to Jesus' brotherhood shared with the saints is rare. This passage parallels the synoptic gospels referenced above as well as Romans 8:29.[427] What should be noticed here in the vertical paradigm is the announcement that Jesus does not feel *shame* over the relationship established. He does not enter into brotherhood with those whom he sanctified begrudgingly. This has a profound effect on the believer as he or she becomes more aware that they, in fact, were "the joy set before him as he endured the cross, despising the shame" (Heb. 12:2). The relationship that the brother or sister of Christ is rid completely of sin and its consequences includes shame in every aspect. Thus, without PSA, Christ could not call us "brothers" because of the *"shame"* that would be introduced to the relationship. DeSilva writes marvelously of the relational impact accomplished:

> The author is creating a sense of the esteem in which Jesus, the exalted Son, holds believers. He does not fear that association with them, *owning them as his own family,* will bring disgrace upon him. This indicates that Jesus' beneficence toward the hearers is accompanied by Jesus' estimation of them as *people of worth*, judging them to be suitable beneficiaries and reliable clients who will not disappoint or bring shame upon him.[428]

The vertical relationship is one in which sin is atoned for and wrath now absent has resulted in the child of God relating to the Father as *Abba* and now the Son as the unashamed older *Brother*. Our older Brother is not only unashamed of those he has made holy, but he also sympathizes with them.

Jesus: The Sympathetic Older Brother

The writer of the epistle to the Hebrews continues:

> Since then we have a great high priest who has passed through the heavens, Jesus, the Son of God, let us hold fast our confession. For we do not have a high priest who

---

[426] O'Brien, *Hebrews,* 122. See also S. J. Kistemaker, "Atonement in Hebrews: 'A Merciful and Faithful High Priest,'" in *The Glory of the Atonement,* ed. C. Hill and F. James III., esp. 165-167, and Jeffery, Ovey, and Sach, eds., *Pierced,* 82-85.

[427] Leon L. Morris, *Hebrews: Bible Study Commentary* (Grand Rapids, MI: Zondervan Publishing, 1983), 27-8. Bruce comments: "Since those who are sanctified to God through his death are sons and daughters of God, the Son of God is not ashamed to acknowledge them as his brothers and sisters–not only as those whose nature he took upon himself, but those whose trials he endured, for whose sins he made atonement, that they might follow him to glory on the path of salvation which he himself cut," F. F. Bruce, *NICNT: The Epistle to the Hebrews* (Grand Rapids, MI: Eerdmans, 2012), 81.

[428] DeSilva, *Hebrews,* 115, emphasis mine.

is unable to sympathize with our weaknesses, but one who in every respect has been tempted as we are, yet without sin. Let us then with confidence draw near to the throne of grace, that we may receive mercy and find grace to help in time of need (Heb. 4:14-16).

Of interest here is Jesus, the Son of God, the "brother" who is "not ashamed" of his siblings, being declared to be *"sympathetic"* towards those he has redeemed. This too, is extremely important within the vertical relational paradigm. The experience of Christ can be defined as *"συμπαθέω*: to share someone's feeling in the sense of being sympathetic with—'to be sympathetic toward, to have sympathy for...' In a number of languages the closest equivalent of 'being sympathetic with' may be 'to understand completely how one feels' or 'to feel in one's heart just like someone else feels.'"[429]

Though Jesus is declared to be the brother of the redeemed, the writer goes further to elaborate stating that Jesus is currently able to *sympathize* in our present weaknesses. McKnight writes,

> The Eastern church's emphasis, along with atonement's further centrality in Anselm, the Reformers, and Anglican thought, gets it right: atonement requires that God becomes human. Without engaging the endless debates about persons and natures and hypostases, it can be said that one thing the incarnation tells us is that Jesus Christ *identifies with us* in our human condition, yet without sin.[430]

This is the second time that the writer of the epistle makes reference to the incarnation of Christ and the profound relational implications. Jesus is not an impersonal, unknowable, disassociated mediator, merely performing mechanical functions. Rather, "his identification with us has not ceased because he has passed into the heavenly sanctuary."[431] This is ever so important for Christians to remain grounded in the reality that though physically in heaven and out of visibility, Jesus most definitely identifies with the present state of hardship his followers currently endure. Lane notes the *γάρ* conjunction at the beginning of verse 15 stating, "It is intended to guard against the mistaken inference that the exalted nature and position of the heavenly high priest will detract in any way from his ability to identify with the weariness and defenselessness of the church in a hostile world."[432]

Lane is also careful to note that the semantic range of the word *συμπαθέω* "extends beyond the sharing feelings (i.e., compassion). It always includes the element of active help."[433] The writer of Hebrews has already declared that Jesus has "become a merciful

---

429 Louw and Nida, Greek-English Lexicon, 293.

430 McKnight, Community Called Atonement, 108.

431 Hughes, Hebrews, 171.

432 William Lane, Word Biblical Commentary, vol. 47a, Hebrews 1-8 (Nashville, TN: Thomas Nelson Publishers, 1991) 107, fn.

433 Lane, Hebrews, 114. Also "sympathy with the sinner in his trial does not depend on the experience of sin but on the experience of the strain of the temptation to sin which only the sinless can know in its full intensity. He who falls yields before the last strain." B. F. Westcott, The

and faithful high priest," and that he was "made like his brothers in all respects, thus "he is able to help those enduring trial" because "he himself endured trial and suffering" (2:17f). The author is concerned about this relational dynamic being understood by followers of Christ – namely that Jesus as a mediator has identified completely with the plight of his people and that the he relates *now* with "sympathy and a gentle disposition."[434] The relational implication of having wrath averted, reconciliation accomplished is one's knowledge that "There is no question of any incapacity on his part to sympathize with our weaknesses, for it was precisely our weaknesses that he embraced and made his own when he took our nature upon himself."[435]

The older brother not only *sympathizes* with the saints but also loves the family beyond measure. Though mentioned throughout the New Testament, one place in which the immeasurable love of Christ is emphasized is in Paul's letter to the Ephesians.

Jesus: The Older Brother's Immeasurable Love

The Apostle Paul prays,

For this reason I bow my knees before the Father, from whom every family in heaven and on earth is named, that according to the riches of his glory he may grant you to be strengthened with power through his Spirit in your inner being, so that Christ may dwell in your hearts through faith—that you, being rooted and grounded in love, may have strength to comprehend with all the saints what is the breadth and length and height and depth, and to know the love of Christ that surpasses knowledge, that you may be filled with all the fullness of God (Eph. 3:14-19).

This passage is written not to an individual but to a community and has major *horizontal* implications which will be discussed in the next chapter. For "the true understanding of Christ's love is not then an individual experience but takes place in the community."[436] With the doctrine of PSA effectively accomplishing its purpose, thus having the wrath of God averted in the death of Jesus, Jesus' role of judge is now met alongside his brotherhood of the saints, and another dimension of the gospel opens to all who receive salvation. We now turn the kaleidoscope to look briefly at the immeasurable love of Christ for his people expressed in a prayer by the Apostle Paul.

Due to the wording in this prayer, scholars differ about *what* specifically Paul could be referencing here regarding the four dimensions (breadth, length, height, and depth). N. Dahl offers helpful insight as he says "If one pays attention to the rhetorical form and

---

Epistle to the Hebrews, (United Kingdom: Macmillan and Co, 1902; Logos Bible Software, for Mac, 2015) 124.

[434] DeSilva, *Hebrews*, 182.

[435] Hughes, *Hebrews*, 171.

[436] Harold Best, *Ephesians: An Exegetical Commentary* (Grand Rapids, MI: Baker Academic, 2002), 167.

asks for the function rather than the precise meaning of the passage"[437] – correct interpretation of the passage depends on this approach. The majority believe that Paul is speaking directly about the love that is *in* Christ due to the definite article used.[438] The reason for this is that "the context itself is about Christ who dwells deeply in believers' hearts (v. 17) and believers who are to know the love of Christ (v.19)."[439] As the believer turns the kaleidoscope in order to see even more of the relational change that occurs vertically between oneself and Christ, the believer experiences the immeasurable *love* of the older Brother, the Lord Jesus. In reference to the four-dimensional love of Christ, Lincoln states that these are "a totality which evokes the immensity of a particular object."[440] Or as Abbott states, "The four words seem intended to indicate, not so much the thoroughness of the comprehension as the vastness of the thing to be comprehended."[441] Best repeats that "this love is without limits and is ultimately *immeasurable*."[442] Even Paul's choice of words are intended to elicit an emotional response in the early church due to the fact that he's using "Asiatic epidictic rhetoric, for which no degree of high praise and hyperbole is too grand when the subject is the work of God and its benefit and blessing to humankind."[443] Furthermore, Witherington continues noting the word choice of Paul by saying, "it is not just the content of the phrases but the sound of the words. The four dimensional terms all end in *-os*, which adds impact and emotional force to the discourse."[444] In reference to the atonement and the love of Jesus that Paul experienced, he wrote, "who loved me and gave himself for me" (Gal. 2:20b). Bruce highlights the vertical relationship that is established between Christ and his family in this Ephesian prayer by saying,

> The disclosure of the eternal mystery is no object of merely intellectual comprehension, although it calls for all the intellectual power at one's command; it requires *personal acquaintance* with the revealer, whose nature is perfect love. To

---

[437] N. A. Dahl, "Cosmic Dimensions and Religious Knowledge (Ephesians 3:18)" in *Jesus and Paulus: Festschrift for Werner Georg Kümmel's 70th Birthday*, ed. E. E. Ellis and E. Grasser, (Gottingen, Germany: Vandenhoeck und Ruprecht, 1975), 74.

[438] O'Brien notes some examples such as the power of God, (See also Clinton Arnold, *Power and Magic: The Concept of Power in Ephesians* (Eugene, OR: Wifp & Stock, 2001), 93-96), "The Mystery of Salvation" in Rudolph Schnackenberg, *The Epistle to the Ephesians* (Edinburgh, England: T&T Clark, 2001), 171-2). "The Manifold Wisdom of God" (Dahl, "Cosmic," 74–75) in Peter Thomas O'Brien, *The Pillar New Testament Commentary: The Letter to the Ephesians* (Grand Rapids, MI: Eerdmans, 1999), 261-3.

[439] Hoehner, *Ephesians*, 488.

[440] Andrew Lincoln and Alexander Wedderburn, *The Theology of the Later Pauline Letters* (Cambridge, England: Cambridge University Press, 1993), 212.

[441] T. K. Abbott, A Critical and Exegetical Commentary on the Epistles to the Ephesians and to the Colossians (Edinburgh, England: T&T Clark, 1969), 99.

[442] Best, *Ephesians*, 167, emphasis mine.

[443] Ben Witherington III, A Socio-Rhetorical Commentary: on the Captivity Epistles, The Letters to Philemon, the Colossians, and the Ephesians (Grand Rapids, MI: Eerdmans, 2007), 276.

[444] Witherington III, *Captivity*, 276.

know the love of Christ is to know Christ himself, in ever widening experience, and to have his outgoing and self-denying love reproduced in oneself.[445]

As the Christian, now reconciled to the Son of God, turns the kaleidoscope of the vertical paradigm, one experiences the older Brother as sympathetic, loving, and may rest in the reality that he or she is protected from all harm either from Satan and demons (angel-culture) or even from one's own conscience that voices condemnation. We now turn to examine Jesus: the older Brother as the Advocate of the younger siblings. This vertical relational aspect too, is grounded in PSA.

Jesus: The Older Brother as Advocate

John writes, "My little children, I am writing these things to you so that you may not sin. But if anyone does sin, we have an advocate with the Father, Jesus Christ the righteous. He is the propitiation for our sins, and not for ours only but also for the sins of the whole world" (1 John 2:1-2).[446]

In writing to the family of God ("children"), John not only highlights Jesus as the *"advocate"* but also his *"propitiatory"* sacrifice he offered in the place of/for sinners. The vertical relational dynamic is increased as one considers the nature of the *advocacy* that Jesus provides before the Father. The Apostle writes words of *comfort* to the church as he creates a scenario "if one sins" (2:1). This implies that someone who is a child of God has been reconciled to the Father by the sacrifice of the Son and yet has still yielded to temptation to sin. The relationship, though marred through sin, is *not* destroyed in the slightest. The child of God is comforted in the reality that the older Brother not only paid the atoning price for the sin committed but presently *advocates* before the Father on behalf of the sinner who is simultaneously a saint. Even the flow of thought of John must be understood here: peering through the kaleidoscope, one can see PSA and the relational dynamics interacting, creating the ongoing understanding of the gospel and experience of regeneration within the family of God. John speaks of "sin," the "righteousness" of Jesus, before the "Father," and "propitiation."

The word for *advocate* here is the word παράκλητος. The present context certainly implies a "legal context"[447] which is surely fitting given the forensic nature of PSA. The word παράκλητος is used five times in the New Testament, all by John. In the gospel of John he uses the word each time in referrence to the coming Holy Spirit and yet, here he uses the word specifically to refer to Jesus.[448] Some, however, would argue differently. For example, Zodhiates says, "the word must not be understood as applying to Christ in the same sense as in 1 John 2:1 where it refers to our substitutionary Advocate who

---

[445] F. F Bruce, NICNT: The Epistles to the Colossians, to Philemon, and to the Ephesians (Grand Rapids, MI: Eerdmans, 1984), 329, emphasis mine.

[446] Other important passages that emphasize Jesus' role as mediator are Romans 8:34 and Hebrews 7:25.

[447] Howard Marshall, *NICNT: The Epistles of John* (Grand Rapids, MI: Eerdmans, 1976), 116.

[448] See John 14:16, 26; 15:26; 16:7. Furthermore, it "is used in connection with his function in heaven." Colin Kruse, *The Letters of John*, 72.

pleads our cause with the Father. It should rather be taken as He who pleads God's cause with us (see John 14:7–9)."[449] Kistemaker comments,

> Our defender is Jesus Christ, whom John describes as the Righteous One (compare Acts 3:14). As sinners, we have the best possible helper because he is righteous. That is, in his human nature Jesus is our *brother* (Heb. 2:11), is acquainted with our frailties (Heb. 4:15), saves us (Heb. 7:25), and is our intercessor. He is also God's Messiah, the Christ, who fulfilled the demands of the law for us and therefore has been given the title *Righteous One*. As a sinless lawyer he represents us in court.[450]

Those who would oppose PSA would interject here by pointing out what would be a perceived weakness in the courtroom metaphor (which is Scriptural and not bound to Anselm's era) by way of pointing out that God appears to be unwilling to forgive sin and thus "forgiveness has to be wrested by the advocate for sinners." But it must be emphasized again that, "It is God himself who is faithful and just and forgives our sins, and in 3:9ff. he adds his powerful voice to the New Testament chorus which declares that it was God the Father who gave Jesus his Son to be the atoning sacrifice for our sins. It is God himself who provides the means of our forgiveness and pays the cost of it."[451] The sin that brought about the judgment of one's soul that is due wrath is averted in the penal sacrifice of the Son. The atonement is something accomplished in *cooperation* between the Father and the Son. Early Church father Chrysostom said,

> Can you see how great God's love is for us? Who was the offended party? He was. Who took the first steps toward reconciliation? He did. Some will say that he sent the Son in his place, but this is a misunderstanding. Christ did not come apart from the Father who sent him. They were both involved together in the work of reconciliation.[452]

Moreover, the older Brother stands to comfort, console, and encourage the younger brothers and sisters in the family of God. It is from here that we now turn our attention to the third member of the Trinity who functions as a judge and through the doctrine of PSA now establishes the relationship of "Comforter" in the life of the Christian.

---

[449] Zodhiates, *Dictionary*, advocate=παράκλητος.

[450] Simon Kistemaker, *New Testament Commentary: James, Epistles of John, Peter, and Jude* (Grand Rapids, MI: Baker Books, 1996), 252, emphasis mine.

[451] Marshall, *John*, 119. However, Marshall mistakenly continues, "The language of advocacy is thus ultimately inadequate to express the paradox of the offended God who himself pardons our offenses by giving his own Son to be our Savior." To state that John uses "inadequate" language is to charge the beloved disciple with being mistaken about the Lord whom he walked with personally and was under the inspiration of the Holy Spirit as he penned this letter. Certainly "Advocate" isn't the only word to describe the relational dynamic between the Brother Jesus and the family of God. Indeed, "mediator" is one that is very similarly employed throughout the book of Hebrews.

[452] Thomas Oden, ed., "Chrysostom," in *Ancient Christian Commentary on Scripture: 1-2 Corinthians* (New York, NY: Routledge, 1999), 248, NPNF 1 12:333.

The Holy Spirit as God

The Bible is unmistakably clear that the Spirit of God is "Holy" because he *is God*. It is important to remember that the very word "Holy" beckons one to acknowledge that God is completely set apart from and unlike anything or anyone in all of creation (i.e., the doctrine of aseity). The role of the Holy Spirit develops throughout Scripture. "From the first page of Genesis, the Spirit of God is spoken of, but the content of this term remains imprecise throughout the entire Old Testament. The Spirit is a power originating in God that invades a man, enabling him to complete God's plans."[453] Barth says that "the Holy Spirit... is God himself, in as so far as he is able, in an inconceivably real way, without being less God, to be present to the creature, and in virtue of this presence, to vouchsafe life to the creature."[454] McIntyre defines the Holy Spirit as "God himself relating himself to the specific details of human existence within the natural process and world history."[455] More succinctly here, Berkhof says that the Holy Spirit "is the personal God himself in relation to us."[456] As Trinity, God is a theo-culture and he is holy entering into a relationship with the fallen human. Graham McFarlane is correct as he notes that the opposite of holy is not sin. Rather, the opposite of holiness is *familiarity*.[457] This is what makes the doctrine of the indwelling Holy Spirit within believers all the more astonishing. One's wonder increases as the relational kaleidoscope is turned, only to behold the supernatural person and work of the third member of the Trinity. First, it will do well to briefly establish that the Scriptures emphasize the Divinity of the Holy Spirit.

The Holy Spirit is referenced eighty-eight times in the Old Testament,[458] two hundred sixty-four times in the New Testament, and never once is the Spirit referred to being any less than the other two members of the Godhead.[459] He is found at the beginning and is involved in creation (Gen. 1:2). Even as Jesus speaks of the Holy Spirit, he does so in a way that equates the Holy Spirit with himself and the Father (John 14:16). The Spirit is not merely the power of God, as though it were an impersonal force, rather a Person. As Wayne Grudem notes in his *Systematic Theology: An Introduction to Biblical Doctrine*, a number of texts would simply lose their meaning if

---

[453] Gonzalo Haya-Prats, Empowered Believers: The Holy Spirit in the Book of Acts (Eugene, OR: Wipf & Stock, 2011), 4.

[454] Karl Barth, *Church Dogmatics*, vol. 1, *The Doctrine of the Word of God*, translated by G. W. Bromiley (Peabody, MA: Hendrickson Publishers, 2010), 515.

[455] John McIntyre, The Shape of Pneumatology: Studies in the Doctrine of the Holy Spirit (Edinburgh, England: T&T Clark, 2004), 173.

[456] Hendrikus Berkhof, *The Doctrine of the Holy Spirit* (Louisville, KY: Westminster John Knox Press, 1986), 116.

[457] Graham McFarlane, Why Do You Believe What You Believe About the Holy Spirit? (Eugene, OR: Wipf & Stock, 2009), 19.

[458] W. H. Griffith Thomas, *The Holy Spirit of God* (London, England: Longmans, 1913), 9.

[459] William Edward Biederwolf and William Moorehead, *A Help to the Study of the Holy Spirit* (Whitefish, MT: Literary Licensing, 2013), 17.

the Holy Spirit were merely a force or "power."[460] Heron writes that the "Spirit is used to speak of God as present and active in the world and in particular among human beings ... The Spirit of God is not detachable from God himself. The Spirit is his living impact here and now."[461]

One passage that pertains to our discussion here is Acts 5:1-11, in which Peter explicitly describes the Holy Spirit not only as God, the Holy Spirit also functions as "Judge." In keeping with the turning of the kaleidoscope, once again the role of "judge" within the Trinity surfaces, now with focus on the Person and Work of the Holy Spirit.

The Holy Spirit as Judge

Luke writes,

> But a man named Ananias, with his wife Sapphira, sold a piece of property, and with his wife's knowledge he kept back for himself some of the proceeds and brought only a part of it and laid it at the apostles' feet. But Peter said, "Ananias, why has Satan filled your heart to lie to the Holy Spirit and to keep back for yourself part of the proceeds of the land? While it remained unsold, did it not remain your own? And after it was sold, was it not at your disposal? Why is it that you have contrived this deed in your heart? You have not lied to man but to God." When Ananias heard these words, he fell down and breathed his last. And great fear came upon all who heard of it. The young men rose and wrapped him up and carried him out and buried him. After an interval of about three hours his wife came in, not knowing what had happened. And Peter said to her, "Tell me whether you sold the land for so much." And she said, "Yes, for so much." But Peter said to her, "How is it that you have agreed together to test the Spirit of the Lord? Behold, the feet of those who have buried your husband are at the door, and they will carry you out." Immediately she fell down at his feet and breathed her last. When the young men came in they found her dead, and they carried her out and buried her beside her husband. And great fear came upon the whole church and upon all who heard of these things (Acts 5:1-11).

In this passage the Divinity of the Holy Spirit is emphasized as he is referred to as "God" (v.4). But not only is his divinity made explicitly clear, his role as functioning *judge* is also observed in this text.[462] The Scripture depicts judgment in two different ways. One is in judgment happening here and now in the present tense on the earth as

---

[460] Wayne Grudem, *Systematic Theology*, 232-3.

[461] Alasdair Heron, The Holy Spirit: The Holy Spirit in the Bible, in the History of Christian Thought, and Recent Theology (Louisville, KY: Westminster John Knox, 1963), 7-8.

[462] "Many have sought to see the reference to Ananias's lying to the Spirit as indicating the "unforgivable sin" of blasphemy against the Spirit (Mark 3:28–29), but Ananias was not guilty of that, which is to attribute the works of God to Satan. Ananias was guilty of duplicity, lying, greed, hypocrisy—but not of blasphemy." See P. Menoud, "*La Mort d'Ananias et de Saphira* (Acts 5: 1–11)," in *Aux Sources de la Tradition Chrétienne: Melanges offerts à M. Maurice Goguel* (Neuchatel, Germany: Delachaux et Niestlé, 1950), 146–54, in Polhill, *Acts*, 156.

is described in the passage above. The other is, of course, final judgment (Rom. 14:10-12; 2 Cor. 5:10; Heb. 9:27). Furthermore, the Scriptures reveal that the role of final judgment is ultimately carried out by the Father and the Son, as stated above. Interestingly, the Scriptures do not speak about the role of the Holy Spirit in the final judgment. Nevertheless, what the Scriptures *do* indicate is that God (the Holy Spirit!) does occasionally judge believers here in the present. For example, though the apostle Paul does not explicitly state that *"the Holy Spirit judged* and brought believers to death" in Corinth (1 Cor. 11:27-32), it is not a stretch theologically to make such a conclusion; for Paul had been addressing at length the reality that believers are now living as temples of the Holy Spirit (1 Cor. 3:16-17). Thus, Paul calls believers to thoroughly examine themselves (1 Cor. 11:29) lest they fall under "judgment."[463] Concerning this passage in Acts, Bruce comments,

> What he [Luke] is concerned to emphasize is the reality of the Holy Spirit's indwelling presence of the church, together with the solemn practical implications of that fact. So early was it necessary to emphasize the lesson later formulated by Paul: "Do you not know that you are God's temple and that God's Spirit dwells in you? If anyone destroys God's temple, God will destroy him. For God's temple is holy, and that temple you are (1 Cor. 3:16-17)" ... A lie told to Peter as a private man might've been relatively venial, but this–whether Ananias knew it or not–was a lie told to God, something prompted by none other than the great adversary of God and humanity.[464]

It must be repeated that there is a marked difference between what is said to be prescriptive and descriptive in the reading of the book of Acts. How should Christians today go about a relationship with the Holy Spirit? And how does the doctrine of PSA interact in this particular context? As one turns the kaleidoscope, one can see that PSA addresses this question. The wrath of God is most certainly satisfied in the death of Jesus as he dies in the place of the sinner; as the believer is regenerated (Titus 3:5) and brought into the family of God, the relationship changes and this is seen as one peers through the relational kaleidoscope. Interestingly, the child of *Abba*, the sibling of the older Brother, need not fear final judgment and wrath. Even so, the Christian today is not excused from walking in the fear of the Lord as this passage clearly teaches. Polhill comments, "just as with God there is both justice and mercy, so with his Spirit there is also an underside to his blessing. There is his judgment. This Ananias and Sapphira experienced. The Spirit is not to be taken lightly."[465]

---

[463] Fee states that "Most likely Paul is here stepping into the prophetic role; by the Spirit he has seen a divine cause and effect between the two otherwise independent realities: the present illnesses of man, which in some cases have led to death, and actions of some at the Table of the Lord who are despising the church and humiliating the "have-nots" by "going ahead with their own private meals," Gordon Fee, *NICNT: The First Epistle to the Corinthians* (Grand Rapids, MI: Eerdmans Publishing, 1987), 565.

[464] F. F. Bruce, *NICNT: Acts* (Grand Rapids, MI: Eerdmans, 1988), 104-5.

[465] Polhill, *Acts*, 160.

As the kaleidoscope turns and the various attributes of God resurface, the holiness and justice of God as well as the summons to obedience comes back into focus. Scripture repeatedly declares that God disciplines his children (Prov. 3:12; Heb. 12:6; Rev. 3:19) and in some cases, it is quite severe.[466] And yet, one's salvation is never in jeopardy nor is the wrath of God expected to be inherited (1 Cor. 3:15; 5:5; 11:28-29). Again, the disciplined of God in his own covenantal community even to the point of occasionally losing their lives, find that their salvation is secure. As one turns the relational kaleidoscope and the holiness of God is brought back into the picture, one can also see simultaneously that one's childhood, adoption into the family, brotherhood of Christ, and comfort by the Holy Spirit cannot be undone. Jesus described the Holy Spirit as primarily the *Comforter* who also performs many other roles in the life of a disciple. It is here that we will examine the nature of the comfort the Holy Spirit provides as well as briefly examine three roles he performs in the life of a disciple, namely, how he guides, convicts, and empowers the people of God.

The Holy Spirit as Comforter

Though there are many pneumatological facets that could be explored here, this example is limited.[467] Therefore, for the sake of highlighting the *relational dynamics* at work between the life of the believer and God the Holy Spirit, the study will be restricted to discussing briefly the third person of the Trinity as *Comforter.* Kostenberger and Swain highlight the great filial relationship Jesus establishes with the children of God through the Spirit:

> The Spirit rests and remains upon the Son *and* upon those who, by receiving and abiding in the Son, have become "children of God" and "brothers" of Jesus (John 1:12; 20:17). Jesus' God has become their God, Jesus' Father, their Father (20:17), Jesus Spirit, their Spirit. Indeed, viewed in this light, we may see the Son's reception of the Spirit at his baptism as an anticipation of his brothers' reception of the same Spirit (1:32-33; 7:39; 20:22). This is the great blessing that Jesus the anointed Son

---

466 "Scripture reveals similar incidents in which God punished sinners with sudden death. For instance, when Aaron's sons Nadab and Abihu who presented fire that God had not prescribed, God struck them with fire so that they died instantaneously (Lev. 10:1-2). When Uzziah tried to steady the ark of God that was placed on an ox-drawn cart instead of carried by priests, God struck him so that he died beside the Ark (2 Sam. 6:7)." Simon J. Kistemaker, *New Testament Commentary: Exposition of the Acts* (Grand Rapids, MI: Baker Books, 1990), 184. In each of these instances, God is the one carrying out capital punishment, not men.

467 "The Spirit's personhood appears from the verbs of personal action – hear, speak, witness, convince, show, lead, guide, teach, command, forbid, desire, give speech, help, intercede with groans – that are used to tell us what he does (John 14:26; 15:26; 16:7-15; Acts 2:4; 8:29; 13:2; 16:6-7; 21:11; Rom. 8:14, 16, 26, 27; Gal. 4:6; 5:17-18; Heb. 3:7; 10:15; 1 Pet. 1:11; Rev. 2:7, 11, 17, 29, et al.)," J. L Packer, *God Has Spoken: Revelation and the Bible* (Grand Rapids, MI: Baker Books, 1994), 193.

brings – *a share in his filial relationship with the Father by the indwelling of the Holy Spirit.*[468]

Kostenberger says, "The Spirit will come to believers per Jesus' request of the Father – striking a Trinitarian note; and once the Spirit comes, it is as if Jesus himself (and the Father, John 14:23) were to take residence "in" believers, analogous to his presence "among" his followers while physically present with them."[469] Again, one must see as the relational kaleidoscope turns, the utterly profound accomplishment in the doctrine of PSA. For believers now enjoy a relationship with the Trinity that otherwise was impossible.

The Gospel of John is usually broken into two parts: the Book of Signs (1:19-12:50); the Book of the Passion (13:1-20:31).[470] Thiselton notes the emphasis of the Holy Spirit in John's gospel as he writes, "The most distinctive teaching in John concerns the five sets of sayings about the Paraclete in John 14-16 (John 14:15-17; 14:25-26; 15:26; 16:7-11, and 16:12-15)."[471]

> If you love me, you will keep my commandments. And I will ask the Father, and he will give you another Helper, to be with you forever, even the Spirit of truth, whom the world cannot receive, because it neither sees him nor knows him. You know him, for he dwells with you and will be in you (14:15–17).

> These things I have spoken to you while I am still with you. But the Helper, the Holy Spirit, whom the Father will send in my name, he will teach you all things and bring to your remembrance all that I have said to you (14:25–26).

> But when the Helper comes, whom I will send to you from the Father, the Spirit of truth, who proceeds from the Father, he will bear witness about me (15:26).

> Nevertheless, I tell you the truth: it is to your advantage that I go away, for if I do not go away, the Helper will not come to you. But if I go, I will send him to you. And when he comes, he will convict the world concerning sin and righteousness and judgment: concerning sin, because they do not believe in me; concerning righteousness, because I go to the Father, and you will see me no longer; concerning judgment, because the ruler of this world is judged (16:7–11).

---

[468] Andreas Kostenberger and Scott Swain, *New Studies in Biblical Theology*, vol. 24, *Father, Son and Spirit: The Trinity and John's Gospel,* ed by D. A. Carson (Downers Grove, IL: Intervarsity Press, 2008), 146-47.

[469] Andreas Kostenberger, A Theology of John's Gospel and Letters: The Word, the Christ, the Son of God (Grand Rapids, MI: Zondervan, 2009), 240-41.

[470] Max Turner, *The Holy Spirit and Spiritual Gifts Then and Now* (Grand Rapids, MI: Baker Academic, 1997), 76.

[471] Anthony Thiselton, The Holy Spirit in Biblical Teaching, Through the Centuries, and Today (Grand Rapids, MI: Eerdmans, 2013), 131.

I still have many things to say to you, but you cannot bear them now. When the Spirit of truth comes, he will guide you into all the truth, for he will not speak on his own authority, but whatever he hears he will speak, and he will declare to you the things that are to come. He will glorify me, for he will take what is mine and declare it to you. All that the Father has is mine; therefore I said that he will take what is mine and declare it to you (John 16:12–15).

Certainly, the doctrine of the indwelling Holy Spirit does not rest entirely upon these passages. However, the context in which Jesus speaks these ever so important (vertical, relational) words is at the Last Supper, on the night of his betrayal and are helpful here as they are given in the context of his penal sacrifice (i.e., consider the "wrath" he spoke of in 3:36, for example). The disciples were most certainly fearful about the events to follow and Jesus offers the words of comfort about the Comforter. The word παράκλητος has a wide semantic range. It is used here in the gospel of John, each time referring to the Holy Spirit and as stated above, in 1 John 2:1 in reference to Christ himself. Historically, in some situations the term was used in a more forensic sense. However, recent translations of παράκλητος "tend to render the Greek as "Counselor," nonetheless the nuance of the more traditional "Comforter" should not be abandoned."[472] Louw and Nida disagree stating that "the principal difficulty encountered in rendering παράκλητος is the fact that this term covers potentially such a wide area of meaning."[473] They continue "the traditional rendering of 'Comforter' is especially misleading because it suggests only one very limited aspect of what the Holy Spirit does."[474] However, for our purposes here, the study is limited to "Comforter." Moreover, McIntyre states, "'Comforter' carries over from the Old Testament its description of the Messiah as *menachem,* comforter. It represents a tenderness, a closeness, concern and caring ... one who comforts us when for one reason or another life has become difficult, dark, meaningless, or just a very lonely place."[475]

Newbigin writes, "By using the name *Parakletos* John is identifying the source of all this calling and comforting and exhorting and beseeching and consoling as no human achievement but as a gift from the Father, a gift whose coming is made possible by the

---

[472] Ryken, Wilhoit, Longman, eds., "Comfort," in *Dictionary of Biblical Imagery,* 161.

[473] Louw and Nida, Greek-English Lexicon.

[474] A term such as "Helper" is highly generic and can be particularly useful in some languages. In certain instances, for example, the concept of "Helper" is expressed idiomatically, for example, "the one who mothers us" or, as in one language in Central Africa, "the one who falls down beside us," that is to say, an individual who upon finding a person collapsed along the road, kneels down beside the victim, cares for his needs, and carries him to safety, Louw and Nida, *Greek-English Lexicon.* Morris agrees with this as well in Morris, *John,* 589. N. H. Snaith presses on the meaning "'Convincer,' i.e., He who convinces men of the things of God, and accomplishes in them a change of heart," N. H. Snaith, "The Meaning of 'the Paraclete.'" *Expository Times* 57, no. 2 (1945-6): 50. Morris, however, in light of the Greek Fathers who "normally" translated the word in the active sense, "counselor," "comforter" ... finds that the Greek Fathers in this particular case... are "incorrect." Morris, *John* 588.

[475] McIntyre, *Pneumatology,* 267.

intercession of Jesus."[476] The Holy Spirit, is to be understood as the *gift* given from the Father and the Son only after the Son would suffer, die, rise, and ascend back to the Father. Beasley-Murray states that "the Spirit is to be 'sent' by the Father in the name of Jesus, a remarkable declaration which binds the Spirit closely to Jesus ... the Spirit no more comes in his own name than Jesus came in his own name." Beasley-Murray also notes, "an interesting parallel, in content though not in language" found in Galatians 4:4-6.[477] In line with the section on *"Abba"* above, Rabens states that Paul's words "you have received the Spirit of adoption" (Rom. 8:15) was based on nonverbal, identity-forming experiences of the Spirit of the Son crying *"Abba!* Father!" The Spirit, together with the human spirit, bearing witness of one's being a child of God (8:16). These individual and communal experiences of the love and closeness of God also include emotions.[478] Within the kaleidoscope one finds that the glory of PSA – the wrath of God has been averted and no longer "remains on" (John 3:36) the now child of God – the Holy Spirit can move in closely to the child of God and extend comfort. This particular understanding of the Holy Spirit "is as satisfactory as any, if it is taken in the fullest sense of one who not only consoles but also strengthens, helps, and counsels, with such authority as a legal advocate has for his client."[479]

The Comforter Who Is "Present"

Another incredible dimension revealed is the ongoing *presence* of the Holy Spirit in the life of the believer. The Holy Spirit does not come and go, rather remains with, abides with, the child of God "forever" (John 14:16). The ongoing comfort supplied not only in wrath being averted through the penal substitution of Christ, but also the ongoing presence with the believer provides followers and family members of Christ peace and security. The redeemed never need "worry" about being "left alone as orphans" in the world (14:18). The comforting words spoken by Jesus to the disciples are two-fold. First, he states that he is going to prepare a place for them that they may dwell with him forever. Secondly, he sends the comforter who does not leave. Jesus addressed the subsequent anxiety and worry that accompanied the early disciples in a world that "hates" Jesus and thus his followers (15:18, 20). Morris states,

> Jesus' bodily Presence was about to be withdrawn from them. Never again would they know the warm intimate companionship of the days of his earthly ministry. Another "Counselor" will be with them ... The Counselor will be with the disciples

---

[476] Leslie Newbigin, *The Light Has Come: An Exposition of the Fourth Gospel* (Grand Rapids, MI: Eerdmans, 1987), 187.

[477] George R. Beasley-Murray, *Word Biblical Commentary,* vol. 36, *John,* 2nd ed. (Nashville, TN: Thomas Nelson Publishers, 1990), 261.

[478] Volker Rabens, "Power from In Between: The Relational Experience of the Holy Spirit and Spiritual Gifts in Paul's Churches," in *The Spirit and Christ,* ed. I. H Marshall, V. Rabens, and C. Bennema, 154.

[479] Douglas Tenney, "Advocate," in *New International Bible Dictionary* (Grand Rapids, MI: Zondervan, 1999), 20.

"forever." The new state of affairs will be permanent. The Spirit once given will not be withdrawn.[480]

It is important to understand that the Sprit does not "replace" Jesus. "Rather, the Spirit discloses the presence of the risen Jesus and his Father to the community of faith."[481] Kostenberger and Swain state,

> the role the Spirit plays in relation to the disciples is analogous to the role he played in relation to Jesus during his earthly ministry. The Spirit, along with the Father, remained with/indwelled Jesus (John 1:32-33; 10:38; 14:10-11); the Spirit, along with the Father and Jesus, remains with/indwells the disciples (14:16-17, 20-23). The Spirit empowered Jesus to speak the words of God (3:34; 6:63); the Spirit empowers the disciples to speak the words of God revealed in Jesus (to be discussed below) (15:26-27; 16:12-15). The Father gave the Spirit to Jesus because he loves him (3:34-35); the Father will give the disciples the Spirit because he loves them, too (14:21, 23).[482]

The Comforter who "Guides"

> I still have many things to say to you, but you cannot bear them now. When the Spirit of truth comes, he will guide you into all the truth, for he will not speak on his own authority, but whatever he hears he will speak, and he will declare to you the things that are to come. He will glorify me, for he will take what is mine and declare it to you. All that the Father has is mine; therefore I said that he will take what is mine and declare it to you (John 16:12–15).

Another relational dynamic of the Holy Spirit is that he "guides" his people. "The Spirit is the divine presence when Jesus' physical presence is taken away from his followers."[483] Koester states that the word ὁδηγέω is a compound word which is based on the words "way" (hodos) and "lead" (agein).[484] Louw and Nida define it as to "guide or to direct, with the implication of making certain that people reach an appropriate destination."[485] This again, beckons attention to the very close, intimate, personal, intentional, filial relationship that he has with believers (vertical paradigm). Just as Jesus spent years teaching and training the twelve, so too, in the passage above, we learn that the Holy Spirit is given to the first disciples and all who would come after them as followers of Jesus. Much like the Father who provides wisdom (above),

---

[480] Morris, John, 576-77.

[481] Craig Koester, The Word of Life: A Theology of John's Gospel (Grand Rapids, MI: Eerdmans, 2008), 148.

[482] Kostenberger and Swain, Father, Son, and Spirit, 146.

[483] Leon Morris, Jesus is the Christ: Studies in the Theology of John (Grand Rapids, MI: Eerdmans, 1989), 159.

[484] Craig Koester, Word of Life, 155.

[485] Louw and Nida, Greek-English Lexicon, 204.

Trinitarian theology is highlighted again here as the Holy Spirit is said to be the one who is doing the *guiding*. Rather than external commands, written on tablets that stand over and against sinners, the Holy Spirit now comes alongside and within the believer to *teach* disciples.[486] Noting again the doctrine of PSA here will be helpful. Having broken fellowship with God through sin and having our minds plunged into the noetic effects of sin, human beings are lost and in need of a guide. Through the suffering death of Jesus in the place of those who have no guidance nor ability to carry out the law of God, wrath is averted and the gospel is magnified in the giving of God the Holy Spirit. Calvin comments, "The purpose of the gospel is the restoration in us of the image of God which had been canceled by sin and that this restoration is progressive and goes on during our whole life, because God makes his glory to shine in us little by little."[487]

The Holy Spirit guides disciples into the truth found in Jesus (John 14:26). He quickens the memories of the disciples in order "to understand plainly the full import and meaning of that revelation."[488] Being in the family of God implies that Christ did not leave his followers as orphans without direction. Rather, the Holy Spirit comforts the siblings of Christ in providing his guidance into life in Christ and with one another.

Specifically, the Holy Spirit guides into the truth. Throughout the gospel of John the "truth" is how God is often characterized. A person who knows and lives by the truth is the person who knows the God who is himself *true* (5:32; 7:28; 8:26).[489] This is also closely tied to the atonement that Christ makes. Koester states,

> [B]efore the Spirit leads people in the way, Jesus must go "the way" of the cross and resurrection. What this means will not be understood at the time, but afterward the Spirit will lead the community to the truth of what Jesus' death and resurrection mean and what these actions convey about God. This is the crucial point. If Jesus has already revealed and embodied God's truth, then the Spirit enables believers to discern what this truth means for them.[490]

Indeed, the truth into which disciples are lead is not a full knowledge of all truth in all subjects. Rather, it is specifically about the person and work of Jesus.[491] Lastly, a brief comment on the *empowering* of the Holy Spirit will conclude the chapter.

---

[486] "'Remaining' and 'indwelling' probably should be viewed as complementary rather than sharply distinct ways of describing the Spirit's work (cf. 14:10, where both terms are used to describe the Father's indwelling relationship to the Son)," Kostenberger and Swain, *Father, Son, and Spirit,* 146, n. 61.

[487] John Calvin, *Commentary on II Corinthians* (Grand Rapids, MI: Baker Books, 1974), 47. See also Stephen Moroney, "Calvin's Teachings on Reason and the Noetic Effects of Sin," in *The Noetic Effects of Sin: A Historical and Contemporary Exploration of How Sin Affects Our Thinking* (Lanham, MD: Lexington Books, 1995), 1-26.

[488] Calvin, II Corinthians, 47.

[489] Craig Koester, *Word of Life,* 155.

[490] Craig Koester, *Word of Life,* 155.

[491] Morris, *John,* 623, n. 38.

The Comforter Who "Empowers Transformation"

As we continue to turn the kaleidoscope and observe that as PSA removes the threat of facing God as "judge," we turn to see that the Holy Spirit, now *empowers* the transformation of the members of the family of God. This can be said even in the context of Ananias and Sapphira who sinned against the Holy Spirit and lost their lives (Acts 5:1-10). The context in which the Holy Spirit judged them does not indicate that they would face the wrath of God in final judgment. As Turner states that the Spirit reserves the right to stand "over and against the community in the sense that he announces judgments that instill the fear of the Lord."[492]

The Holy Spirit empowers believers to do many things, such as to uniquely serve the Church (1 Cor. 12:4-11), proclaim the Gospel (Luke 24:45-49; 1 Pet. 2:9 and will be explored later), and remain in communion with God through prayer (Rom. 8:26). Returning to the subject at hand with penal substitution as the atonement model employed in the establishment of the relational paradigm (vertical), it is helpful to look again at the Epistle to the Galatians. Noted earlier under the section, "The Tree: Becoming a Curse," Paul articulates the cross of Christ in terms of penal substitution (Gal. 3:13). Then, in the following chapter (as referenced above) he writes, "And because you are sons, God has sent the Spirit of his Son into our hearts, crying, 'Abba! Father!' So you are no longer a slave, but a son, and if a son, then an heir through God" (4:6-7).

As he continues demonstrating the relationship between the law and the gospel theologically, Paul does not do so without repeatedly (thirteen times) referencing the person and the work of the Holy Spirit (Gal. 3:2, 3, 5, 14; 4:6, 29; 5:5, 16, 17, 18, 22, 25; 6:8). It is the Spirit who is involved in accomplishing the ongoing empowering and transformation of the believer. For, as Turner notes,

> Receiving Christ and receiving the Spirit are simply ways of speaking of essentially the same reality, for Christ cannot be received except in the gift of the Spirit who brings him, and the Spirit comes as the Spirit of Christ, to unite us with Christ, and to lead us deeper into Christ, and *empower* us to serve Christ until finally the Spirit conforms us fully to Christ in resurrection.[493]

Paul writes,

> But I say, walk by the Spirit, and you will not gratify the desires of the flesh. For the desires of the flesh are against the Spirit, and the desires of the Spirit are against the flesh, for these are opposed to each other, to keep you from doing the things you want to do. But if you are led by the Spirit, you are not under the law. Now the works of the flesh are evident: sexual immorality, impurity, sensuality, idolatry, sorcery, enmity, strife, jealousy, fits of anger, rivalries, dissensions, divisions, envy, drunkenness, orgies, and things like these. I warn you, as I warned you before, that

---

[492] Turner, *Holy Spirit,* 157.

[493] Max Turner, "Receiving Christ and Receiving the Spirit: In Dialogue with David Pawson," *Journal of Pentecostal Theology* 7, no. 15 (Winter 1999): 30, emphasis mine.

those who do such things will not inherit the kingdom of God. But the fruit of the Spirit is love, joy, peace, patience, kindness, goodness, faithfulness, gentleness, self-control; against such things there is no law. And those who belong to Christ Jesus have crucified the flesh with its passions and desires. If we live by the Spirit, let us also keep in step with the Spirit. Let us not become conceited, provoking one another, envying one another (Gal. 5:16-26).

Paul's admonition to Christians to "walk" is "a common Hebraism for 'conducting one's life' and thus is synonymous with 'living.'"[494] This ongoing transformation is thus *relational*. It is not only a response to God in what he has accomplished in the gospel, but it is experienced via a daily *walk* in which the indwelling Holy Spirit is active. The Holy Spirit now guides the child of God and is thus a sign that the prophecy of Jeremiah, regarding the new covenant, has been inaugurated. Throughout the entire Old Testament, the people of God experienced the Law of God as it was inscribed on stone tablets, yet now the children of God know his law through it being written on their hearts (Jer. 31:31-34; Heb. 8:8-12); "God's will is now an inward principle, the result of the leading of the Spirit within the believer. To 'walk by the Spirit' means to be under the constant, moment-by-moment direction, control, and guidance of the Spirit."[495] Additionally, it is imperative to note the present tense of περιπατέω which implies a *continuous* action.[496]

This continuous walking in and by the Spirit is relational though it is not without great opposition as Paul notes in this passage. Rather, the flesh is juxtaposed against the Spirit and wills contrary to the things of God. These are the things for which Christ gave himself as a penalty bearing substitute (Gal. 3:13). And yet the "conflict" (5:17) is still very present and the decision of the child of God who now by the Spirit cries, "*Abba! Father!*" (4:6) is faced with the decision to not only cry to the Father but also to be "led by the Spirit" (5:18). The ongoing willingness to "be led by the Spirit" is not one in which the believer is passive. "The active leading of the Holy Spirit does not signify the believer's being, so to speak, led by the nose willy-nilly; on the contrary he must let himself be led by the Spirit–that is, actively choose to stand on the side of the Spirit over against the flesh."[497] Repeating Dunn here is appropriate, "To know God is to worship him ... to know God is to be known by him, a two-way relationship of acknowledgement and obligation (Gal. 4:9)."[498] Indeed, in this two-way relationship, the child of God is saved by grace, through faith in the person and work of Jesus. He is filled with the Holy Spirit (Eph. 5:18) and is *empowered* to carry out the will of God through abiding in Christ (John 15:1-5), being led by the Spirit (Gal. 5:18), unto the glory of God in all things (Rom. 11:33-36).

---

[494] Ronald Fung, *NICNT: The Epistle to the Galatians* (Grand Rapids, MI: Eerdmans, 1988), 248.

[495] Fung, *Galatians*, 248-49.

[496] George Ladd, *A Theology of the New Testament* (Grand Rapids, MI: Eerdmans, 1993), 475.

[497] Fung, *Galatians*, 251.

[498] James Dunn, "The Body of Christ," 47.

This chapter has sought to establish the relational paradigm vertically and demonstrate how PSA provides the ability to now relate to the Triune God as children who receive wisdom, tenderness, and grace from *Abba*. sympathy, advocacy, and love from the older Brother, and presence, guidance, and empowerment to transform through the Comforter. It is now that we turn our attention to examine some of the relational implications of PSA in a horizontal paradigm.

Summary

Chapter Five has established some of the primary relational implications derived and available to Christians as a result of the doctrine of PSA. In moving from enemies of God to adopted children, the children of God understand the members of the Trinity now in more familial terms and relate to the members of the Godhead as such. Because the wrath of God is averted in the death of Christ, the children of God now relate to the Father as "*Abba*," the Son as "Brother," and the Holy Spirit as "Comforter."

CHAPTER 6

PSA AND THE HORIZONTAL RELATIONAL PARADIGM

Introduction

Thirty years ago Vern Poythress published the first edition of his *Symphonic Theology: The Validity of Multiple Perspectives in Theology*. Therein, he writes, "We use what we have gained from one perspective to reinforce, correct, or improve what we understood through another. I call this procedure 'symphonic theology' because it is analogous to a blending of various musical instruments to express the variation of a symphonic theme."[499] Indeed, he seeks to demonstrate how one might go about harmonizing various theological ideas so as to provide the Christian thinker with a broader approach to doing theology. The metaphor of the kaleidoscope finds itself with a similar intention. In this chapter, the subject focus will be upon the application of the doctrine of PSA to a relational paradigm as a model that can assist disciples in light of the cross and in the local church. Additionally, the present chapter lends itself in the direction of *theological ontology:* because we are examining both the Triune God and his image bearers in relation to himself (vertical) and human-to-human (horizontal) relationships through the penal substitutionary atonement of Christ. This calls to mind Barth's understanding of human beings as "beings-in-relation."[500] When Enoch Wan defines *relational realism* ontologically he does so by saying that it is "the systematic understanding that 'reality' is primarily based on the 'vertical relationship' between God and the created order and secondarily horizontal relationships within the created order."[501] Hence, this is why in the previous chapter, we first established the vertical paradigm so as to now logically discuss the horizontal.

In the magnanimous Philippian hymn, to be discussed below, the Apostle Paul captures much of the essence of the atoning work of Christ. The meaning of the text is better understood when considering the *"cultures"* involved in the reconciliation of God and human beings and human-to-human reconciliation. That is to say that Paul uses the atoning work of Christ to speak not only of *justification* but that he speaks of it as the "lens" by which believers are to see themselves, others, and the world with strong *relational* implications ("humility," "attitude," etc.). More precisely, he speaks of believers having a certain *"mind"* (Phil. 2:5) within them that is directly informed by the self-emptying Christ who suffered on the cross. There will be more on this below as we apply the metaphor of the kaleidoscope to the horizontal paradigm. However, first a

---

[499] Vern Poythress, Symphonic Theology: The Validity of Multiple Perspectives in Theology (Phillipsburg, NJ: P&R Publishing, 2001), 43.

[500] Deddo, *Barth's*, 99.

[501] Enoch Wan, "Relational Theology and Relational Missiology," *EMS Occasional Bulletin* 21, no.1 (Fall 2007), 2.

comment on the gospel and three categories of thought regarding Christian anthropology will be helpful as the three cultures will be continually referenced in the kaleidoscopic diagram.

It is important to keep in mind both Christian anthropology and ontology as we examine some of the relational implications of PSA. In the atoning work of Christ, we observe the second member of the Trinity (supra-culture, Culture A) descending *(kenosis!),* being "born in the likeness of men" (human culture, Culture C) to the lowest class ("servant"),[502] and suffering the death of a criminal ("the cross"!).[503] The act of the atonement and the resurrection of Christ with "his name exalted far above every name" brings about the bending knees and confessing tongues of all relational beings in cultures B and C. God did not send an angel (angel culture, Culture B) rather, sent his Son who is equal with the Father (Culture A) to the lowest level of human culture (Culture C) for the salvation of humankind. Following Wan's line of thinking regarding "relational realism" it is first and foremost important to spend more space establishing this *vertical* aspect of PSA and then move on to the subject at hand.

The doctrine of PSA not only speaks clearly to the vertical relationship extended to and established by the Triune God in the transformation and adoption of people into his family (Gal. 4:6); PSA also has incredible *horizontal* relational implications on the lives of those to whom God is now reconciled. This chapter will interact with a few selected texts extrapolating this reality. The following diagram serves as an aid in understanding what this chapter expounds upon: the horizontal relational implications of PSA applied through the metaphor of a kaleidoscope.

---

[502] This could also be described as "Culture C-2," due to how slaves were viewed in the first century Roman context.

[503] For diagrams of this concept, see Wan, "The Christian Response to Chinese Folk Religion," in *Christian Witness in Pluralistic Contexts*, 190.

Figure 10 – Kaleidoscope: The horizontal relational implications of PSA

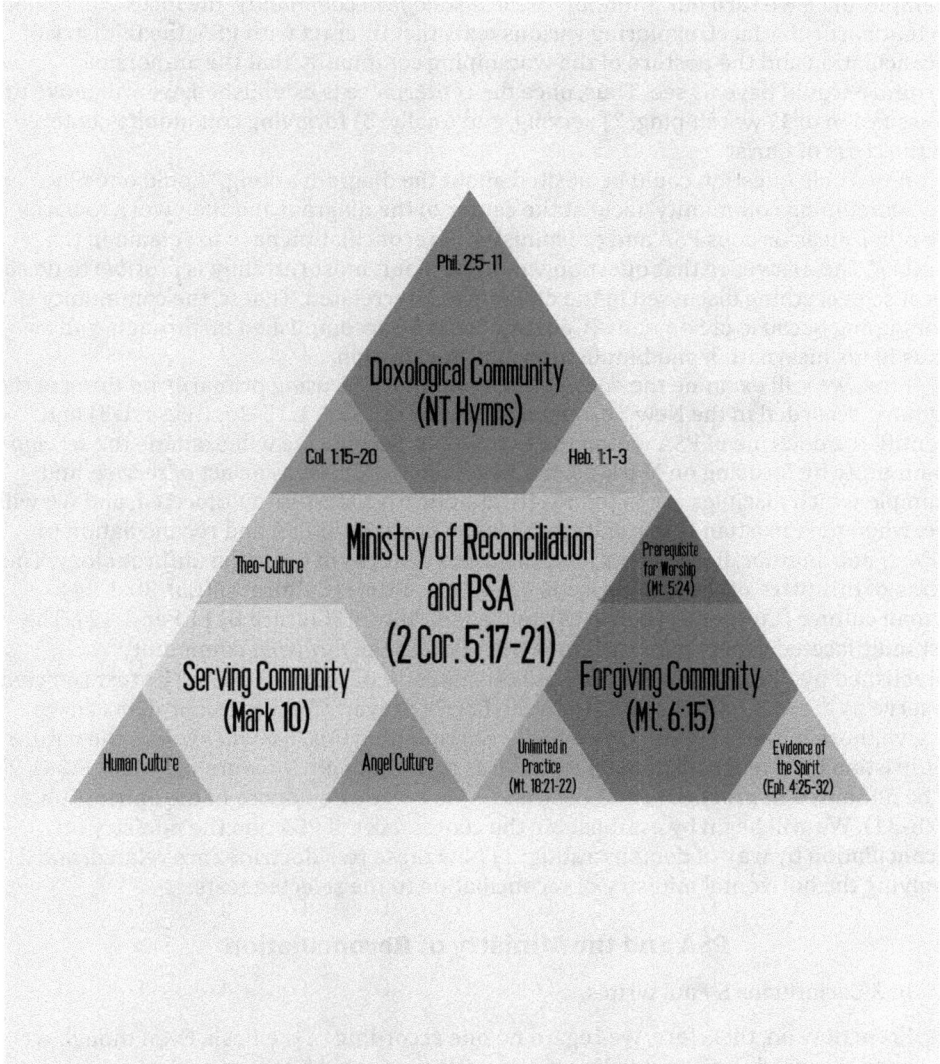

This chapter will begin by establishing the centerpiece of the kaleidoscope, expounding upon the relationship between the doctrine of PSA and the "ministry of reconciliation" that Paul speaks about in 2 Corinthians 5:18. From there, we will explore three major facets of the *kind* of *community* that understands the doctrine of PSA and the ministry of reconciliation that these truths create.[504] Indeed, each of the

---

[504] McKnight refers to this as "A Community Called 'Atonement.'"

three selected facets, like a kaleidoscope, are also multi-faceted. Therefore, as an example, once we turn our attention to the *doxological community*, the focus will remain on that particular facet, exploring various texts that interact with PSA, the ministry of reconciliation and the posture of the worshiping community that the authors of Scripture would have us see. Thus, once the centerpiece is established, we will move to a discussion of 1) worshiping, 2) serving, and finally, 3) forgiving community centered on the cross of Christ.

A possible question could be posited about the diagram asking, "Could one place the 'worshiping community' facet at the center of the diagram and then work towards the other ideas or does PSA and the ministry of reconciliation have to remain in the center?" The answer to that question would be that it most certainly is *possible* to do so because everything discussed in the diagram is interrelated. That is, the community is worshiping because of Someone (God) and what he accomplished in, through, and as Jesus in his incarnation and humiliation and glorification.

First, we will examine the *doxological* community focusing primarily on three of the "hymns" recorded in the New Testament (Phil. 2:5-11; Col. 1:15-20; Heb. 1:1-3) and identify the doctrine of PSA within those contexts. Second, we will examine the *serving* community by focusing on Mark 10, the atonement of Christ as an act of *service*, and example which disciples are to follow. In addition, this facet is multifaceted, and we will see, when the Christian community applies the doctrine of PSA and reconciliation to *serving* one another, it actually affects the three cultures in Christian anthropology. The facets of this piece of the kaleidoscope are Theo-culture (Culture A) (Col. 3:23-24), human culture (Culture C) (Gal. 5:13), and angel culture (Culture B) (1 Pet. 1:12). The last multifaceted aspect of this chapter will address the *forgiving* community established by Christ in light of PSA and the ministry of reconciliation. The text selected to serve as the foundation comes from the Lord's prayer: "forgive us our debts as we forgive those indebted to us" (Matt. 6:12). Surrounding this, we will explore the nature of Christian forgiveness as it is: 1) to serve as a prerequisite for worship (Matt. 5:24), 2) to be unlimited in practice (18:21-22), and 3) to serve as evidence of the Spirit (Eph. 4:28-31). We will begin by establishing the center facet of PSA and the ministry of reconciliation by way of demonstrating: 1) how these two doctrines are related, and 2) applying the horizontal ministry of reconciliation to the selected texts.

PSA and the Ministry of Reconciliation

In 2 Corinthians 5 Paul writes,

From now on, therefore, we regard no one according to the flesh. Even though we once regarded Christ according to the flesh, we regard him thus no longer. Therefore, if anyone is in Christ, he is a new creation. The old has passed away; behold, the new has come. All this is from God, who through Christ reconciled us to himself and gave us the ministry of reconciliation; that is, in Christ God was reconciling the world to himself, not counting their trespasses against them, and entrusting to us the message of reconciliation. Therefore, we are ambassadors for Christ, God making his appeal through us. We implore you on behalf of Christ, be reconciled to God. For our sake he made him to be sin who knew no sin, so that in him we might become the righteousness of God (2 Cor. 5:16-21).

PSA and the ministry of reconciliation are closely related. As we examine the centerpiece of the kaleidoscope,[505] we observe Paul's statement, "He [God] made him [Christ] to be sin who knew no sin (cf. Heb. 4:15), so that in him [Christ] we might become the righteousness of God" (2 Cor. 5:21). This is what Luther famously coined as the "great exchange." Ralph Martin writes of this section of Scripture:

> The lengthy, weighty passage in vv.16-21 has many facets but one master theme. In it Paul is setting down the Christian conviction that in the Christ event a new world has been born and a new age has supervened on world history. Phrases like "a new creation," "reconciliation," and "righteousness of God" are all virtual synonyms for this new eon which has radically affected *both* divine-human *and* all earthly relationships.[506]

Thus, the doctrine of justification is not a cold, impersonal, disconnected proposition. Instead, it is close, intimate, warm, and relational. Not only in terms of the vertical relationship, but also horizontally, *"all earthly relationships"* are affected. Briefly recalling what was covered earlier in the book under "Becoming the Curse" will be helpful here. Marshall reminds us that Jesus' death "took away their sin and liability to judgment/wrath in order to become righteous. The consequences of sin, specifically death, are borne by Christ when he is made one with sinners, and, in that sense, the substitution is penal."[507]

---

[505] Gloria L. Schabb uses the metaphor of the kaleidoscope as well and wonderfully describes the metaphorical usage of it as follows: "The kaleidoscope (Greek: 'beautiful-form-to-see') is a contoured structure that, through the use of mirrors and lenses set at different angles, creates a multiplicity of symmetrical patterns from fragments of various materials, illuminated by a source of light. The materials that produce the patterns are commonly shards or fragments of shattered stained glass. However, while these shards are the stuff of which the image is formed, the mirrors of the kaleidoscope are its heart. These mirrors or modes of reflection vary in quality, quantity, and angles of placement. The better the quality of the mirror, the sharper and clearer the ultimate reflection; the greater the number of mirrors, the more diverse the shape of the image; and the narrower the angle of placement of the mirror, the greater the number of reflections produced. When directed toward an external entity and rotated, the object case, which contains the shards of various forms, colors, and densities, produces, in interaction with the mirrors, a 'beautiful form to see.' As a result, a mandala is created, a circular design of concentric forms, a 'sacred circle with a centerpoint' that is a universal image of oneness and wisdom. Obviously, while each of the elements of the kaleidoscope can be defined and discussed independently, it is only in their collaboration that the beauty, clarity, and variety of patterns can be produced." Gloria L. Schabb, "Feminist Theological Methodology: A Kaleidoscopic Model." *Theological Studies* 62, no. 2 (May 2001): 342.

[506] Ralph Martin, *Word Biblical Commentary*, vol. 40, *2 Corinthians* (Nashville, TN: Thomas Nelson, 1985), 158.

[507] Marshall, *Aspects*, 48.

Some such as Hooker would argue that in this context, Christ is presented not as our substitute but rather our *representative*. She writes, "It is as man's *representative,* rather than as his substitute, that Christ suffers, and it is only as one who is fully human that he is able to do anything effective for mankind, by lifting man, as it were, into an obedient relationship with God."[508] Certainly, this is what is meant by becoming the "righteousness of God." However, she is overlooking the significance of words like "made," "sin," and "for" in this verse which speaks of the wrath of God. For Christ to be "made" into *"sin"* on the cross *"for"* those who are *reconciled* to God speaks of *substitution* and not merely representation. "Paul is not focusing on Jesus' human life but on his inglorious death. Christ experienced the consequences for human sin. The one who lived a sinless life died a sinner's death, estranged from God and the object of (averting!) wrath. He was treated as a sinner in his death."[509] Thus, in becoming the righteousness of God, Christians are not only reconciled to God but also have been "given the ministry of reconciliation" (τὴν διακονίαν τῆς καταλλαγῆς). This speaks to the incredible *relational* implications of PSA in the Christian community and sheds light on so much of *how* to go about life together, with the wrath of God poured out on Christ rather than one another. Indeed, Milbank is right when he says, "the main stress is that, upon the basis of the rejected one, a new sort of *community* is to be built."[510]

To now be reconciled with God, the Christian understands that her sins "are not counted against" her (vertical). Following the vertical relationship, Paul's immediate *application* of this reality is *horizontal* (Wan), for, Paul uses the word "ambassador" (πρεσβεύομεν).[511] Historically, the term *ambassador* was extremely significant. "To reject the representations of an envoy was to reject the one who sent him. To ignore Paul at this point would have been to ignore the Christ on whose behalf he spoke."[512] Not only are Christians to understand themselves as *ambassadors* but the relational aspect is heightened as Paul declares that *"God"* is speaking – making his appeal through us. This implies that the ongoing relationship that believers have with God (vertical) now breaks into communication with others (horizontal)! Thus, the reconciliation is both *vertical* and *horizontal*; God-to-human and human-to-human relationships are now characterized through the atonement and experienced as "reconciled."

Scot McKnight's comments here are weighty and should be quoted at length:

---

[508] Morna D. Hooker, "Interchange in Christ," *Journal of Theological Studies* 22, no. 2 (October 1971): 358.

[509] Garland, *2 Corinthians,* 301.

[510] Milbank, *Reconciled,* 98 (emphasis mine).

[511] "To be an ambassador in the ancient world (Greek, Roman, or Jewish), as in modern times, involved three things: (1) a commissioning for a special assignment; (2) representing the sender; and (3) exercising the authority of the sender. It was universally expected that an ambassador, whatever his message and however delicate or risky his mission, would be treated with respect and dignity, accorded appropriate hospitality, and guaranteed a safe exit."[511] See M. J. Harris, *A Commentary on the Greek Text: The Second Epistle to the Corinthians* (Grand Rapids, MI: Eerdmans, 2005), 445).

[512] Barnett, *2 Corinthians,* 310.

To be forgiven, to be atoned for, to be reconciled – synonymous expressions – is to be granted a *mission* to become a reciprocal performer of the same: to forgive, to work atonement, and to be an agent of reconciliation. Thus, atonement is not just something done to us and for us, it is *something we participate in–in this world, in the here and now.* It is not just something done, but something that is being done and something that we do as we join God in the *missio Dei.*[513]

It is with this centerpiece of the kaleidoscope diagram established that we "turn the cylinder" so to speak and observe the wisdom of God displayed through the reconciled community. First, we will examine the doxological community as we direct our attention to the first facet above the centerpiece.

The Doxological Community

The doxological community is focused on the reflective worship and glory due to God in light of Christ's actions as the one who averts the wrath of God. The Aposlte Paul writes to the Ephesisans and instructs them in that they are to address "one another in psalms and hymns and spiritual songs, singing and making melody to the Lord with your heart" (Eph. 5:19). To the Colossians he says, "Let the word of Christ dwell in you richly, teaching and admonishing one another in all wisdom, singing psalms and hymns and spiritual songs, with thankfulness in your hearts to God" (Col. 3:16). In writing to emperor Trajan in 111 A.D., Pliny states that Christians "were in the habit of meeting on a certain fixed day before it was light, when they sang in alternate verses a hymn to Christ, as to a god."[514]

There is much debate about whether or not the "hymns" recorded in the New Testament were actually used by Christians prior, and thus quoted by Paul and others in their writings, or that the writings were original to the authors. The three passages that will be examined are Philippians 2:5-11, Colossians 1:15-20, and Hebrews 1:1-3.[515] Larger debate surrounds the Philippian hymn and less debate around the others examined here.[516] There is incredibly rich discussion and volumous material available on the historical-context, linguistic-structure, and overall exegetical insight available on these passages. For our purposes here, however, the focus will remain on the major themes found within these Christological-hymns as they relate to the horizontal

---

[513] McKnight, *Community Called Atonement,* 31-32, (emphasis mine).

[514] Pliny, "Letter 10.96," accessed March 31, 2016, http://faculty.georgetown.edu/jod/texts/pliny.html.

[515] Other similar "minor" passages are 1 Tim. 3:16 and 1 Pet. 3:18-22.

[516] For lengthy discussions around the history of the "hymns" or "Christ-hymns" of the New Testament see Jack Sanders, *The New Testament Christological Hymns: Their Historical Religious Background* (Cambridge England: Cambridge University Press, 1971); Robert Karris, *A Symphony of New Testament Hymns* (Collegeville, MN: Liturgical Press,1996).

relational implications of PSA. The major themes within the hymns are: 1) Preexistence of Christ, 2) Incarnation of Christ, and 3) Exaltation of Christ.[517]

The Philippian Hymn (Phil. 2:5-11)

To the Philippian church Paul wrote,

Have this mind among yourselves, which is yours in Christ Jesus, who, though he was in the form of God, did not count equality with God a thing to be grasped, but emptied himself, by taking the form of a servant, being born in the likeness of men. And being found in human form, he humbled himself by becoming obedient to the point of death, even death on a cross. Therefore God has highly exalted him and bestowed on him the name that is above every name, so that at the name of Jesus every knee should bow, in heaven and on earth and under the earth, and every tongue confess that Jesus Christ is Lord, to the glory of God the Father (Phil. 2:5-11).

In this passage Paul admonishes the believers to have a *mindset* (v.5) about them, one of "humility" (v.8) towards one another. Then Paul proceeds to cite the early "hymn." There are lengthy discussions both in favor of this section being original to Paul as well as those who favor him quoting an early Christian hymn used in corporate worship gatherings. One of the reasons why some would argue that it is not original to Paul is the fact that the pericope does not contain an explicit presentation of the doctrine of redemption, which would be typical of Pauline theology. Rather, here, the hymn speaks of the cross in more *exemplary* terms. Thus, it highlights the humility and obedience of Jesus to the Father. Paul sees this as the context to provide the grounding and motivation for love, humility, selflessness (vv.1-4) to be expressed toward one another in the worshipping community. However, that is not to say that the idea of *substitution* and wrath are totally absent from Paul's thought amongst the Phillipians either. A brief excurses at this point will support this last statement and then we will return for a moment to the Philippian Christ-hymn.

In the following chapter Paul writes,For many, of whom I have often told you and now tell you even with tears, walk as enemies of the cross of Christ. Their end is destruction, their god is their belly, and they glory in their shame, with minds set on earthly things (Phil. 3:18-19). This is the only other explicit mention of the cross in the letter to the Philippian church. Here, there is discussion surrounding *who* are the "enemies of the cross of Christ."[518] Martin sees this passage as falling within the framework of PSA. In defining the "message of the cross," he says,

---

[517] Donald Guthrie, *New Testament Theology: A Thematic Study* (Downers Grove, IL: IVP, 2013), 345.

[518] "Plainly they were persons inside the Christian Church, although probably not at Philippi." See George Kennedy, *New Testament Interpretation Through Historical Criticism* (Chapel Hill, NC: University of North Carolina Press, 1984), 461. Others, such as Martin press one to think that these were Judaizers (though he doesn't use the term) amongst the early churches with a false gospel. "Paul... considered it necessary to warn against them simply because he knew of their numbers (πολλι, "many") and the zeal with which they propagated their religion." Additionally, he

it is nothing other than the gospel, indeed an exhaustive statement of the content of the gospel, namely that Christ must be crucified, that the *Messiah had to die in order for sinners to be forgiven by God*–was the very thing that scandalized the Jews and was treated as folly by the Greeks (1 Cor. 1:23). The gospel was an "offense" to them and "foolishness" because in the cross God did precisely the opposite of what they expected him to do.[519]

It is important to recall what was expounded upon in the previous chapter regarding the judgment of enemies and the adopting of family members in the present discussion. The "enemies of the cross," first look to their eternal condition; their end being one of "destruction." Destruction does not necessarily mean *loss of existence* since its opposite is salvation (Phil. 1:28).[520] Thus, the enemies of the cross, if not in right relationship with God (reconciled), face their "eschatological end"[521] ("*telos*") of "destruction." This is important when reading the Christ-hymn, that in the Philippian church the wrath of God was understood to be present in the cross of Christ though not stated explicitly in the worship-hymn.

Returning to the Christ-hymn in the horizontal paradigm Paul is helping the body grow in their discipleship as the community is admonished to express the virtues of love, humility, and selflessness. The "mindsets" of both 2:5 and 3:19 are particularly important. One mindset is *doxological*, focused on the person and work of Christ (Preexistence, Incarnation, and Exaltation). Whereas the mindset of the "enemies" is one set on "earthly things." A doxological community is one that is presently focusing upon the "eschatological end" – grounded in the work of Christ upon the cross that ought to be one that exhibits the virtues of love, humility, and selflessness rather than following the "god(s)" of their "bellies," "glory(ing) in shame," and "minds set on earthly things." In keeping with the kaleidoscope as a suitable metaphor, we now turn to see the work of the cross in creating a doxological community in the city of Colossae.

---

writes, "These people may have been, and probably were, very religious, honest, sincere Christians. But if their 'goodness' and the religious acts that they faithfully performed in any way tended to keep them from casting themselves wholly upon God and asking for the righteousness that he supplies only through Jesus Christ, if their beliefs and practices set them in opposition to the gospel of salvation by Christ alone and its outworking in a life of obedience and earnest moral endeavor, if their doing the law threatened the exclusiveness of the forgiveness of sins by faith in Christ, then, for Paul, their conduct was indeed 'evil' because it brought ultimate harm both to themselves and to others." Ralph Martin, *Tyndale New Testament Commentaries: Philippians* (Downers Grove, IL: IVP, 2008), 222.

[519] Martin, *Philippians,* 223 (emphasis mine).

[520] Richard Melick, *The New American Commentary,* vol. 32, *Philippians, Colossians, Philemon* (Nashville, TN: Broadman & Holman Publishers, 1991), 143.

[521] Gordon Fee, *NICNT: Paul's Letter to the Philippians* (Grand Rapids, MI: Eerdmans Publishing, 1995) 370n34.

The Colossian Hymn (Col. 1:15-20)

Paul wrote to the Colossian church, praying that all of the "saints" and faithful brothers in Christ" (1:2) would be "filled with knowledge of the will of God" (v.9), and "understanding" (v.9), "walking worthy of the Lord" (v.10), performing "good works" (v.10), full of "strength and power with patience and joy" (v.11), with hearts of "thanks" (v.12) because God had "delivered them from the domain of darkness and transferred them to the kingdom of his beloved Son, in whom we have redemption, the forgiveness of sins" (Col. 1:13-14). Thinking along the lines of the horizontal relationships, Paul longs for the community to be one of *wisdom* (1:9, 28; 2:3; 3:16; 4:5). However, in order to implement the horizontal, Paul first establishes what God has done in Christ (vertical). It is here that we look at our second "hymn."

> He is the image of the invisible God, the firstborn of all creation. For by him all things were created, in heaven and on earth, visible and invisible, whether thrones or dominions or rulers or authorities—all things were created through him and for him. And he is before all things, and in him all things hold together. And he is the head of the body, the church. He is the beginning, the firstborn from the dead, that in everything he might be preeminent. For in him all the fullness of God was pleased to dwell, and through him to reconcile to himself all things, whether on earth or in heaven, making peace by the blood of his cross (Col. 1:15-20).

Bruce states that these six verses are cast in a form of "rhythmical prose which is found in much early Christian hymnody."[522] Indeed, Martin also affirms that the weight of scholarly opinion today considers this to be a hymn. However,

> In describing the passage this way it should be noted that the term "hymn" is not employed in the modern sense of what we understand by congregational hymns with metrical verses. Nor are we to think in terms of Greek poetic form. The category is used broadly, similar to that of "creed" and includes dogmatic, confessional, liturgical, polemical, or doxological material.[523]

Again, in this "hymn" we find the preexistence, incarnation, and exaltation of Christ being emphasized in a *doxological* fashion for the community. Thus, this facet, too, fits well within the kaleidoscope diagram. In addition to his preexistent state and his role in creation, the hymn confesses Christ to be in authority over all ontological cultures understood from Christian anthropology (Theo culture, Angel culture, and human culture). And yet, the hymn *closes* with a reference to peace-making "by the blood of his cross" (v.20). Interestingly, Paul speaks of the cross here and in 2:14 with both including an emphasis on PSA alongside a *Christus Victor* model of the atonement. The shedding of Christ's "blood" is what brings "peace" and extinguishes the war, enmity,

---

[522] Bruce, *Colossians, Philemon, and Ephesians*, 54. He also then references in n. 73 over twenty important articles that affirm this.

[523] Peter T. O'Brien, *Word Biblical Commentary* vol. 44, *Colossians, Philemon* (Nashville, TN: Thomas Nelson, 1982), 34-35.

and wrath between God and human beings. "Reconciliation and making peace (which includes the notion of pacification) are used synonymously to describe the climatic work of Christ effected on the historical plane in and through his death on the cross."[524] It is worth noting here that in Ephesians 2:13-16, the same horizontal themes of reconciliation related to the atoning work of Christ are repeated. Paul writes,

> But now in Christ Jesus you who once were far off have been brought near by the blood of Christ. For he himself is our peace, who has made us both one and has broken down in his flesh the dividing wall of hostility by abolishing the law of commandments expressed in ordinances, that he might create in himself one new man in place of the two, so making peace, and might reconcile us both to God in one body through the cross, thereby killing the hostility (Eph. 2:13-16).

The reconciliation of the Jewish and Gentile peoples results in one new humanity as Paul addresses alienation, through the "cross" as *killing* the hostility (enmity!) and has "made peace" between God and humans *and* has established the grounding, the context, and the ability, to see peaceful, harmonious living occurring within once hostile relationships. Hendriksen writes,

> The meaning is that Christ's atoning death had achieved its purpose: the proper relation between the Ephesians and their God had been established. By grace those estranged from God, having heard and accepted the gospel, had laid aside their wicked alienation from God and had entered into the fruits of Christ's perfect atonement. This miracle had been achieved "through the cross," that very cross which to the Jews was a stumbling-block and to the Gentiles folly (1 Cor. 1:23). It was by means of Christ's death on the cross that the curse had been borne, and, having been borne, had been lifted off the hearts and lives of all believers (Gal. 3:13). The miracle of Calvary, however, was even more thrilling, for, *through the strange instrument of the cross,* the Sufferer not only reconciled to God both Jews and Gentiles but also slew the deeply-rooted antipathy that had existed for so long a time between the two groups.[525]

Again, in the letter to the Colossians, Paul states explicitly the doctrine of PSA by referencing the debt that was paid by Christ to God on the cross. Paul writes to the Colossian community "And you, who were dead in your trespasses and the uncircumcision of your flesh, God made alive together with him, having forgiven us all our trespasses, by canceling the record of debt that stood against us with its legal demands. This he set aside, nailing it to the cross" (Col. 2:13-14). This reconciliation was not to be understood in individual terms only. For Paul continues by way of calling attention to the horizontal-relational application of the penal sacrifice of Christ begun in the hymn, he continues by saying,

---

524 O'Brien, Colossians, Philemon, 62.
525 William Hendriksen, New Testament Commentary: Galatians, Ephesians, Philippians, Colossians, and Philemon (Grand Rapids, MI: Baker Books, 2002), 135-36.

On account of these the wrath of God is coming. In these you too once walked, when you were living in them. But now you must put them all away: anger, wrath, malice, slander, and obscene talk from your mouth. Do not lie to one another, seeing that you have put off the old self with its practices and have put on the new self, which is being renewed in knowledge after the image of its creator. Here there is not Greek and Jew, circumcised and uncircumcised, barbarian, Scythian, slave, free; but Christ is all, and in all (Col. 3:6-11).

Paul now, in light of the doxological community, applies the work of the cross not only in penal terms that addresses the coming "wrath of God," he speaks as well to the ongoing discipleship that plays out practically in relating to one another. In turning the kaleidoscope, we observe that what God has done in Christ is *directly* related to the community as believers are to put away "anger," "wrath," "malice," "slander," "obscene talk," and "lying." Melick notes,

> The sins are mentioned in a group of five. In contrast to the former list, this list is more social in nature. These sins destroy *social relationships* and are more expressive of attitudes than specific actions ... Since the new life is to be lived *corporately with all Christians, positive Christian social relationships are mandatory* ... These five, then, are mentioned not so much because they are more typical of Christians than of non-Christians, but because they are necessary to *harmonious relationships* in the body of Christ. Respect for all persons should characterize all Christians, but there must be a special regard for the church.[526]

Moreover, the sins are not only to be put away, but the positive virtues that bless and build up the community of Jesus are also listed. We are to "bear with one another" (Col. 3:13), "forgive one another" (3:13), "teach one another" (3:16), and "admonish one another." It is clearly seen here that when the apostle Paul speaks of the wrath bearing of the son of God on his cross, he does not do so in a way that privatizes one's Christian faith but rather has a transforming effect on the heart and mind of the individual and thus the community experiences grace. It is here, as we turn the kaleidoscope, we see the third selected hymn come into focus.

The Hebrew Hymn (Heb. 1:1-3)

As referenced above, the word "hymn" here is applied loosely.[527] However, as Attridge says, "The rhetorical artistry of this exordium surpasses that of any other

---

[526] Melick, Philippians, Colossians, Philemon, 293.

[527] "When the writer quotes Ps 110:1 in v.13, he follows the Old Greek version in reading the genitive ἐκ δεξιῶν, but when he alludes to this passage in v.3 he writes the dative ἐν δεξιᾷ, rather than the genetive ἐκ δεξιῶν. A probable explanation for this variation is that the allusions are based on a liturgical confession rather than the text of the psalm (Hay, *Glory*, 35,41) " quoted in Lane, *Hebrews*, 7.

portion of the New Testament."[528] The writer of the Epistle to the Hebrews opens with these lines:

> Long ago, at many times and in many ways, God spoke to our fathers by the prophets, but in these last days he has spoken to us by his Son, whom he appointed the heir of all things, through whom also he created the world. He is the radiance of the glory of God and the exact imprint of his nature, and he upholds the universe by the word of his power. After making purification for sins, he sat down at the right hand of the Majesty on high (Heb. 1:1-3).

The manner in which *Auctor* (the Latin word for source which is sometimes used amongst scholarship) begins the letter is one of remarkable Biblical theology that is distinguished in its own right within the New Testament by brilliantly articulating comparisons, parallels even, between the old and the new, the former and the present, the *was* and *is* with a knowledge of the *not yet* but sure *to be*.[529] In this set of parallels the writer establishes the salvation-historical pattern found throughout Scripture as he picks up on "types and trajectories" (redemptive-historical) hermeneutics. The prologue easily ranks amongst some of the highest Christological claims in all of Holy Scripture.[530] In essence, the writer of the Epistle offers no shortage of imagery coupled with pointed theological assertions as his *"kaleidoscopic"* handling of the Old Testament as examined in the wake of such events as the incarnation, humiliation, resurrection, and ascension of the Messiah.

This hymn, as the others examined above, speaks to the preexistence of the Son as well as his incarnation, and his exaltation. What concerns us here is verse 3, the *"purification for sins,"* and the effect it carries on the doxological community addressed. First, it must be stated that "purification" here does not speak directly to PSA in explicit terms. Rather, as in the other hymns, it does establish that in the early worshiping community, the centrality of the cross in Christian worship and practice remained steadfast. In addition, this reference to "purification" provides grounding for later discussions of the work of Christ on the cross, and some of these, in fact, do speak to PSA and have horizontal relational implications. O'Brien writes, "Later [in the Epistle],

---

[528] Attridge, *Hebrews*, 36.

[529] Ancient rhetoricians believed that the opening words of a public address should colorfully introduce the topic. The anonymous author of *Rhetorica ad Herennim* said: "We shall have attentive hearers by promising to discuss something important, new and unusual matters, or as such as pertain to the commonwealth, or to the hearers themselves, or to the worship of the immortal gods; ... and by enumerating the points we are going to discuss." (1.4.7 trans. Caplan, 1954) cited in James Thompson, *Padeia Commentaries on the New Testament: Hebrews* (Grand Rapids, MI: Baker Academic, 2008), 32. Further, "Some have suggested that the author deliberately omitted the introduction, but this is doubtful. The beautifully balanced literary classical sentence with which Hebrews does begin has all the earmarks of the original introduction," David Allen, "The Authorship of Hebrews: Historical Survey of the Lukan Theory," *Criswell Theological Review* 8, no. 2 (Spring 2011): 3-4.

[530] Neighboring passages to see would be John 1:1-4,14; Colossians 1:15-20; Philippians 2:5-11; Revelation 1:9-20 to name a few with weighty emphasis to high Christological statements.

Christ's superior offering *for sin* under the new covenant will be expanded fully (Heb. 9:1-10:18)."[531] The cross will be elaborated on in 7:27; 10:12; 12:2 as well as the Day of Atonement, blood of the covenant, ashes of the red heifer and sacrifices in the remainder of the letter (esp. 9:1-10:18) as the cultic rituals serve as a precursor to the work of the Son. The Greek, καθαρισμός is a relatively rare word used in the NT as it pertains to the self-sacrifice of Jesus, appearing only in 2 Peter 1:9. Yet it is common in the LXX and the Old Testament for cultic purification.[532] The doctrine of expiation is highlighted here but should not be seen as divorced from propitiation either.[533] Nicole points out that the word *kippur* is used over 100 times in the Old Testament and that it is used 80 percent of the time in reference to *ritual* purity.[534] "Purification for sin" here is an affirmation of the fact that sin has stained humankind, thus they are under the judgment of God, Christ has accomplished the gracious act of reconciliation between God and his people, and this, too, has effect on the relational dynamics of the doxological community. Recalling the diagram, as we turn the kaleidoscope, one can observe PSA and the ministry of reconciliation understood within the community in the Epistle to the Hebrews. For example,

> For it was indeed fitting that we should have such a high priest, holy, innocent, unstained, *separated from sinners*, and exalted above the heavens. He has no need, like those high priests, to offer sacrifices daily, first for his own *sins* and then for those of *the people*, since he did this once for all when he offered up himself (7:26-27).

Here we see the sinless Christ who offered himself up *"for ... the people."* Or again,

> When he said above, "You have neither desired nor taken pleasure in sacrifices and offerings and burnt offerings and sin offerings" (these are offered according to the

---

[531] O'Brien, *Hebrews,* 58 (emphasis mine).

[532] Attridge, *Hebrews,* 46. In the LXX, cf. Exod. 29:36; Lev. 15:13; Prov. 14:9. Attridge notes, "The description of the expiation ceremony on Yom Kippur at Ex. 30:10 is particularly important.

[533] Because of the nature of the Epistle to the Hebrews with the cultic background serving as a shadow and not the substance, and in this instance both Yom Kippur and the Passover address both propitiation and expiation, one comment is necessary regarding *propitiation*. It has been recently noted by penal substitutionary advocates that in the Passover, there is something quite unique between the first nine plagues and the tenth, namely that the tenth plague had a *condition* to it. For, a lamb must be slaughtered and the blood applied to the door of the home in order for the firstborn to be spared. "Thus the lamb becomes a substitute for the firstborn son, dying in his place," Jeffery, Ovey, Sach, *Pierced,* 37. Therefore, "the effect of blood sacrifice in the averting of judgment is clear." Christopher Wright, "Atonement," 73. Because of the atoning sacrifice made by the Israelites, many of the other terms highlighted by Averbeck came into effect such as forgiveness, cleansing, consecration, or redemption, see Richard Averbeck in *NIDOTTE,* vol. 2, 689-710.Yet, "in each case the bottom-line connotation of the result [atonement] is the same: preventing the outbreak of Yahweh's wrath." Groves, "Isaiah," 66.

[534] Emile Nicole, "Pentateuch," 47-8.

law), then he added, "Behold, I have come to do your will." He does away with the first in order to establish the second. And by that will we have been sanctified *through the offering of the body of Jesus Christ once for all.* And every priest stands daily at his service, offering repeatedly the same sacrifices, which can never take away *sins.* But when Christ had offered for all time *a single sacrifice for sins,* he sat down at the right hand of God, waiting from that time until his enemies should be made a footstool for his feet. For by a single offering he has perfected for all time those who are being sanctified (Heb. 10:8-14).

Again, PSA is here demonstrated by the repeated emphasis on the "offering ... *for sins.*" Relationally, the believers who trust in the person and work of Christ for salvation are admonished to *"encourage one another"* twice in the Epistle (3:13, 10:25) as well as to "gather together" (10:25), and to "spur one another on to love and good works" (10:24).

Therefore, brothers, since we have confidence to enter the holy places *by the blood of Jesus,* by the new and living way that he opened for us through the curtain, that is, *through his flesh,* and since we have a great priest over the house of God, let us draw near with a true heart in full assurance of faith, with our hearts sprinkled clean from an evil conscience and our bodies washed with pure water. Let us hold fast the confession of our hope without wavering, for he who promised is faithful. And *let us consider how to stir up one another to love and good works,* not *neglecting to meet together,* as is the habit of some, but *encouraging* one another, and all the more as you see the Day drawing near (Heb. 10:19-25).

Considering, Stirring, and Provoking Love and Good Works

In light of the blood shed by Christ who cleansed us of our sins and reconciled us to God, the writer of the epistle draws the implication that the community is to give careful thought and attention to "stirring up one another to love and good works." The word here for "consider" (κατανοέω) means "to give very careful consideration to some matter—'to think about very carefully, to consider closely.'"[535] O'Brien states that the believers are "being urged to focus their minds and energies on the needs of their fellow members in order to spur, even provoke, them to love and good deeds. For believers to fulfill this responsibility presupposes that they possess a care and practical concern for one another."[536] This goes beyond *reminding* one another of the content of the gospel and seeks to apply it in practical acts of "love and good deeds." DeSilva states,

The exhortation pertains more to doing good works and showing love as the addressees look around at their fellow believers, observing their situations and persons attentively. The author may, moreover, seek to establish an emulative environment: "paying attention to one another" will not only lead to seeing and responding to need, but also will involve seeing one's sisters' and brothers' noble

---

[535] Louw and Nida, *Greek-English Lexicon,* vol. 1, 349.
[536] O'Brien, *Hebrews,* 369-70.

deeds and becoming zealous to emulate them, such that doing good stimulates more well-doing. The author approaches the congregation first by urging them *to look at each other, to see each other, to notice one another.* He does not merely exhort them to preach well-doing, but to be engaged in it first, and then perchance to stimulate it and be stimulated to well-doing by mutual example. This connects with the author's exhortations throughout Hebrews (3:12-14; 12:15-17; 13:1-3, 16) to create the sort of *intragroup relationships* and support structures that make it possible, even preferable, to put up with the snubbing hostility from without rather than give up on the love and mutual regard that exist within.[537]

The relationships within the body are to be treated with the utmost honor, respect, love, and intentionality. Anything less reduces the gospel implications to a privatized, individualized version of Christianity, and resembles nothing within the pages of the New Testament.[538]

Encouraging One Another

In addition to considering one another, spurring one another on, and provoking one another towards love and good deeds, the writer of Hebrews paints the picture of a community that is committed to ongoing encouragement in two places (3:13 and 10:25). The first time "encouragement" surfaces the believers are told, "Take care, brothers, lest there be in any of you an evil, unbelieving heart, leading you to fall away from the living God. But exhort one another every day, as long as it is called "today," that none of you may be hardened by the deceitfulness of sin" (Heb. 3:12-13). The second time the admonishment to encourage one another is found in chapter 10 as referenced above. "not neglecting to meet together, as is the habit of some, but encouraging one another, and all the more as you see the Day drawing near" (Heb. 10:25).

The very word for *encouragement* is understood as "to call to one's side." In each of these texts the concepts of sin and evil and neglecting the body of Christ are all present. The wrath of God no longer threatens those who are in Christ in final judgment as discussed in the previous chapter. However, the temptations and deceitfulness of sin threaten to dissuade the believer from persevering in the faith. Thus, the need for ongoing, daily *encouragement* from the body is essential. The context of Hebrews 3 cited above is one that specifically highlights the wrath of God. Quoting Psalm 95:7-11,

---

[537] DeSilva, *Hebrews,* 341-342 (emphasis mine).

[538] Newbigin powerfully reminds us that "The community that confesses Jesus is Lord has been, from the beginning, a movement launched into the public life of mankind. The Greco-Roman world in which the New Testament was written was full of societies offering to those who wished to join a way of personal salvation. There were several commonly used Greek words for such societies. At no time did the church use any of these names for itself ... it used with almost total consistency the name *ecclesia* – the *ecclesia theou,* the assembly called by God ... The Church could have escaped persecution by the Roman Empire if it had been content to be treated as a *cultus privatus.*" Leslie Newbigin, *The Open Secret: An Introduction to the Theology of Mission* (Grand Rapids, MI: Eerdmans, 1995), 16.

the writer of Hebrews reminds the early Christians of the wrath of God that forbade the Israelites from entering into the promised land due to their *unbelief*. DeSilva reminds readers that the early church stood at the same kind of threshold as the ancient Israelites: God had come to them, God had given them good news, God had liberated them, God had promised an inheritance. They need only to persevere for "a little while" (10:35-39). "They need to be reminded that God's patronage enables fearlessness in the face of human opposition (13:5-6), but also that God's promise demands faithfulness and firmness."[539] Yet this is not to be done in isolation. Rather the entire community is called to action as everyone is understood to be responsible *to* and *for* one another.

Furthermore, believers must consider the urgency of the "today" referenced by the Psalmist and repeated here in Hebrews. "The psalm allows for the author to heighten the urgency of how one will respond to the word 'today' by calling attention to the Christian cultural knowledge that there are a limited number of 'todays' left before God tears into the fabric of human history to execute judgment and bestow rewards" (cf. 10:25, 37-39; 12:26-28).[540]

When speaking of the horizontal relationships expressed in this community, sociologist Peter Berger coins the communal idea presented here as a "plausibility structure."[541] DeSiliva expounds by saying, "Sustaining beliefs, values, and hopes requires social reinforcement, particularly when other social groups seek to reinforce different beliefs and values."[542] Filson writes,

> He wants them to show solidarity … in regular assembling for common worship … He knows they need to keep the bond of Christian brotherhood strong especially in times when hostility from without actively besets them. They need the inner resources *that can come only through common worship and mutual encouragement*.[543]

The atoning work of Christ that creates the family of God, the brotherhood, has profound horizontal implications as demonstrated in this first facet of the horizontal, relational paradigm. We have observed that the Philippian church is to be filled with love, humility, selflessness (Phil. 2:5-11). In Colossae (Col. 1:15-20), the believers are to put away anger, wrath, malice, slander, obscene talk, and lying (3:8-9) from among them and are to "forgive" (v.13), "teach" (v.16), and "admonish" (3:16) one another. In Hebrews, we observed that the family of God is to "encourage" one another in perseverance as well as to "spur one another on to love and good works" (Heb. 3:12; 10:25) and are to gather together regularly for worship (10:25).

---

[539] DeSilva, *Hebrews*, 147.

[540] DeSilva, *Hebrews*, 149.

[541] Peter Berger, The Sacred Canopy: Elements of a Sociological Theory of Religion (New York, NY: Anchor, 1995), 45.

[542] DeSilva, *Hebrews*, 149.

[543] Floyd V. Filson, *Yesterday: A Study of Hebrews in Light of Chapter 13*, Studies in Biblical Theology, second series 4 (London, England: SCM 1967.), 69 (emphasis mine).

What can be observed by these three examples drawn from what many consider to be New Testament hymns is that the New Testament churches are to offer themselves up to God in doxological fashion that blesses and builds up one another simultaneously. It is here that we reference the diagram again, turn the cylinder, and bring the "serving community" into focus.

A Serving Community (Mark 10)

Mark 10:35-45 is one of the more famous passages in the gospels for several reasons. The conversation between Jesus and the brothers, James and John, surrounds the subjects of power, serving, and one very important aspect as to how Jesus understood his atoning sacrifice ("ransom") as an act of service that was intended to then be emulated amongst those who would come after him as obedient disciples. Mark records,

> And James and John, the sons of Zebedee, came up to him and said to him, "Teacher, we want you to do for us whatever we ask of you." And he said to them, "What do you want me to do for you?" And they said to him, "Grant us to sit, one at your right hand and one at your left, in your glory." Jesus said to them, "You do not know what you are asking. Are you able to drink the cup that I drink, or to be baptized with the baptism with which I am baptized?" And they said to him, "We are able." And Jesus said to them, "The cup that I drink you will drink, and with the baptism with which I am baptized, you will be baptized, but to sit at my right hand or at my left is not mine to grant, but it is for those for whom it has been prepared." And when the ten heard it, they began to be indignant at James and John. And Jesus called them to him and said to them, "You know that those who are considered rulers of the Gentiles lord it over them, and their great ones exercise authority over them. But it shall not be so among you. But whoever would be great among you must be your servant, and whoever would be first among you must be slave of all. For even the Son of Man came not to be served but to serve, and to give his life as a ransom for many" (Mark 10:35-45).[544]

The brothers' request to be seated in a place of future eschatological glory is met with a question by Jesus regarding *"baptism"* and *"the cup."* As referenced earlier in the book, the "cup" that Jesus refers to here is one picture in the Old Testament which repeatedly speaks of the "wrath of God" (Jer. 25:15-17; 49:12; 51:7; Ps. 75:8; Zech. 12:2-3; Lam. 4:21; Hab. 2:16). In the apocalypse, John also references *"the cup"* as in direct relation to the wrath of God (Rev. 14:10; 18:16). The disciples clearly do not understand the metaphor and answer Jesus, "We are able" (10:39). Jesus then instructs the disciples teaching them that greatness in the community of God is not accomplished through lording authority over others as the notorious pagan Gentiles. Instead, greatness is measured in terms of service to others. Jesus then punctuates his point by

---

[544] This same account is also recorded in Matthew 20:20-28.

directing attention to his cross: "For even the Son of Man came not to be served but to serve, and to give his life as a ransom for many" (10:45).

The use of the word *ransom* here has been the subject of much debate and oftentimes been used to speak inaccurately about the meaning of the death of Christ. To whom was this price, this *ransom*, paid? Origen, in the 3rd century popularized the idea that the ransom was, in fact, paid to Satan. Russell summarizes Origen's thoughts succinctly.

> In order to rescue us from Satan's power without violating justice, God was obliged to pay the Devil a ransom. The only ransom the Devil would accept was a perfect man, so when God offered him Christ, he seized him eagerly, and in turn handed him to vicious humans to torment and kill him. Death and the Devil exulted in their triumph, but only for a flicker of a moment, for the ransom was a trick. Since Christ was God, the Devil could not hold him, and since Christ was without sin, it was a violation of justice to try to hold him, a violation that annulled Satan's claim to keep the rest of us in bondage. The slate, wiped clean, meant that we were free. Satan had been duped, gulled, cheated, and made a fool of.[545]

This theory, however, is greatly flawed. Edwards responds to this theory exposing the flaws therein and sustains the penal view.

> Satan ... is not mentioned in v.45, nor even in Mark's passion account. Satan was last mentioned in 8:33, and there he attempts to *avert* Jesus from suffering and death! The death of the Son of Man on behalf of "the many" is a sacrifice in obedience to God's will, a full expression of his love, and a full satisfaction of God's justice.[546]

Thus, Jesus anchors his penal sacrifice in the context of teaching the disciples about what true servant hood looks like. Edwards hones in on the Greek text of verses 43-44 and offers profound insight. He says:

> the best textual evidence suggests that it is the present of the verb "to be" (Gk. *estin*), not the future (Gk. *estai*), that is, "It is not the way among you," as opposed to "It shall not be this way among you." V.43a is thus not an admonition to behave in a certain way as much as a description of the way things actually are in the kingdom of God, and even among disciples of the kingdom. Thus, to fail in being a servant is

---

[545] Jeffery Russell, *Satan: The Early Christian Tradition* (Ithaca, NY: Cornell University Press, 1987), 140.

[546] Edwards, *The Gospel According to Mark*, 328. Lane writes in his commentary, "The Son of Man takes *the place* of the many and there happens to him what would have happened to them (cf. Ch.8:37: what no man can do, Jesus, as the unique Son of Man, achieves)." William Lane, *NICNT: The Gospel of Mark* (Grand Rapids, MI: Eerdmans Publishing, 1974), 384; italics in original. See also Jeffery, Ovey, and Sach, *Pierced*, 67-73 for details surrounding Jesus' death in the dark, the cry of dereliction and his prediction of his own suffering and death, thus emphasizing the ransom paid to God is indeed a penal substitution.

not simply to fall short of an ideal condition but to stand outside of an existing condition that corresponds to the kingdom of God.[547][##]

Therefore, the serving community that Jesus establishes is not merely a moral population with a virtuous ethic attached to it. Rather, love is made manifest with the acts of service that flow out of the position the community *already* exists within: namely, the kingdom of God.[548] The juxtaposition to the Romans in the text is also very important. For "In the Greek world 'service,' was the opposite of happiness, as Plato says: 'How can one be happy when he has to serve someone?' Jesus has effectively introduced his upside down kingdom through his sacrificial serving nature and actions."[549] Dan Le correctly asserts, "When faced with the problem of sin, a model cannot only focus on placating God's anger; neither can it focus on victory for an example and omit how reconciliation happens between humanity, God, and creation, which is a result of the gracious activity of God at work through Christ."[550] Graham McFarlane of London School of Theology helpfully writes,

> This is the great power of the Christian gospel – and evangel in which God deals with God on our behalf. Yet to stop here is to do serious damage to the Gospel. Inheriting eternal life, according to Jesus, also demands engagement with our neighbor. And to do this demands a pneumatic dimension – where life through the Spirit is hypostatized and first informs wherein Neighbor is reconciled with Neighbor and togetherness maybe demonstrated *en carne* in the here and now as an anticipatory expression of what is to come in fullness.[551]

It is here that we now direct our attention to the three cultures cited in the diagram (Theo-culture, human culture, and angel culture) as defined by Wan with an emphasis on looking at how the actions of Christian *service* uniquely impact the relationship between each culture.

---

[547] Edwards, The Gospel According to Mark, 325.

[548] Chrysostom proclaimed, "You see how humbling of himself did not make him have less but produced countless benefits, countless deeds of virtue, and made his glory shine forth with greater brightness. God wants for nothing and has need of nothing. Yet, when he humbled himself, he produced such great good, increased his household, and extended his kingdom. Why, then, are you afraid that you will become less if you humble yourself?" Chrysostom, "What Lowliness Accomplished," in *On the Incomprehensible Nature of God*, 8.46 – 47, vol. 2 of *Mark: Ancient Christian Commentary*, ed. Thomas Oden and Christopher Hall (Downers Grove: IVP, 2005),143.

[549] Craigh A. Evans, *Word Biblical Commentary,* vol. 34b, *Mark 8:27-16:20* (Nashville, TN: Thomas Nelson Publishers, 2001), 119.

[550] Dan Lé, The Naked Christ: An Atonement Model for a Body-Obsessed Culture (Eugene, OR: Wipf & Stock, 2012), 216.

[551] McFarlane, "Togetherness," 327.

Theo-Culture (Culture A)

This brief section will focus on ontological realism and Christian cultural anthropology applied to final judgment. As mentioned earlier in the book, Matthew's gospel highlights PSA from very early on: "You shall call his name Jesus, *for* he will save his people from their sins" (1:21). Moreover, at the Last Supper, Jesus then takes the cup and said to the disciples, "Drink of it, all of you, for this is my blood of the covenant, which is poured out for many for the forgiveness of sins" (26: 27b-28). In different places in the New Testament, Jesus himself makes it abundantly clear that he identifies so *closely* with his people that when they are blessed, neglected, or persecuted he makes their suffering his very own. The "abiding" (John 15:5) and "oneness" (17:20-26) that he speaks of is not something that is to be entered into at the *parousia* but is in existence in the present day. The judgment scene that Jesus describes recorded in Matthew's Gospel is probably the best-known passage that speaks to his present experiences with his followers.[552]

The word "pericope" used to describe Matthew 25:31-46 is a more appropriate term than "parable" though some are inclined to read it as such.[553] The metaphors of "sheep" and "goats" fall to the wayside as Jesus makes clear that he is speaking of them as people facing the final judgment.[554] Christ (Culture A) and his angels (Culture B) joyfully welcome the "righteous" (Culture C) and condemn the wicked (Culture C) alongside the devil (Culture B) and his angels (Culture B). Matthew writes:

> "When the Son of Man comes in his glory, and all the angels with him, then he will sit on his glorious throne. Before him will be gathered all the nations, and he will separate people one from another as a shepherd separates the sheep from the goats. And he will place the sheep on his right, but the goats on the left. Then the King will say to those on his right, 'Come, you who are blessed by my Father, inherit the kingdom prepared for you from the foundation of the world. For I was hungry and you gave me food, I was thirsty and you gave me drink, I was a stranger and you welcomed me, I was naked and you clothed me, I was sick and you visited me, I was in prison and you came to me.' Then the righteous will answer him, saying, 'Lord, when did we see you hungry and feed you, or thirsty and give you drink? And when did we see you a stranger and welcome you, or naked and clothe you? And

---

[552] Another text that highlights this same reality is found at the confronting and conversion of Saul. For when Saul is found persecuting the Church (people, not an impersonal institution), the Lord Jesus appears: "And falling to the ground, he heard a voice saying to him, 'Saul, Saul, why are you persecuting me?' And he said, 'Who are you, Lord?' And he said, 'I am Jesus, whom you are persecuting'" (Acts 9:4-5). Marshall comments, "'*Why do you persecute me?*' is a question aimed directly at the immediate purpose of Paul and indicates that while he thought that he was merely attacking a group of men for their heretical way of worshipping God, he was in reality attacking a group who had a heavenly spokesman and representative; *to attack the Christians was to attack this heavenly figure.*" Howard Marshall, *An Introduction and Commentary*, vol. 5, *Acts* (Downers Grove, IL: IVP 1980), 179, (emphasis mine).

[553] Joachim Jeremias, *The Parables of Jesus* (London, England: SCM Press, 2003), 206, for example.

[554] Blomberg, *Matthew*, 375.

when did we see you sick or in prison and visit you?' And the King will answer them, 'Truly, I say to you, as you did it to one of the least of these my brothers, you did it to me.'

"Then he will say to those on his left, 'Depart from me, you cursed, into the eternal fire prepared for the devil and his angels. For I was hungry and you gave me no food, I was thirsty and you gave me no drink, I was a stranger and you did not welcome me, naked and you did not clothe me, sick and in prison and you did not visit me.' Then they also will answer, saying, 'Lord, when did we see you hungry or thirsty or a stranger or naked or sick or in prison, and did not minister to you?' Then he will answer them, saying, 'Truly, I say to you, as you did not do it to one of the least of these, you did not do it to me.' And these will go away into eternal punishment, but the righteous into eternal life" (Matt. 25:31-46).

Much can be discussed about the nature of justification here in this passage alone.[555] What Matthew records does not immediately strike one as sounding Pauline in a traditional sense regarding salvation being one accomplished by grace through faith rather than works. In this pronouncement, Jesus is very concerned with what was committed or omitted regarding whether or not the "least of his brothers" had their needs met or not through acts of simple compassion, generosity, and service. Moreover, the idea of a works-based salvation or damnation appears to be heightened based on the *"then he will say"* statements of verses 34 and 41. France is helpful in noting,

> A systematic theologian can devise a scheme whereby justification by grace through faith and judgment according to works are together parts of a greater whole, but Matthew is not writing a systematic theology, and the present passage brings its fullest expression his conviction that when the Son of Man comes he will "repay every person according to what they have done" (16:27). This is the ultimate outworking of the Matthean motif of reward for those who have lived according to the will of God (see on 5:12). And that will is here spelled out in terms of the way people have responded to the needs of 'these my smallest brothers and sisters.'[556]

A few observations about this scene are necessary before addressing *serving* and the three cultures (Theo, human, and angel) mentioned in this text. First, Jesus describes himself here as the "Son of Man" and this harkens to mind the Danelic scene of judgment (Dan. 7:9-14). Daniel describes the judgment scene and provides the backdrop centuries prior to the arrival of Jesus and Jesus then carries these same tones into his statements in Matthew. Second, when Jesus references "the smallest of his brothers and sisters" he is *likely* speaking of those who profess to follow him. This is

---

[555] See Carson, *Matthew,* 518-520; Hagner, *Matthew 1-13*, 740-741; France, *Matthew,* 957-960; Roger Morhlang, *Matthew and Paul: A Comparison of Ethical Perspectives* (Cambridge, England: Cambridge University Press, 2004), 67-71.
[556] France, *Matthew,* 959.

because of how Jesus speaks in Matthew 12:46-50 and in 28:10 regarding those who would be his disciples. Thus, the followers of Christ are the "brothers and sisters" and not merely any particular person in suffering, though simple Christian charity extended to anyone is certainly not excluded. Interestingly, Solomon says, "the person who is kind to the poor lends to the LORD" (Prov. 19:17). This truth is now extended here and the Lord Jesus' "identification with his people goes further: their experiences are his experiences, and what is done to them is done to him."[557]

Third, the response of both the "sheep" and the "goats" are essentially the same; both are *surprised* when Jesus speaks about acts of service and compassion being extended or withheld. The "righteous" were unaware that their kindnesses were "done unto" Jesus himself. Then "those on his left" (Culture C) claim ignorance of Christ's hiddenness in the suffering of his brothers and sisters and therefore face the damnation "prepared for the devil and his angels" (Culture B). Therefore, it stands that because of the close identification Jesus (Culture A) shares with his brothers and sisters (Culture C) that the "righteous" ones (Culture C) serving "the least of these" (Culture C) in fact, serve not only humans but God himself. It is here that we turn the kaleidoscope, noting the ministry of reconciliation a bit more and observe the nature of *serving* human-to-human (Culture C) come into focus.

Human Culture (Culture C)

As shown above, in his Epistle to the Galatians, Paul emphasizes PSA (3:10-13) and the resulting intimate *Abba*-child relationship (3:26) experienced between the justified (Culture C) and God (Culture A), (4:6, cf. Rom. 8:15).[558] As we turn the kaleidoscope and continue through the Epistle, we observe Paul highlight the nature of Christian freedom, the admonition to resist an antinomian lifestyle, and to rather "through love *serve* one another" (5:13b). He states, "For you were called to freedom, brothers. Only do not use your freedom as an opportunity for the flesh, but through love serve one another" (5:13). Because the Galatian Christians were justified and had experienced firsthand the "ministry of reconciliation" between God and one another (2 Cor. 5:17-21), new responsibilities now accompany these early disciples.

First, Paul reviews for the Galatians that they are family members by reminding them of their *brotherhood (adelphoi)*. This would have been extremely noteworthy to have Paul, the converted Jew, so closely identifying with this Gentile church. Secondly, the "freedom" given in Christ is not to be used as an "opportunity" (lit. "springboard") for more sin. Third, he states that freedom rightly understood and applied is expressed through loving acts of service to the Christian community *(ἀλλὰ διὰ τῆς ἀγάπης δουλεύετε ἀλλάλοις)*. Bruce comments:

> As Paul himself is the δοῦλος of Christ (1:10) and of his converts (2 Cor. 4:5), so his converts should be δοῦλοι one of another. But this is a completely different form of slavery from that against which he otherwise warns them. It is as though he said, "If

---

557 France, *Matthew*, 965.
558 Note Wan's remarks about establishing the vertical paradigm first and then the horizontal paradigm takes shape.

you must live in slavery, here is the form of slavery in which you may safely indulge—the slavery of practical love for one another."[559]

The "freedom" of the justified works itself out practically in a united community devoted to serving one another. Bruce continues by saying, "The liberty of the gospel is not to be exercised in isolated independence. The Christian does not emulate the self-sufficiency of the Stoic, *in se ipso totus teres atque rotundus* (Horace, *Satire* 2.7.86); his sufficiency is in Christ, and he is involved in the interdependent and loving fellowship of the people of Christ."[560] The reconciled community does not view the command to serve one another as "a restriction on freedom but rather the very means of its actualization."[561] The community which is truly free from the curse of the law (3:10) is the community that is free to love and serves one another. Or as Martin Luther stated: "A Christian is free and independent in every respect, a bond servant to none. A Christian is a dutiful servant in every respect, owning a duty to everyone."[562] It is now that we turn our attention to the last facet of this particular piece of the kaleidoscope and briefly examine the angel culture (Culture B) and the *curiosity* provoked by the salvation and serving lifestyle exhibited in the churches addressed by the Apostle Peter (Culture C).

Angel Culture (Culture B)

Thus far, we have examined Theo Culture (Culture A) and human culture (Culture C) in regards to the reconciled community (2 Cor. 5:17-21) which understands that the atoning work of Christ was an act of service which summons the followers of Christ into the same lifestyle of loving service (Mark 10:45). The Apostle Peter reminds us that the nature of service within the household of faith through the centuries not only profoundly impacts the Church (Culture C) and simultaneously glorifies God (Culture A) but that even the angels (Culture B!) are *intrigued* by the work of God in and through his *serving* community. Peter writes,

> Concerning this salvation, the prophets who prophesied about the grace that was to be yours searched and inquired carefully, inquiring what person or time the Spirit of Christ in them was indicating when he predicted the sufferings of Christ and the subsequent glories. It was revealed to them that they were serving not themselves but you, in the things that have now been announced to you through those who

---

[559] F. F. Bruce, *NIGTC: The Epistle to the Galatians* (Grand Rapids, MI: Paternoster and William B. Eerdmans Publishing, 1988), 241.

[560] Bruce, *Galatians*, 241.

[561] Timothy George, *The New American Commentary*, vol. 30, *Galatians* (Nashville, TN: Broadman & Holman Publishers, 1994), 378.

[562] Gerhard Ebeling, *Luther: An Introduction to His Thought* (Philadelphia, PA: Fortress, 1972), 212. Or as Barrett writes, "The opposite of flesh is love ... love that looks away from the self and its wishes, even its real needs, to the neighbor, and spends its resources on his needs." Charles K. Barrett, *Freedom and Obligation: A Study of the Epistle to the Galatians* (London, England: SPCK, 1985), 72–73.

preached the good news to you by the Holy Spirit sent from heaven, things into which angels long to look (1 Pet. 1:10-12).

It is here we observe that Peter states explicitly that those who prophesied about the coming of Christ "were not *serving* themselves" and were rather *serving* the future Church (Culture C). Indeed, Christ himself, "the Spirit of *Christ*" predicted his own sufferings for centuries prior to his moment of sacrifice on Good Friday. And it was in his revelation to the Old Testament prophets that they were aware that their *service* was to the future children of God. Peter then makes the ever so interesting remark about angels (Culture B); he states that the good news proclaimed to the church contains "things into which angels long to look."

This "salvation" Peter speaks of refers to being saved from the judgment and wrath of God as well as the destruction of the devil. Peter writes, "For Christ also suffered once for sins, the righteous for the unrighteous, that he might bring us to God" (3:18). Indeed, Jesus *suffered* for his people. Peter continues, "For it is time for judgment to begin at the household of God; and if it begins with us, what will be the outcome for those who do not obey the gospel of God?" (4:17). Peter clearly understands the atoning work of Christ to be the means which spares the children of God from his just judgment and wrath due to their *sins*. Moreover, he states that the children of God are to be saved from the destruction of Satan (Culture B). He writes, "And be sober-minded; be watchful. Your adversary the devil prowls around like a roaring lion, seeking someone to devour" (5:8). It is this salvation that the "angels long to look into" implying a lack of knowledge.

Angels (Culture B) are not omniscient. That attribute belongs to God alone (Culture A) (cf. Mark 13:32; Eph. 3:10). Marshall writes, "We should presume that angels are ignorant of certain things (Mark 13:32; Rom. 16:25; 1 Cor. 2:6-9), and that they long to know more as they see the fulfillment of God's purposes (Luke 15:10; Rom. 8:19)."[563] Additionally, there are a number of places in the New Testament that emphasize the fact that the angels are "not superior to believers (1 Cor. 6:3; Heb. 1:14; 2:16)."[564] Scot McKnight helpfully notes, "The angels are brought in here, not to invite us (Culture C) to speculate about their (Culture B) activities, but to press on our minds (Culture C) the privileges of salvation; neither the prophets (Culture C) nor the angels (Culture B) experience what the church (Culture C) assumes and enjoys."[565] Thus, the wrath from which Christians are spared was an act of incomprehensible *service* by Christ (Mark 10:45). Indeed, the service of Christ was something so great that prophets longed to experience it (but served anyway!) and angels long "to look into it." Understanding the death of Jesus as an act of service (Mark 10:45) and a summons for his followers to emulate can be understood to glorify God (Culture A), serve others without condition or reservation (Culture C), and thus, this serving-laden-gospel even intrigues the angels

563 Howard Marshall, *IVP New Testament Commentary: 1 Peter* (Downers Grove, IL: IVP, 2011), 47.

564 Norman Hillyer, *New International Biblical Commentary: 1 and 2 Peter, Jude* (Grand Rapids, MI: Baker Books, 1991), 42.

565 Scot McKnight, *1 Peter* (Downers Grove, IL: Zondervan, 1996), 74.

(Culture B). It is here that we look to the diagram, turn the kaleidoscope, and examine the *forgiving* community that is created in relation to the ministry of reconciliation.

Forgiving Community

The doctrine and practice of forgiveness both vertically and horizontally finds itself being highlighted in a number of places in the Gospel of Matthew. In the Sermon on the Mount, Jesus makes an extremely bold statement about forgiveness amongst those who would claim to know and follow God. He says, "For if you forgive others their trespasses, your heavenly Father will also forgive you, but if you do not forgive others their trespasses, neither will your Father forgive your trespasses" (Matt. 6:14-15).

Understanding the nature of forgiveness, the atoning work of Christ, and the *relational* implications are immensely important to one's discipleship and the ongoing mission of God expressed in the ecclesial community. As Colin Gunton states, "Our sinfulness ... is not conceived *mathematically* as the accumulation of wrong acts, but *relationally* as that which universally qualifies human existence in the flesh."[566] The places in which forgiveness of sins and PSA most clearly surface in Matthew's gospel are found in the birth and passion narratives as noted above.[567] The angel comes to Joseph in a dream and instructs him, "you shall call his name Jesus, for he will save his people from their sins" (1:21). Rutledge reminds us that "the Evangelist does not explain *why* the people need to be saved; it is presupposed."[568] Carson informs readers that "the verb 'save' can refer to deliverance from physical danger (8:25), disease (9:21-22), or even death (24:22); in the NT it commonly refers to the comprehensive salvation inaugurated by Jesus that will be consummated at his return."[569]

The majority of Jews in the first century held that the Davidic Messiah would be primarily concerned with bringing about political justice and freeing the people of God from the rule of the Romans. This does not mean that *all* Jews felt this way, however. For the Pharisees would have been concerned with sin (see Pss. Sol. 17:21-46). France states that at this announcement, about the messiah being one "who will save his people from their sins," the indication is that "the angel's words thus signal at the start that any political euphoria which may have been evoked by the Davidic and royal theme of the 'book of origin' is wide of the mark of what Jesus' actual mission is to be."[570]

In Matt. 20:28, Jesus repeats what is covered above as he speaks of giving his life as a "ransom for many." Shortly after this account, Matthew records that at the Last Supper, Jesus says of his blood, "this is my blood of the covenant, which is poured out for many for the forgiveness of sins" (26:28). Thus, the point of Christ's death is one

---

[566] Colin E. Gunton, Father, Son, and Holy Spirit: Toward a Fully Trinitarian Theology (New York, NY: T&T Clark, 2003), 192.

[567] Hagner, Matthew 1-13, 19.

[568] Flemming Rutledge, *The Crucifixion: Understanding the Death of Jesus Christ* (Grand Rapids, MI: Eerdmans, 2015), 186, (emphasis mine).

[569] Carson, *Matthew,* 76.

[570] France, *Matthew,* 54.

which directly confronts and defeats sin and its consequences and ushers in *forgiveness*. France comments,

> the final phrase, "for the forgiveness of sins," not only recalls the servant's death for the sins of his people (Isa. 53:5-6, 8,10,11,12) but also further reinforces the allusion to Jeremiah's new covenant prophecy, where the basis of this new *relationship* is that "I will forgive their wickedness, and will remember their sins no more"; it also recalls to the reader the original statement of Jesus' mission in 1:21, to "save his people from their sins.[571]

This covenant-establishing relationship that Jesus speaks of cannot be accomplished without the shedding of blood and forgiveness of sin being extended to his people, whom he came to save. Treat argues,

> Yet while Christ died to reconcile sinners into a relationship with their Creator, it is not a generic, undefined relationship. Rather, Christ's atoning work reconciles sinners into a *covenant* relationship with God, a relational bond that makes two parties as close as family. Reconciliation has always been the aim of atonement, but reconciliation has a covenantal ring.[572]

The vertical aspect is again found here in grounding, informing, and empowering the horizontal application of the atonement.[573]

Scot McKnight's excellent work entitled, *A Community Called Atonement*, is one that beckons a close listening ear and reading eye as it pertains to the horizontal implications of the atoning work of Christ. McKnight is careful not to reduce the atonement to only one model and is content with the tension of holding multiple models at once. His points are nonetheless extremely relevant as pertaining to this facet of the kaleidoscope. McKnight's case is simple yet profound: God intends his community to become a community of atonement-in-praxis (horizontal) as a result of atonement first understood and applied by God, in Christ, through the Holy Spirit (vertical). This is all couched within the rubric of the *Mission of God*. One important piece of his thought is sparked by what McLaren calls the "secret message of Jesus." The secret being that the atonement is not something to be experienced privately with no practical implications on Christian relationships. Instead, the redeemed community is to practice atonement. This must be quoted at length here especially as it pertains to Jesus' statement in the Sermon on the Mount,

---

[571] France, *Matthew*, 994, (emphasis mine).

[572] Jeremy Treat, "Atonement and Covenant," in *Locating Atonement: Explorations in Constructive Dogmatics*, ed. Oliver Crisp and Fred Sanders (Grand Rapids, MI: Zondervan, 2015), 108.

[573] We would be remiss to not call to mind what Luke records in the actual crucifixion of Jesus, as he prayed specifically for the forgiveness of others. "Father, forgive them for they know not what they do" (23:34) again greatly underscores the nature of atonement and forgiveness first demonstrated vertically and with profound implications for those who would come after Jesus to be applied horizontally.

Forgiveness, then, is reciprocal. Thus, "atonement" itself is *reciprocal* performance; it is praxis. As the follower of Jesus forgives others their debts and sins–this is, of course, the import of the classical statement to Peter that divides the Protestant from the Roman Catholic (Matt. 16:19)–so the follower of Jesus is an agent of atonement ... God reconciles us to himself and he does this "through Christ" (vertical). And then that reconciliation is given to us (horizontal) so we can have a "ministry" (*ten diakonian*) of "reconciliation." And this is done by being an "ambassador" (*presbuomenon*) of Christ–that is, as his personal agent of representation. "Ambassadors" are *Eikons* of Christ in this world. As ambassadors, they are extending the reconciling/atoning work of God to others. That work involves "not counting their trespasses against them." The term "trespasses" here is similar enough to tie Paul's words to Jesus' words (at some level). And this forgiveness is at the same time a relational reconciliation with God: "be reconciled to God" (2 Cor. 5:20).[574]

McKnight is highlighting something *very* important here. He is not downplaying or minimizing sin in the ecclesial community. Nor is he implying that sin is against God exclusively. Instead, McKnight is calling for Christians to acknowledge sin, the cross of Jesus, then to appropriate and practically apply the work of Christ's cross in the ministry of reconciliation, namely through *forgiveness* of one another's sins. It is here that we continue to turn the kaleidoscope and introduce the concept that reconciliation is to be made as a *prerequisite* to worship.

Prerequisite to Worship

The colors of the kaleidoscope continue to intensify as the ministry of reconciliation is practiced in light of the cross of Jesus. The children of God are reconciled to God and are no longer under his wrath. And yet, the family of God is imperfect, sins, and many times finds *anger* or strife present within the community. Jesus demonstrates the seriousness of reconciliation and it being something that his "brothers" are to practice as he makes a drastic statement regarding the "remembrance" of an offense at the time one appears before the "altar." The "altar," of course, would be located in Jerusalem, some 80 miles distance from where he preached this in Galilee.[575] In keeping with what Jesus says about praying for God's forgiveness and the worshiper extending that same forgiveness to those who have sinned in 6:14-15, he desires those who have been reconciled to God and would approach him in worship (vertical) would be consistent in character by maintaining unity and pursuing reconciliation with one another (horizontal). In the Sermon on the Mount Jesus says,

> "You have heard that it was said to those of old, 'You shall not murder; and whoever murders will be liable to judgment.' But I say to you that everyone who is angry with his brother will be liable to judgment; whoever insults his brother will

---

[574] McKnight, Community Called Atonement, 31.
[575] France, *Matthew*, 202.

be liable to the council; and whoever says, 'You fool!' will be liable to the hell of fire" (Matt. 5:21-22).

And then he follows this with two short "parables"[576] both of which communicate the *urgency* that is to accompany the situation, one of which pertains to our subject at hand. The parable (or example) is, "So if you are offering your gift at the altar and there remember that your brother has something against you, leave your gift there before the altar and go. First be reconciled to your brother, and then come and offer your gift" (5:23-24).

First, we must note that Jesus addresses the "anger" that would give rise to "murder" and condemns the former saying that the one who is angry would be liable to "judgment" (*krisis*). Indeed, "Jesus presses beyond behavior specifically punished by law to the kind of heart that generates such behavior. Anger that would generate murder if unimpeded is the spiritual equivalent of murder."[577] It is important to remember God's offense at forgiveness. Stott states, "Since no human court is competent to try a case of inward anger ... Not only are anger and insult equivalent to murder, he said, but the punishment to which they render us liable is nothing less than the divine judgment of hell."[578]

Similar to McKnight, Hauwerwas understands that the community that is reconciled with the Father becomes "a community of reconciliation, a community of peace."[579] Jesus does not forbid one experiencing the emotion of anger with another. Rather, what he forbids is one who would profess to be a disciple to knowingly persist in unreconciled relationships while simultaneously continuing to approach God in worship. This would be consistent with the prophets who called for purity of heart and relationships within the worshiping community (e.g., Isa. 1:10-17; Jer. 7:8-11; Amos 5:21-24; Mic. 6:6-8; cf. Ps. 24:3-4). "The *gift* is presumably an animal sacrifice, to offer which a layman was allowed to enter the Court of the Priests where the *altar* stood. Jesus' instruction to interrupt such a solemn occasion indicates the importance of the demand."[580]

Alison helpfully calls attention to the concepts of murder and sacrifice in the context of worship and reconciliation with the story of Cain and Abel.[581] He is *convinced*

---

[576] France, *Matthew*, 202

[577] Craig Keener, *A Socio-Rhetorical Commentary: The Gospel of Matthew* (Grand Rapids, MI: Eerdmans, 2009), 183.

[578] John Stott, The Message of the Sermon on the Mount (Matthew 5-7, Christian Counter Culture) (Downers Grove, IL: IVP, 1985), 85.

[579] Stanley Hauwerwas, *Matthew* (Grand Rapids, MI: Brazos Press, 2015), 68.

[580] France, *Matthew*, 120-121.

[581] Dale Alison, *Studies in Matthew: Interpretation Past and Present* (Grand Rapids, MI: Baker Books, 2012), 65-72. Alison states "Not only does the passage quote the Decalogue ("You will not murder," Exod. 20:13 = Deut. 5:17) and summarize the legislation in Gen. 9:6; Exod. 21:12 = Lev. 24:17; Num. 35:12; and Deut. 17:8-13 (murder merits the death penalty), but it also expands its meaning and lends force to its argument by tacit recall of Genesis and its famous story of fratricide." Alison, *Matthew*, 67.

that Jesus had the brothers of Genesis 4 in mind as he admonished his disciples to leave the altar and first be *reconciled* to one another. Alison first affirms Cyprian's interpretation of Jesus' statement:

> God does not receive the sacrifice of a person who is in disagreement but commands him to go back from the altar and first be reconciled to his brother, so that God also may be appeased by the prayers of a peacemaker. Our peace and brotherly agreement is the greater sacrifice to God – and a people united as one in the unity of the Father, Son, and Holy Spirit. For even in the sacrifices that Abel and Cain first offered, God looked not at their gifts, but at their hearts, so that he was acceptable in his gift who was acceptable in his heart. Abel, peaceable and righteous in sacrificing in innocence to God, taught others also, when they bring their gift to the altar, thus to come with the fear of God, with a simple heart, with the law of righteousness, with the peace of concord.... The quarrelsome and disunited and he who has not peace with his brothers ... will not be able to escape the crime of fraternal dissension, because, as it is written, "He who hates his brother is a murderer" (1 John 3:15), and no murderer attains to the kingdom of heaven nor does he live with God.[582]

Therefore, the reconciliation accomplished by the cross of Christ is both vertical and horizontal in nature. As we continue to turn the kaleidoscope, we now arrive at the question of exactly "how much forgiveness is to be extended within the ecclesial community?" This was first asked by none other than the Apostle Peter himself. And Jesus' answer far surpasses any other religious ideas of the day as he calls one to place no limit on forgiveness, grounded in God's forgiveness.

Unlimited in Practice

Jesus does not expect a community to form around him that would immediately and completely part with sin as will happen in the glorified state in the eschaton. Rather, he envisions his people who can appropriate the atoning work of the cross and apply it not only individually but to one another as well. In Matthew 18:15-20 Jesus gives specific relational instructions on how he expects his disciples to go about what happens "if your brother *sins* against you" (v.15). This is where the Church develops her understanding of church discipline. But then Peter interjects, and the following conversation transpires: "Then Peter came up and said to him, 'Lord, how often will my brother sin against me, and I forgive him? As many as seven times?' Jesus said to him, 'I do not say to you seven times, but seventy-seven times'" (vv.21-22).

Jesus illustrates his point by telling a shocking parable; to use McKnight's phrase "reciprocity" is what is expected of any disciple.[583] Indeed, what we learn here is that the "exhortation to forgive without limit is undergirded by a parable which compares God's forgiveness and ours; it is because there is no limit to God's generosity to his

---

[582] Cyprian, *De dom. orat.* 23-24 (CSEL 3, ed. G. Hartel, p. 285). Cf. also Cyprian, *De zel. et liv.* 17-18 (CCSL 3A, ed. M. Simonetti, 85).

[583] McKnight, Community Called Atonement, 29.

undeserving people that they in their turn cannot claim the right to withhold forgiveness from their fellow disciples. A community of the forgiven must be a forgiving community."[584]

"Therefore the kingdom of heaven may be compared to a king who wished to settle accounts with his servants. When he began to settle, one was brought to him who owed him ten thousand talents. And since he could not pay, his master ordered him to be sold, with his wife and children and all that he had, and payment to be made. So the servant fell on his knees, imploring him, 'Have patience with me, and I will pay you everything.' And out of pity for him, the master of that servant released him and forgave him the debt. But when that same servant went out, he found one of his fellow servants who owed him a hundred denarii, and seizing him, he began to choke him, saying, 'Pay what you owe.' So his fellow servant fell down and pleaded with him, 'Have patience with me, and I will pay you.' He refused and went and put him in prison until he should pay the debt. When his fellow servants saw what had taken place, they were greatly distressed, and they went and reported to their master all that had taken place. Then his master summoned him and said to him, 'You wicked servant! I forgave you all that debt because you pleaded with me. And should not you have had mercy on your fellow servant, as I had mercy on you?' And in anger his master delivered him to the jailers, until he should pay all his debt. So also my heavenly Father will do to every one of you, if you do not forgive your brother from your heart" (Matt. 18:23-35).

In this parable we are informed "about the indissoluble connection of being embraced by God's grace so that it unleashes a cycle of humans' embracing others with grace."[585] The question by the Apostle Peter is very interesting in the kaleidoscope when considering PSA. Peter's concern is with *"sin against me"* as this is precisely what God deals with in PSA though the sin was against *Him*. Hagner helpfully notes that the verb "'ἁμαρτήσειν,' 'sin,' is left general, presumably in order to include as a wide a variety of phenomena as possible."[586] France notes, regarding Jesus' statement in Matt. 6:14-15, "the principle is clear, but its practical outworking still needs to be clarified, since its open-ended demand may easily be *exploited* by a manipulative fellow disciple; surely there must be a limit?"[587]

Peter's suggested forgiveness be extended "seven times" was intended to be extremely generous. For "In rabbinic discussion the consensus was that a brother might be forgiven a repeated sin three times; on the fourth, there is no forgiveness."[588] Jesus reveals to Peter that Peter's understanding of how frequent forgiveness should be extended falls short compared to God's. The plea for unlimited forgiveness is not

---

[584] France, *Matthew*, 702.

[585] McKnight, Community Called Atonement, 30.

[586] Donald Hagner, *Word Biblical Commentary: Matthew 14-28* (Grand Rapids, MI: Zondervan, 1995), 537.

[587] France, *Matthew*, 700, (italics mine).

[588] Carson, Matthew, 405. See b. Yoma 86b-87a.

carelessness that omits discipline (i.e., Matt. 18:15-20). But "rather he teaches that forgiveness of fellow members in his community of 'little ones' (brothers) cannot possibly be limited by frequency or quantity; as the ensuing parable shows, all of them have been forgiven far more than they will ever forgive."[589] It cannot be overlooked that the one who would receive the forgiveness of the king (God) and then withhold forgiveness for a brother results in the "great distress" of other "fellow servants" (v.31). Indeed, the one who has sinned and the one sinned against are not the only parties involved. The horizontal paradigm broadens beyond one to one relationships and takes into account the *community* (the Church) who are also recipients of the grace of God. The onlookers report to the master the inequitable behavior and the master who had shown "mercy" is now filled with "anger" (v.34) and then has the man jailed (tortured). The reference to the "torturers… may hint at eschatological punishment."[590]

Jesus' closing statement about forgiveness coming "from the heart" speaks beyond the unlimited quantity of forgiveness but also to the *quality* of forgiveness that is to be extended.[591] That is to say that what "he expects of his people is not a reluctant or merely verbal concession which leaves the underlying problem unresolved, but a genuine, warm forgiveness 'from the heart' so that the broken relationship is fully restored."[592] It is now that we turn to the final facet within the kaleidoscope and examine the evidence of the Holy Spirit's work in the forgiving community.

Evidence of the Holy Spirit

The metaphor of the kaleidoscope is intentionally designed as an illustrative device that keeps multiple theological ideas present at the same time, causing one idea to be seen in the light of another. Following what has been said about PSA, reconciliation, and the forgiving community, we now turn to look at Paul's words to the Ephesian church (Eph. 4:30-32). However, prior to addressing the forgiving community, it must be established that PSA is in fact in Paul's mind as he writes to this young community of believers.

PSA in Ephesians

In the Epistle to the Ephesians, Paul addresses several things regarding Christian thought and life. He consistently grounds the horizontal, relational implications of the gospel in the vertical axis of being reconciled to God. In 1:7, we read, "In him we have *redemption through his blood*, the *forgiveness* of our *trespasses*." This redemption would

---

[589] Carson, *Matthew,* 405. Or as Hagner aptly states, "Unlimited frequency of forgiveness goes with the unlimited scope of what is to be forgiven. This emphasis on the extravagant character of forgiveness is taken up in the parable that follows, which places the disciple's forgiveness of others squarely upon the foundation of God's forgiveness of the disciple" (vv. 33, 35), Hagner, *Matthew 14-28,* 537.

[590] Hagner, *Matthew 14-28,* 540.

[591] France reminds readers of "the 'heart' as expressing a person's true inward nature cf. 5:8, 28; 6:21; 12:34; 15:8, 18-19." France, *Matthew,* 708, fn. 29.

[592] France, *Matthew,* 708, fn. 29.

otherwise not have existed; for it came through the self-giving sacrifice of the Son's "blood."

In Ephesians 1:7 the redemption which we have in the Beloved has been procured *through his blood.* This abbreviated expression is pregnant with meaning, and signifies that Christ's violent death on the cross as a sacrifice is the *means* by which our deliverance has been won (cf. Rom. 3:25). It was obtained at very great cost. The *redemption* in view is equated with, or at least in apposition to, *the forgiveness of sins,* for it involved a rescue from God's just judgment on our trespasses. As a result we now have free access to our heavenly Father, knowing that we have been redeemed and forgiven.[593]

Then we read that the followers of Jesus formerly "were *dead* in the *trespasses* and *sins* in which we [you] once walked (2:1a) and that we "were by nature *children of wrath*" (2:3). Thus, the "children of wrath" now understand that their relationship with God and the covenantal community was formerly couched in terms of being "separated," "alienated," not familial, but instead, "strangers" (2:12). And now, those who were "children of wrath" (2:3, also mentioned in 5:6) are indeed "blameless and holy sons" (1:5) … "Who were once far off have now been brought near by the *blood* of Christ" (v.13). Such is the redemptive work of Christ when applied to the child of God.

The wrath of God is certainly present in the mind of Paul as it is mentioned explicitly in 2:3 and 5:6. It must be repeated that the wrath of God is not merely leaving sinners to experience the consequences of sin in a cause-and-effect type of system. Instead, the wrath of God can be seen as *personal.* Dodd argues that God's wrath is impersonal, "and does not… describe the attitude of God to man, but rather… describe[s] the inevitable process of cause and effect in a moral universe."[594] Yet, as Gaffin points out,

These views simply do not do justice to Paul. Rather, what we find in 5:3-6 is that "because of such things" … "Wrath here is distinct from these things; it is God's response to ("because of") them, his (surely personal) reaction against them, provoked by them. On its negative side, it involves exclusion from "any inheritance in the kingdom of Christ and of God" (Eph. 5:5), an exclusion that, in view of its terms, deprivation of eschatological attitude, is surely the punitive payback for sin. Similarly, God's wrath will result, on "the day of the Lord," in "sudden destruction" coming upon the unrepentant (1 Thess. 5:2-3, 9).[595]

Paul then reminds the Ephesians that "nearness" to God that came through Christ's blood "through the cross" (2:16) resulted in "*killing* the hostility" that existed between one another. The vertical profoundly shapes how the horizontal is to be lived and experienced. As O'Brien states, "the focus of attention, in the first instance, is not on

---

593 O'Brien, *Ephesians,* 106.

594 Dodd, *Romans,* 23.

595 Gaffin, "Scandal," 151.

peace with God as such, although verses 16–18 will show that this vertical peace is foundational to the restoration of relationships between Jews and Gentiles."[596]

Sealing by and Grieving of the Holy Spirit

This community that is now reconciled to God and to one another and invited to go before God with their granted "access to him" in "One Spirit" (2:18) are admonished in very clear terms as to how to live life amongst the redeemed community and to live in the Holy Spirit who has "sealed" them. "And do not grieve the Holy Spirit of God, by whom you were sealed for the day of redemption. Let all bitterness and wrath and anger and clamor and slander be put away from you, along with all malice. Be kind to one another, tenderhearted, forgiving one another, as God in Christ forgave you (4:30-32).

The first time Paul mentions the Person of the Holy Spirit in the letter to the Ephesians he writes, "In him you also, when you heard the word of truth, the gospel of your salvation, and believed in him, were *sealed* with the promised Holy Spirit" (1:13). Interestingly, in describing salvation Paul does not use the word "saved" that would naturally follow one's believing but rather uses the word "sealed" which is only used one other time prior in the New Testament (2 Cor. 1:22). Discussions abound concerning whether or not Paul is linking the *sealing* here with water baptism.[597] Arnold rightly states,

The principal idea here is that God has bestowed his Spirit on believers and that this occurs after people hear the gospel and put their faith in its message. In spite of the fact that the image of sealing occurs in the texts of some of the early church fathers to speak of the Spirit's coming after baptism, it is best here to stay with the explicit words of the text and link the coming of the Spirit with the exercise of faith. Nowhere in the NT is "sealing" used as a metaphor of the baptism in the Spirit; this usage appears only later.[598]

With this in mind, we call attention to 4:25-32, especially verses 30-32. Here we read that in the larger pericope Paul is concerned with the community's "social virtues"[599] displayed in fidelity to the gospel in and through the Holy Spirit who is

---

[596] O'Brien, *Ephesians*,194).

[597] See A. T. Lincoln, World Biblical Commentary, vol. 42, Ephesians (Nashville, TN: Thomas Nelson, 1990) 37-40; G. Lampe, The Seal of the Spirit: A Study of Baptism and Confirmation in the New Testament and the Fathers (London, England: Longmans Green,1951), 5; G.R. Beasley-Murray, Baptism in the New Testament (Grand Rapids, MI: Eerdmans, 1973), 174; Best, Ephesians, 29-31.

[598] Arnold, *Ephesians*, 92. Lincoln writes, "As regards acceptance of the Christian gospel, believing can be seen to be the vital link between hearing the word and receiving the Spirit. When they believed, the readers of this Epistle were sealed with the Spirit. Cattle and slaves were branded with their owner's seal, and so the seal was a mark of ownership and of preservation as the owner's property," Lincoln, *Ephesians,* 39.

[599] Arnold, *Ephesians*, 296.

indeed, personal[600] (able to be *grieved*). Specifically, he focuses on the community's application of the gospel in addressing "truth" (v.25), "anger" (v.26), "theft" (v.28), "honest work" (v.28), "corrupt talk" (v.29), "encouragement" (v.29), "bitterness" (v.31), "wrath" (v.31), "anger" (v.31), "clamor" (v.31), "slander" (v.31), and "malice" (v.31). Lincoln notes that the grieving of the Holy Spirit (vertical) occurs in direct response to the misconduct within the redeemed community (horizontal). He says,

> It is not a question of some offense aimed *directly at the Spirit* but rather that believers by committing the sort of sins that have been mentioned in earlier sentences, sins which disrupt communal life, are hereby *disrupting and opposing* the work of the Sprit in building up the Church (cf 2:22; 4:3,4 cf. also Halter *Taufe*, 261).[601]

Paul then appeals to the believers to cultivate the virtues of, "kindness" (v.32), "tenderheartecness" (v.32), and "forgiveness" (v.32) and that these are intended to be ongoing. He is "not addressing a specific situation in the community, but is rather giving foundational teaching for life together as believers."[602]

Of particular concern here is the "forgiveness" that Paul desires the church to practice amongst themselves. In this passage he does not specifically have unbelievers in mind as his "emphasis is on enhancing the community life of the believers."[603] Paul's line of thinking is as follows: The sealing of the Spirit (1:13) for the day of redemption accomplished by the sacrificial work of Christ on the cross (2:13) is not to be hoarded to oneself or neglected in practice but is to be applied to other believers or the Spirit will be "grieved" (4:30). Best notes that the injunction "as God in Christ forgave you" harkens back to the center of the kaleidoscope as 2 Corinthians 5:19, where "God's action in Christ is the basis for Christian behavior."[604]

This chapter has sought to present a model for applying the doctrine of PSA and the ministry of reconciliation to the local church. The community goes before God collectively in light of and because of what God accomplished in the cross of Christ. A community that is single-minded as a result of the cross, doxological, servant-oriented,

---

[600] Arnold helpfully calls to mind that "many theologians have rightly pointed out over the centuries, the fact that the Spirit grieves over sin demonstrates that the Spirit is a person. This is consistent with other attributes of personhood attested about the Spirit in Paul's writings, such as the Spirit's bearing witness (Rom. 8:16), speaking (1 Tim 4:1), interceding for believers (Rom. 8:26), having thoughts (Rom. 8:27), having desires (Gal. 5:17), dwelling in the lives of believers as in a temple (Rom. 8:9, 11; 1 Cor. 3:16; 2 Tim. 1:14), searching and investigating (1 Cor. 2:10), teaching believers (1 Cor. 2:13), leading the people of God (Gal. 5:17-18, 25), and giving divine gifts and abilities to people (1 Cor. 12:9, 11). The Spirit is therefore not an impersonal force or power," Arnold, *Ephesians*, 306.

[601] Lincoln, *Ephesians*, 307, (emphasis mine).

[602] Arnold, *Ephesians*, 308. Indeed, Arnold continues by saying that "the present imperative (γίνεσθε) indicates that Paul wants them to continually strive for the acquisition and display of these virtues."

[603] Arnold, *Ephesians*, 308.

[604] Best, *Ephesians*, 240.

and consistent in extending forgiveness to one another truly grasps what is seen and accomplished in the death of the Son of God.

Summary

This chapter has sought to establish the horizontal paradigm and derive some of the relational implications of the doctrine of PSA and the ministry of reconciliation employing the metaphor of a kaleidoscope. The ecclesial community reconciled to God and to one another through the substitutionary atoning death of the Son of God carries profound relational implications on how the members of the body relate to one another. Some of those implications are becoming doxological, serving, and forgiving people of God.

CHAPTER 7

THE THEORETICAL INTEGRATION OF PSA WITH "HONOR AND SHAME" FROM A RELATIONAL PERSPECTIVE

Introduction

The focus of this work up to this point has been to examine the doctrine of PSA and some of the resulting relational implications (both vertical and horizontal) that result through using the metaphor of a kaleidoscope. However, we would be remiss in bringing the writing to a close without speaking briefly to the relational implications of PSA in honor-shame cultures. Kevin Vanhoozer rightly states the need for humility and relational intentionality among Christians primarily in the West to hear and do systematic theology with those in the East and Global South:

> The moral for systematic theology is clear. No one interpretative community can mine all the treasures of the Word of God by itself. If biblical interpretation is indeed the soul of theology, then theologians had better attend to the global conversation. Reading Scripture with Christians from different parts of the world is invigorating; to be exact, it reinvigorates our tired concepts and categories ... the most important contribution of voices from the global South and East has been rehabilitating the importance of interpreting Scripture with the goal of achieving practical wisdom: performing the text in new contexts, staging new parables of the kingdom of God wherever two or three are gathered in Christ's name.[605]

Cultural anthropologists often note distinctions between fear, guilt, and shame in different societies.[606] These three negative emotional and relational experiences serve to provide culture with a sense of being, belonging, inclusion, and exclusion. One's moral or immoral actions bring about consequences that have real implications on both the individuals and family – impacting both public and private life. Approximately 80% of the world's population lives in honor-shame contexts. Though this is the case there still *remains a significant blind spot in Western culture, theology, and missiology.*[607] As Andrew Walls noted over twenty years ago, what the church in the west needs

---

[605] Kevin Vanhoozer, "'One Rule to Rule Them All?' Theological Method in an Era of World Christianity" in *Globalizing Theology: Belief and Practice in an Era of World Christianity,* ed. Craig Ott and Harold A. Netland (Grand Rapids, MI: Baker Academic, 2006), 122

[606] Alan Silver, Jews, Myth, and History: A Critical Exploration of Contemporary Jewish Belief (Leicester, England: Troubador Publishing, 2008), 161.

[607] Honor-shame contexts and the gospel: accessed October 12, 2018, http://honorshame.com/about/, emphasis mine. For a tremendous resource speaking thoughtfully about honor-shame contexts and the gospel, please see Jayson Georges' Home page: http://honorshame.com.

desperately is to hear from theologians beyond Western, Continental Europe, and North America. His words are worth quoting at length:

> The faith of the twenty-first century will require a devout, vigorous scholarship rooted in the soil of Africa, Asia, and Latin America, [for] the majority of Christians are now Africans, Asians, Latin Americans, and Pacific Islanders.... Christianity is now primarily a non-Western religion and on present indications will steadily become more so .... The most urgent reason for the study of religious traditions of Africa and Asia, of the Amerindian and the Pacific peoples, is their significance for Christian theology; they are the substratum of the Christian faith and life for the greater number of the Christians in the world.[608]

Moreover, as the United States continues to become increasingly diverse with people immigrating, bringing their cultural ideologies intact, including honor-shame, Christians need to be thinking creatively about how to remain faithful to Scripture and lovingly contextualize the gospel message for the newcomers. "The United States has become the religiously most diverse nation on earth.... Nowhere, even in today's world of mass migrations, is the sheer range of religious faith as wide as it is in the United States."[609]

In the West, culture *tends* to operate out of a guilt-innocence base understanding of morality whereas, in many other places around the globe, shame and honor take precedence for how one thinks about herself or is viewed by other family members and the larger society. In honor-shame cultures inward *feelings* of shame serve only as a *part* of the larger picture. In addition to *feeling* honor and shame there are actual *social identities* attached that define one's public standing. Honor and shame are outward, physical statuses and are not merely limited to one's inward, personal conscience. Understanding this is critical for understanding both the world in which the gospel message first was articulated as well as for understanding the majority of the world's modern population. "All cultures include honor among their social values. What distinguishes the ancient Mediterranean world from modern Euro-American culture, in this regard, is the relative value assigned to honor–and honor-seeking–compared with the other social and relational priorities of life."[610] It is noteworthy that honor-shame is thought of, nuanced, expressed, and experienced differently in various contexts. That is to say that Latin Americans, Asians, and Africans, though abiding by an honor-shame model may still express notable differences within each of these contexts. It is wise for Westerners to be mindful of these realities. When conversing with others, asking thoughtful questions, rather than making assumptions, will be beneficial. Indeed, though we use the word "shame"

---

[608] Andrew Walls, "Old Athens and New Jerusalem: Some Signposts for Christian Scholarship in the Early History of Mission Studies," *International Bulletin of Missionary Research* 21, no. 4 (October 1997): 153.

[609] Diana Eck, A New Religious America: How a "Christian Country" Has Become the World's Most Religiously Diverse Nation (New York, NY: Harper Collins, 2001), 4-5.

[610] Joseph H. Hellerman, Embracing Shared Ministry: Power and Status in the Early Church and Why It Matters Today (Grand Rapids, MI: Kregel Publishing, 2013), 57.

we will often be thinking of something different than our friends from the Global South and the East. More often than not, in Western cultures shame is primarily a *private*, *individualistic* experience within oneself rather than being something profoundly connected to family and the larger community.[611] In the ancient Mediterranean world, honor was a public experience. Honor was "functionally the *public* recognition of one's social standing."[612]

The "Blind Spot"

As has been noted, some believe that PSA is virtually incomprehensible in Eastern contexts because of the "recent work in applying what we have learned about cultural anthropology and social psychology to the Scriptures [appears to] reveal how much *more at home* the Bible is in the Japanese context than in a Western society."[613] Thus, the thought follows that the doctrine of PSA will not gain any footing in the mind of the individual. Others echo the same idea stating "the penal substitution model of atonement is the predominant view in the Western church *because* it aligns with cultural understandings of the functions of justice, consequence, and individual responsibility in view of existing legal codes and justice systems in the Western context."[614] Undoubtedly, PSA has flourished more on Western soil than other places around the globe. The reason for this is that generally speaking, here in the West, people tend to operate out of a guilt-innocence based understanding of sin and its consequences. However, to state that Westerners gravitate towards the penal substitution model "*because* it aligns with cultural understandings" is a bit of an overstatement. There are many thoughtful believers who have examined the Biblical-historical material, grasped the theological implications, and considered the hermeneutical challenges of PSA and still remain convinced that though challenging to understand and even offensive to proclaim, the Scripture is clear that the doctrine of PSA is in fact Biblically grounded and stands as God's truth revealed to humankind. The reality is that one's modern cultural context does not negate nor legitimize the truth of Scripture. There are places in Scripture where we see both "Western" *and* "Eastern" ideas presented. The reason for this is because the gospel itself originates in God (Theo-culture) and not humankind. The burden falls on the missionary in finding ways to articulate the Scripture in contexts in which the truth may be presented and embraced though certain concepts will be less "natural" due to the physical location and cultural norms.

In order to explore the articulation of the doctrine of PSA within an honor-shame context using the relational paradigm, we shall call attention to Christ's *humiliation* as he identifies with humanity in the incarnation; specifically observing how his humility

---

611 Honor-shame cultures: accessed November 20, 2018, http://honorshame.com/types-honor-shame-cultures/.

612 Halvor Moxnes, "Honor and Shame," in *The Social Sciences and New Testament Interpretation,* ed. Richard Rohrbaugh (Grand Rapids: MI, Baker Academic, 1996), 20.

613 Green and Baker, *Scandal,* 162.

614 Bud Simon, "Shame and Secularization: A Collateral Rise in American Society with Implications for Evangelism," *Evangelical Missiological Society,* National Conference, Dallas, Texas, 2018: 11, (emphasis mine). https://www.emsweb.org/conference.

spoke to the first-century honor-shame society. As David DeSilva notes, "The social values of honor and dishonor were foundational to first-century culture, whether Roman, Greek, Egyptian, or Judean."[615] In an effort to maintain clarity, attention will be primarily grounded in the Philippian hymn (2:5-11) mentioned above.

Honor–Shame Culture in Philippi

Luke notes that of all the colonies Paul visited, Philippi was particularly "Roman" (Acts 16:12). Roman culture embodied the honor-shame culture. "A person like Paul who came from the east to Philippi entered another world. Roman colonies could be found also in Asia minor, but none was so markedly Roman as Philippi."[616] Roman philosopher, Cicero encapsulated the passionate pursuit of honor by saying that "By nature we yearn and hunger for honor, and once we have glimpsed, as it were, some part of its radiance, there is nothing we are not prepared to bear and suffer in order to secure it."[617] Thus, honor was sought and prized above everything in life. Joseph Hellermann, who has written extensively on honor-shame culture and has brought much to light in recent years to the realm of practical pastoral leadership, notes that

> "Honor–not money (and certainly not love)–was the most prized social commodity in the Roman world during the New Testament era. Beyond the basic necessities of life, persons in antiquity did everything possible to defend and augment their honor in the public sphere. Conversely, they did everything in their power to avoid the shame of public disorder."[618]

Honor was something that was both "ascribed" and "achieved." Ascribed honor, for example, had to do with one's birth. If one was born "into a powerful or wealthy family" that act alone "gives a person certain honor by virtue of that origin; birth into a particular *ethnos* (e.g., Roman or Jewish) means a share in the honor (or dishonor, in some eyes) that attaches generally to whole people." The social status group into which one was born in Philippi determined the quality of one's entire existence, having ramifications in every area of life. Examples of *achieved* honor would be a woman behaving modest and chaste or a man showing great bravery and courage in battle.

Hellerman notes that in the ancient world, "the greatest social chasm in the empire divided the population between what social analysts call elites and non-elites."[619] Thus, this two-class society was one "in which a small percentage of persons controlled both

---

[615] David DeSilva, An Introduction to the New Testament: Contexts, Methods, and Ministry Formation, (Downers Grove, IL: IVP, 2018) 125.

[616] Peter Pillhofer, *Philippi, Band 1: Die erest christliche Gemeinde Europas,* WUNT (Tubingen, Germany: J.C.B. Mohr, 1995), 92, in *Embracing Shared Ministry,* translated by Joseph Hellerman, (Grand Rapids, MI: Kregel Ministry, 2013), 85.

[617] Cicero, Tusculan Disputations, 2.24.58.

[618] Hellerman, *Embracing,* 56.

[619] Hellerman, *Embracing,* 27.

the means of and positions of power and influence."[620] The diagram following shows where everyone stood according to "rank."

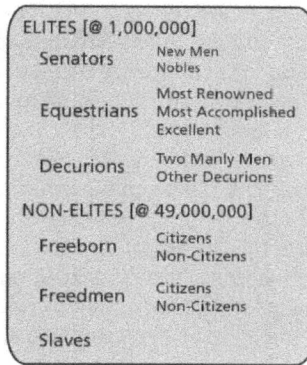

Figure 11 – Rank: Elites and Non-Elites[621]

It is with *this* cultural background in mind that we turn our attention once more to the Philippian hymn to see this great *reversal* that Christ wrought in his incarnation, humiliation, and glorification. From there, we will examine the three people groups present in the public shaming and death of Jesus. Lastly, we shall see how, in his resurrection, Jesus bestows *honor* on those who treated him so shamefully, and that the manner in which the New Testament presents these honors were intrinsic to the anthropological and sociological contexts of each group. Paul writes to the Philippian church:

> Have this mind among yourselves, which is yours in Christ Jesus, who, though he was in the form of God, did not count equality with God a thing to be grasped, but emptied himself, by taking the form of a servant, being born in the likeness of men. And being found in human form, he humbled himself by becoming obedient to the point of death, even death on a cross. Therefore God has highly exalted him and bestowed on him the name that is above every name, so that at the name of Jesus every knee should bow, in heaven and on earth and under the earth, and every tongue confess that Jesus Christ is Lord, to the glory of God the Father (Phil. 2:5-11).

Hellerman offers an interesting insight into this passage that commentators identify as one of the "high Christological passages" of the New Testament (alongside John 1:1-4; Col. 1:15-20; Heb. 1:1-3). He demonstrates that though the hymn clearly has much to say about the subject of Christology, the hymn is first and foremost ecclesiological (viz.

---

620 Hellerman, *Embracing,* 27.
621 Hellerman, *Embracing,* 27.

horizontal). "Or, perhaps, more accurately, what we have in Philippians 2:6-11 is Christology in the service of an overarching ecclesiological agenda."[622] This is because of Paul's opening appeal to the brothers and sisters in Philippi to *"have this mind in you"* (v.5). Jesus' humility in his self-emptying (ἐκένωσεν) involved him stooping lower and lower until he reached the lowest rung of the social hierarchy in the first century. Paul begins his appeal to the church by first calling attention to the *"equality"* that Jesus relinquished. In his self-emptying, Jesus did something mentally – he did not *"count"* his "equality with God" something "to be grasped" (v.6). Thus, his first action in the redemption of humanity was not first in the incarnation, nor his humiliation on Good Friday. Rather, it was in his mind. The Christ, in his *estimating,* concluded that he would temporarily release his rightful place of glory. In order for Paul to appeal to the "mind" of the church, he first appealed to the "mind" of Christ in his "counting" and "considering." In a culture in which honor and status were prized above all, this would have struck the early readers as utterly unfathomable. The Divine Son of God of *his own volition* became a slave. Jesus's entering as a person, in a specific place, assumed the position of the despised.

PSA and Honor–Shame in the Death and Resurrection of Jesus

In the crucifixion and resurrection narratives, themes of shame and honor repeatedly surface. As has been stated repeatedly, PSA is only one model of the atonement and does not exhaust all that Scripture has to say about what the death of the Son of God accomplishes. In the penal model, the wrath of God is averted through the death of Christ, thus the theme of Passover is found and, even Paul himself calls Christ "our Passover" (1 Cor. 5:7). However, in cultures where honor and shame are in focus, one way to move toward articulating the doctrine of PSA is first to examine the *types* of shame Jesus experienced by the disciples who abandoned him, the Jewish authorities who mocked him, and the Romans who executed him in shame.

Moreover, after his resurrection, the New Testament writers demonstrate that the cultures who directly shamed Jesus to death, now by grace, receive *honor* that was intrinsic to their own sociological and cultural values. Below is a kaleidoscopic diagram providing an illustration. Recall that the usage of the kaleidoscope as a metaphor is one way in which we can attempt to keep several events or concepts in mind at the same time, as we consider the various aspects of shame and honor expressed in Christ's substitutionary death and glorious resurrection.

Here is the kaleidoscope that represents Jesus being shamed by three various people groups.

---

[622] Hellerman, *Embracing,* 11.

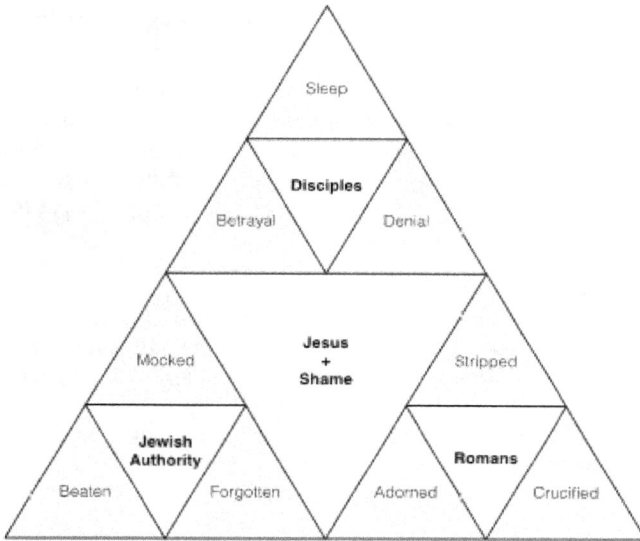

Figure 12 – Jesus and Shame

Sleep, Betrayal, and Denial: The Disciples and the Shame of Jesus

In addition to Jesus's repeated predictions of his death and resurrection (Mark 8:31-33, 9:30-32, 10:32-34) he also predicted his *betrayal* (John 13:18-30). Prior to the betrayal by Judas, Jesus and his disciples go to the garden and he instructed his disciples to watch and pray for him (Matt. 26:36-46). As *disciples*, they were to commit themselves to rigorous obedience to their rabbi. In her monograph on early discipleship, Sylvia Wilkey Collinson writes discipleship was essentially …

> Learning relationships [that] involved close, personal family-like commitment of both teacher and taught to one another, for a significant period of time. It usually entailed communal living. Learners observed and imitated their teachers as they pursued their daily occupations and assisted them in performing their duties. The way of life was prescribed by the master who often *commanded obedience.*
> Together they believe in and worked towards common goals.[623]

---

[623] Sylvia Wilkey Collinson, *Making Disciples: The Significance of Jesus' Educational Methods for Today's Church,* (Eugene, OR: Wipf & Stock Publishers, 2004], 23, emphasis mine. She also rightly notes that the Gospel of Mark "places three of the occasions when Jesus called his disciples

Sleep

Yet, what Jesus found was not diligent, prayerful, sacrificial, loving-concern and obedience but rather disciples giving in to sleep – "for their eyes were heavy" (v.43). Hagner captures the *shame* of the moment:

> When Jesus returns to the three disciples, he finds that they are sleeping and that he has received no support from them. They seem *oblivious* to what he is going through despite the indication of his anguish ... (see Daube for the view that *sleeping* violated the fellowship of the Passover community) ... and becomes a metaphor in the NT for moral failure (cf. 1 Thess. 5:6-7; Eph. 5:14).[624]

Betrayal

In addition to the sleeping during his trying hour, Jesus experienced shame through the betrayal by Judas. Matthew records: "Now the betrayer had given them a sign, saying, 'The one I will kiss is the man; seize him.' And he came up to Jesus at once and said, 'Greetings, Rabbi!' And he kissed him. Jesus said to him, 'Friend, do what you came to do.' Then they came up and laid hands on Jesus and seized him" (Matt. 26:48-50).

Rather than finding honor, courage, and loyalty, Jesus was shamed through Judas' fear and betrayal. The kiss of Judas is particularly striking. Keener helpfully highlights the lack of *honor.*

> A kiss was a sign of special affection among family members and close friends, or of a disciples' *honor and affection* for his teacher. Judas's kiss is thus a special act of hypocrisy (cf. Prov. 27:6). Given ancient values concerning hospitality, friendship, and covenant loyalty, any of Matthew's readers encountering this story for the first time would have been horrified by the narration of the betrayal. Judas appears as the most contemptible of traitors; Jesus appears as one unjustly betrayed.[625]

Denial

The next place we observe Jesus being shamed by his disciples is recorded in the thrice-denying Peter. Luke records

> Then they seized him and led him away, bringing him into the high priest's house, and Peter was following at a distance. And when they had kindled a fire in the middle of the courtyard and sat down together, Peter sat down among them. Then a servant girl, seeing him as he sat in the light and looking closely at him, said, "This man also was with him." But he denied it, saying, "Woman, I do not know him." And

---

immediately after his three passion predictions. This seems more than coincidental. It appears that Mark, at least, believed that the disciples of Jesus should expect their lives to follow a path of suffering similar to that of their master," 31.

[624] Hagner, *Matthew 14-28,* 783, emphasis mine.

[625] Craig Keener, *The IVP Bible Background Commentary: New Testament,* (Grand Rapids, MI: Baker Academic, 1994), 122, emphasis mine.

a little later someone else saw him and said, "You also are one of them." But Peter said, "Man, I am not." And after an interval of about an hour still another insisted, saying, "Certainly this man also was with him, for he too is a Galilean." But Peter said, "Man, I do not know what you are talking about." And immediately, while he was still speaking, the rooster crowed. And the Lord turned and looked at Peter. And Peter remembered the saying of the Lord, how he had said to him, "Before the rooster crows today, you will deny me three times." And he went out and wept bitterly (Luke 22:54-62).[626]

John Nolland captures the shame of these moments as he writes, "The recently confident Peter cannot, once Jesus has been arrested, maintain his allegiance to his master in the face of even the challenge mounted by *a few nameless people of no particular significance* who are sitting around a fire in the courtyard of the high priest's house."[627]

Of particular interest at this moment is the fact that Peter's denials do not come before people of esteemed honor such as a local senator, much less, the Emperor. Instead, Peter denies any affiliation with Jesus before "a few nameless people of no particular significance." The shame intensified all the more on behalf of the disciples. Through their sleeping, betraying, and denying the disciples have abandoned their Master in utter shame. We rotate the kaleidoscope and bring the Jewish leaders into the picture as well.

Mocked, Beaten, and Forgotten: The Jewish Authorities Shame Jesus

After Jesus is betrayed, he is captured by the Romans and taken before Caiaphas the High Priest and is tried. Matthew records:

Then those who had seized Jesus led him to Caiaphas the high priest, where the scribes and the elders had gathered. And Peter was following him at a distance, as far as the courtyard of the high priest, and going inside he sat with the guards to see the end. Now the chief priests and the whole council were seeking false testimony against Jesus that they might put him to death, but they found none, though many false witnesses came forward. At last two came forward and said, "This man said, 'I am able to destroy the temple of God, and to rebuild it in three days.'" And the high priest stood up and said, "Have you no answer to make? What is it that these men testify against you?" But Jesus remained silent. And the high priest said to him, "I adjure you by the living God, tell us if you are the Christ, the

---

[626] "Jesus had predicted Peter's threefold denial in v.34; now Luke recounts the fulfillment of Jesus' prophecy in dramatic fashion punctuated by its staccato-like style. In quick succession, Peter denies that he knows Jesus (v.57, echoing v.34), that he is associated with Jesus' followers (v.58), and finally his association with Jesus from the beginning of the ministry in Galilee (vv.59-60)." See Joel Green, *The Gospel of Luke*, 787.

[627] John Nolland. *Word Biblical Commentary*, vol. 35c, *Luke 18:35-24:53* (Nashville, TN: Thomas Nelson, 1989), 1094, emphasis mine.

Son of God." Jesus said to him, "You have said so. But I tell you, from now on you will see the Son of Man seated at the right hand of Power and coming on the clouds of heaven." Then the high priest tore his robes and said, "He has uttered blasphemy. What further witnesses do we need? You have now heard his blasphemy. What is your judgment?" They answered, "He deserves death" (Matt. 26:57-66).

Mocked

Jesus is shamefully *mocked* by the Jewish authorities both *prior* to his crucifixion as well as *while* he dies on his cross (Matt. 26:67-68, 27:41; Mark 15:31; Luke 22:63, 23:35). The authorities who repeatedly *mock* Jesus publicly do so in an effort to continue to lower Jesus' status in the eyes of all who followed him up to this point. With incredible irony, the Jewish authorities *mock* Jesus in Matthew 27:43 saying "He trusts in God; let God deliver him now, if he desires him. For he said, 'I am the Son of God.'" These are the very words prophesied in Psalm 22:8. Even after he was buried, the Jewish authorities did not relinquish their verbal assault and slander of Jesus. As Jesus lay in his grave,

> ...the chief priests and the Pharisees gathered before Pilate and said, "Sir, we remember how that *impostor* said, while he was still alive, 'After three days I will rise.' Therefore order the tomb to be made secure until the third day, lest his disciples go and steal him away and tell the people, 'He has risen from the dead,' and the last *fraud* will be worse than the first." Pilate said to them, "You have a guard of soldiers. Go, make it as secure as you can." So they went and made the tomb secure by sealing the stone and setting a guard (Matt. 27:62–66).

Thus, what can be observed here is the *intentional* reinforcement of the Jewish authorities' shameful opinion of Jesus, calling him an "impostor" or "fraud."

Beaten

In addition to Jesus being unjustly tried and found guilty of *blasphemy*, no doubt, shaming him, the Son of God, to the highest degree, the Jewish authorities also put him to open shame him by the use of physical violence. Matthew continues, "Then they spit in his face and struck him. And some slapped him, saying, 'Prophesy to us, you Christ! Who is it that struck you?'" (26:67-68). Jennifer Glancy highlights the shame that accompanied physical violence, "Citizen or not, free or slave, a beaten body was a dishonored body; any free person who was publicly stripped and battered with rods suffered an effective reduction in social status."[628]

Forgotten

Lastly, in calling for his "crucifixion" (27:22), the Jewish authorities cry out for the ultimate shaming of Christ. In addition to all of the physical agony mentioned earlier in

---

[628] Jennifer A. Glancy, "Boasting of Beatings (2 Corinthians 11:23-25)," *Journal of Biblical Literature* 123, no. 1 (March 2004): 124.

this work, the Jewish authorities sought to erase even the *memory* of Jesus from all of history. In order to capture the full flavor of the "forgetting," it serves well to quote Richard Bauckham at length:

> Crucifixion was and had to be offensively public. So much the more resolutely was it banished from the literature and culture in which the Roman Empire celebrated its glory. Great generals like Julius Caesar, the great provincial governors like Pliny, who regularly ordered crucifixions wrote up their memoirs with never a mention of the fact. It was not what they wished to remember or be remembered for.
>
> However, a second reason why ancient literature rarely dwelt on crucifixion reinforces the first: the people who were crucified were not people who mattered. Crucifixion was for the lower classes, foreigners, slaves. It was the penalty for political crimes against the state, for violent robbery, and for rebellious slaves. It maintained the authority of the state and the structure of a slave-owning society. It secured peace and prosperity for the majority by barbarous treatment of others. Crucifixion could be forgotten because it was a way of forgetting people, a way of excluding from society those who would disturb its conscience or its security, a way of denying humanity to the "others," a way of reducing their humanity to carrion.
>
> The illusion of a civilized society had to be maintained by forgetting its victims. Crucifixion was the way of removing them, rendering them nothing; and so that they might be well and truly forgotten, crucifixion itself was not discussed.[629]

We now turn the kaleidoscope to observe how Jesus was *shamed* by the Romans in his crucifixion.

Stripped, Adorned, and Crucified: The Roman Authorities Shame Jesus

In keeping with the shame that Jesus underwent as he averts the wrath of God, he continues to absorb the wrath of humankind. The Romans were merciless as they made sport in the shaming of Jesus. Truly, it is beyond comprehension for one to imagine the utter brutality common amongst Romans inflicting pain, shame, and death upon victims.[630] Matthew records that "the soldiers of the governor took Jesus into the

---

[629] Richard Bauckham, *The Bible in Politics: How to Read the Bible Politically,* (Louisville, KY: Westminster, 1989), 147-8.

[630] Dan Lé writes, "In early Rome, victims of civil or military oppression were tied into sacks filled with poisonous vipers, then thrown into the Tiber, or dragged to death behind a chariot. They were also flogged, scourged, burned, beheaded, and crucified. Some prisoners were hung by their genitals or tied while a trained eagle bit and clawed them to death. Martyrs were slowly burned to death, or boiled in cauldrons or put in frying pans. More inventive tortures such as submersing men in a freezing pond until their extremities froze and could be shattered by blows. Girls were sewn naked into the belly of a freshly killed ass with only their head protruding; then the ass was

governor's headquarters, and they gathered the whole battalion before him. And they stripped him and put a scarlet robe on him" (Matt. 27:27-28).

Stripped

The stripping and robing of Jesus, something that can at times be overlooked by many Westerners, is exceptionally vivid to those from Eastern parts of the world, who strongly identify with the honor-shame culture. Dan Lé in his distinguished work, *The Naked Christ: An Atonement Model for a Body-Obsessed Culture,* has written extensively on this subject.

> We may not know exactly how many times the clothing and undressing happened, but what we can be certain of is that Christ was disrobed at the scourging and once again at the cross, when his clothes were divided. The naked scourging was meant to be *shameful,* and the confiscation of property indicates that Jesus' clothes were totally removed. Therefore, he suffered *shame* ..."[631]

Adorned

The gospel of Matthew tells us that in addition to the stripping and robing of Jesus, Pilate's soldiers

> ... took Jesus into the governor's headquarters, and they gathered the whole battalion before him. And they stripped him and put a scarlet robe on him twisting together a crown of thorns, they put it on his head and put a reed in his right hand. And kneeling before him, they mocked him, saying, "Hail, King of the Jews!" And they spit on him and took the reed and struck him on the head. And when they had mocked him, they stripped him of the robe and put his own clothes on him and led him away to crucify him (Matt. 27:27-31).

France helpfully points out that those participating in this part of the shaming of Jesus were technically "Pilate's solders ... rather than Roman legionnaire (there was no legion stationed in Palestine at this time), they are likely to have been drawn from the non-Jewish population of surrounding areas who would have had little sympathy with a supposed Jewish king."[632]

During this private "mock enthronement"[633] Jesus is "robed" by a smaller red cloak that was worn by Roman military. The color of red or "purple" as Mark and John record, no doubt calls attention to what truly "honored" people would wear. Recall Hellerman's

---

exposed to the hot sun until it rotted. The practice of torment that involves nudity is common, one of which involves tying up a honey-smeared naked body for ants and bees to gnaw at the flesh (Mannnix, *The History of Torture,* 26, 38; Scott, *Corporal,* 4-5)." See Lé, *Naked,* 149-150, fn. 4.

[631] Lé, *Naked,* 160-161.
[632] France, *Matthew,* 1061.
[633] France, *Matthew,* 1061.

"Elites vs. Non-Elites" mentioned above.[634] Roman soldiers often played games to pass time: they "carved on the stone pavement of the fortress Antonia, where they were garrisoned on the Temple Mount, and knucklebones used as dice have also been recovered there."[635] They also twisted a crown of thorns and placed it upon the head of Jesus, mocking him as "King of the Jews." The crown was likely from any common spiked plant nearby "even if the intention was primarily mockery rather than physical torture, such a wreath would inevitably be painful."[636] The "stick" or "reed" resembling a king's royal scepter placed in his "right hand" was intentional. "The right side was identified as the place of *honor* (1 Kings 2:19; Ps. 45:9)."[637] Addressing Jesus with "Hail!" mocked his claim as King; for the word "Hail!" echoed whom they held to be the true king, Ave Caesar![638] The spit upon Jesus was something particularly shaming. This is because "Jewish people considered the spittle of non-Jews particularly unclean. The soldiers spitting on Jesus might parody the kiss of homage expected by rulers of the Greek East."[639]

All of the shaming is complete. Jesus has been reduced to almost nothing. All that remains is the dreaded public Roman crucifixion.

Crucified

Crucifixion was nothing less than utter *shaming* of the victim.

> They stripped him of the robe and put his own clothes on him and led him away to crucify him. As they went out, they found a man of Cyrene, Simon by name. They compelled this man to carry his cross. And when they came to a place called Golgotha (which means Place of a Skull), they offered him wine to drink, mixed with gall, but when he tasted it, he would not drink it. And when they had crucified him, they divided his garments among them by casting lots. Then they sat down and kept watch over him there. And over his head they put the charge against him, which read. "This is Jesus, the King of the Jews" (Matt. 27:31-37).

Jesus was dressed in his own clothing for the last time before forced to carry his cross out into the public. Traditionally, the victim would be left naked, but being that this was *Passover* and many Jews were present, clothing Jesus may have occurred in an effort to keep from offending such a massive crowd of Jewish worshipers. The Romans took on the practice of crucifixion and practiced it strictly on slaves (cf. Phil. 2:8-9). The grotesque destruction of human life was always done in a public place, inviting the shaming and taunting crowds as well as to instill fear in the minds of all who would

---

[634] See also Carson, *Matthew,* 573.
[635] Keener, *Background,* 127.
[636] France, *Matthew,* 1062.
[637] Ryken, Wilhoit, Longman III, eds., *Dictionary of Biblical Imagery,* "Right, Right Hand," 728.
[638] Carson, *Matthew,* 573.
[639] Keener, *Background,* 127.

oppose Rome. Keeping crucifixions very public was done so that "observers could rejoice in the punishment of the condemned and learn from their agony not to follow their example."[640] Initially, crucifixion was not a method of killing; rather it was a punishment for misusing the hands and feet on Roman soil.[641] Lé summarizes perfectly the shame accompanied in public crucifixion and is well worth quoting at length:

> The fact that crucifixion was an extreme degradation, a torment and inhumane death, and the most *shameful* death man can suffer, could not be overemphasized. The victim was normally denuded, and insulted physically to the very private parts in the flogging. Then, he would be led naked to the sight of execution. The victim was deprived of his dignity, being turned from a living human being into a feast for scavenging birds, and not to be removed or buried, unless an exception of mercy was granted. While nakedness was the norm for crucifixion, the helpless and agonizing victim could not move, swat flies, or even breathe. Often, victims befouled themselves with their own urine or excrement. Being crucified in different positions, the criminals suffered a death of pain, irritation, itches, painful and humiliating genital mutilations with sadistic mockery in the middle of a public place. In Cunningham's words, "The whole point of Roman crucifixion was to reduce the victim to the status of a thing, stripping him of every vestige of human dignity, in order to discourage any challenge of the might of Rome."[642]

There is certainly so much more that has been and will be said surrounding the shame present in the death of Christ. The above material is an effort to help Westerners who are inclined to overlook the historical aspects of shame present in the gospels that tend to stand out to those coming from honor-shame contexts more naturally. We now provide another kaleidoscope turn and observe the *honor* that Jesus graciously extends and bestows upon those who shamed him to death.

Here is a depiction of the kaleidoscope that represents Jesus extending *honor* to the three various people groups involved in shaming him. Yes, honor that spoke directly to their shame.

---

[640] Melissa Barden Dowling, *Clemency and Cruelty in the Roman World* (Ann Arbor, MI: University of Michigan Press, 2006), 224.

[641] Lé, *Naked*, 152.

[642] Lé, *Naked*, 158-159.

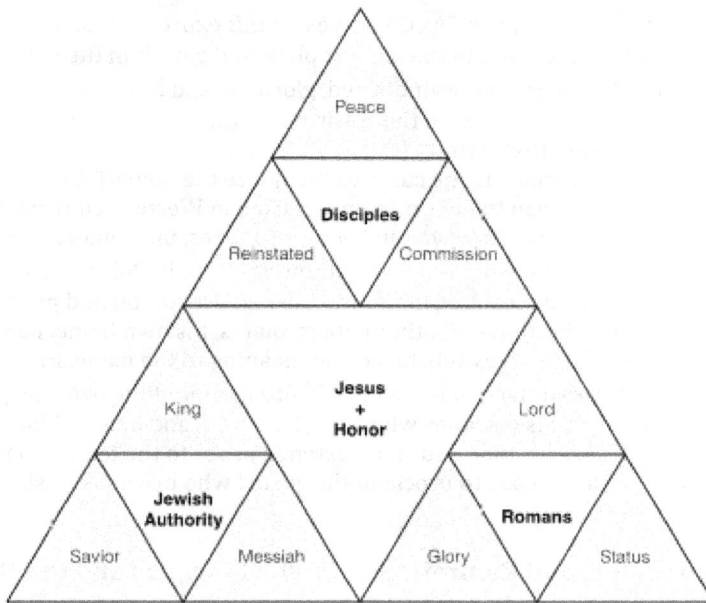

Figure 13 – Jesus and Honor

The Father Honors the Son in Glory

Following along the Philippian hymn we read that after the humiliation of the cross "Therefore, God has highly exalted him and bestowed on him the name that is above every name, so that at the name of Jesus every knee should bow, in heaven and on earth and under the earth, and every tongue confess that Jesus Christ is Lord, to the glory of God the Father" (Phil. 2:9-11).

The hymn transitions from shame to honor as God the Father "is now presented as decisively intervening and acting on his Son's behalf."[643] Though Paul does not mention the resurrection nor ascension back to the right hand of the Father, "these two realities are presupposed by what he *does say*."[644] Paul's usage of "therefore" should not be interpreted as God rewarding Christ for his humiliation or asserting that Jesus has

---

[643] Peter Thomas O'Brien, *NIGTC: The Epistle to the Philippians* (Grand Rapids, MI: Eerdmans, 1991.)

[644] Fee, *Philippians,* 220, emphasis mine.

ascertained a sort of victory over the powers of Rome. Fee insists that "It asserts the divine vindication of Christ's emptying himself and humbling himself in obedience by dying on a cross."[645] He continues, "As God's 'yes' to *this* expression of 'equality with God,' God the Father 'exalted him to the highest place and gave him the name that is above every name.'"[646] Jesus is now vindicated, glorified, and honored above every name on the earth (human culture), in the spirit-realm (angel and demon culture), and now is glorified within the Holy Trinity (theo-culture).

Those coming from honor-shame cultures recognize the powerful words of Paul in reference to *"the name."* When the word "name" is used in Western cultures, we tend to think of someone's first name. However, in Eastern cultures, much more is at stake. The name represents one's character, family, and status.[647] Here in Philippians, we see that the "Father has magnificently exalted his Son to the highest station and graciously bestowed on him the name above all other names, that is, his own name, Lord (= Yahweh), along with all that gives substance and meaning to the name. In his exalted state, Jesus now exercises universal lordship."[648] After triumphing over the grave, Jesus now bestows honor upon his disciples who slept, betrayed, and denied him. As we turn the kaleidoscope, we observe that Jesus now extends peace to the fearful, reinstates the denying, and commissions those to proclaim the gospel who previously "slept for their eyes were heavy."

Peace, Reinstated, and Commissioned: The Disciples and the Honor of Jesus

Peace

After his resurrection, the shamed, fearful, and hiding disciples encounter their resurrected rabbi. John writes,

> On the evening of that day, the first day of the week, the doors being locked where the disciples were for fear of the Jews, Jesus came and stood among them and said to them, "Peace be with you." When he had said this, he showed them his hands and his side. Then the disciples were glad when they saw the Lord. Jesus said to them again, "Peace be with you. As the Father has sent me, even so I am sending you" (John 20:19-21).

John indicates that the reason for their hiding was because of their "fear of the Jews." Certainly, the Jews who had called for the brutal execution of Jesus would show no

---

[645] Fee, *Philippians,* 220, italics in original.

[646] Fee, *Philippians,* 220. See also Honor-shame name, accessed January 18, 2019, http://honorshame.com/biblically-what-is-your-name/.

[647] See Honor-shame name, accessed January 18, 2019, http://honorshame.com/biblically-what-is-your-name/.

[648] O'Brien, *Philippians,* 233.

more mercy to his disciples. Tenney suggests that "they were probably holding a consultation on the best method of withdrawing from the city without attracting the notice of the temple police or the Roman authorities. The doors were locked for fear that the Jews would send an arresting detachment for them as they had for Jesus."[649]

Jesus appeared in the room with the disciples and said "Peace to you" twice; once upon identifying himself, and then again after the disciples examine the wounds in his body. Jesus repeating the word "peace" extended to his disciples is significant in an honor-shame culture. Certainly, the disciples who had slept, betrayed, and denied Jesus were not in right and honorable standing with him! They had failed him in every way possible. And yet, Jesus honors them by extending not a sword or a strong rebuke but "peace." Morris captures the full flavor of the extension of peace when he writes "For the Greeks (as for us) peace was essentially negative, the absence of war. But for the Hebrews it meant positive blessing, especially a right relationship with God. This is to be seen in the Old Testament, and it is carried over into the New.[650] Judas had hanged himself and Peter had wept bitterly. The fear-stricken disciples are taken from a place of shame to being in a "blessed" state; a "right relationship with God" was secure. Jesus installed his disciples in a place of *honor*. We now turn to see Jesus in his reinstatement of Peter who had denied him.

Reinstated

John records, on the evening of the Last Supper, Peter and Jesus talking, "'Lord, where are you going?' Jesus answered him, 'Where I am going you cannot follow me now, but you will follow afterward.' Peter said to him, 'Lord, why can I not follow you now? I will lay down my life for you.' Jesus answered, 'Will you lay down your life for me? Truly, truly, I say to you, the rooster will not crow till you have denied me three times,' (John 13:36-38). The disciple Peter promised Jesus he would follow him to death. And yet, Jesus predicts that Peter will yet deny him three times that evening. He was not ready to die for Jesus, though Jesus was ready to die for Peter.

John records the denials as follows,

Simon Peter followed Jesus, and so did another disciple. Since that disciple was known to the high priest, he entered with Jesus into the courtyard of the high priest, but Peter stood outside at the door. So the other disciple, who was known to the high priest, went out and spoke to the servant girl who kept watch at the door, and brought Peter in. The servant girl at the door said to Peter, "You also are not one of this man's disciples, are you?" He said, "I am not." Now the servants and officers had made a charcoal fire, because it was cold, and they were standing and warming themselves. Peter also was with them, standing and warming himself....

---

[649] Merrill C. Tenney, *The Expositor's Bible Commentary*, vol. 9, *John-Acts*, ed. Frank E. Gaebelein, (Grand Rapids, MI: Zondervan, 1984), 192.

[650]Morris, *John*, 584. Additionally, for an outstanding treatment of the following verse, "And when he had said this, he breathed on them and said to them, 'Receive the Holy Spirit,'" (John 20:22), see Carson's "Without Evidence," 105-118, esp. 112.

they said to him, "You also are not one of his disciples, are you?" He denied it and said, "I am not." One of the servants of the high priest, a relative of the man whose ear Peter had cut off, asked, "Did I not see you in the garden with him?" Peter again denied it, and at once a rooster crowed (John 18:15-18, 25-27).

After his resurrection, Jesus reinstates Peter:

When they had finished breakfast, Jesus said to Simon Peter, "Simon, son of John, do you love me more than these?" He said to him, "Yes, Lord; you know that I love you." He said to him, "Feed my lambs." He said to him a second time, "Simon, son of John, do you love me?" He said to him, "Yes, Lord; you know that I love you." He said to him, "Tend my sheep." He said to him the third time, "Simon, son of John, do you love me?" Peter was grieved because he said to him the third time, "Do you love me?" and he said to him, "Lord, you know everything; you know that I love you." Jesus said to him, "Feed my sheep. Truly, truly, I say to you, when you were young, you used to dress yourself and walk wherever you wanted, but when you are old, you will stretch out your hands, and another will dress you and carry you where you do not want to go." (This he said to show by what kind of death he was to glorify God.) And after saying this he said to him, "Follow me" (21:15-19).

Presumably, we can imagine that Jesus and Peter are on a walk together after breakfast, not in public, but in private. While alone, the question "Do you love me more than these?" is a bit vague. The reader is not certain whether or not Jesus has in mind the other disciples or whether he might be speaking about some other persons or things. Nonetheless, Peter was grieved, his heart was deeply saddened in regret over his denials. Peter was aware of his own weakness and Jesus repeatedly asked him about his love and commitment. And yet, for each denial that preceded the crucifixion, there now was an affirmation of *love* for his living and triumphant "Lord."[651] Jesus then instructs this same dishonorable Peter to now tend and feed Jesus' sheep. In yet another reversal from a place of shame to a place of honor, Peter is reinstated!

There can be little doubt but that the whole scene is meant to show us Peter completely restored to his position of leadership. Three times he had denied his Lord. Now he has three times affirmed his love for him, and three times he has been *commissioned* to care for the flock. This must have had the effect of a demonstration that, whatever had been the mistakes of the past, Jesus was restoring Peter to a place of trust.[652]

We rotate the kaleidoscope and see Jesus bestowing honor on the disciples as he *commissions* them.

---

[651] F. F. Bruce, *The Gospel and Epistles of John* (Grand Rapids, MI: Eerdmans, 1983), 404.
[652] Morris, *John* 772.

Commissioned

In the Great Commission in Matthew's epilogue, we find Jesus declaring exactly how much glory, how honorable he is in the cosmos: "And Jesus came and said to them, 'All authority in heaven and on earth has been given to me'" (Matt. 28:18).

Jesus is now exalted above every ruler, including the Emperor as well as every angel and demon. Again, consider Hellerman's observations on honor-shame culture.[653] Matthew records the final words of his gospel coming from the mouth of the resurrected Jesus and not the disciples. Jesus then commissions his disciples saying, "Go therefore and make disciples of all nations, baptizing them in the name of the Father and of the Son and of the Holy Spirit, teaching them to observe all that I have commanded you. And behold, I am with you always, to the end of the age" (vv.19-20).

France notes the intentionality of Jesus in this scene being one that is profoundly *relational*.

> We do not have merely words "Jesus said" but rather a combination of three verbs: he "came to" them, "spoke to" them, and "said." This rather fulsome introductory clause not only emphasizes the climactic role of this speech but also responds to the disciples' hesitation: Jesus' "coming to" his frightened disciples is an act of *reassurance*, ... he "speaks to" them to restore the broken relationship, and the words he will not utter will leave their failure far behind, *swallowed up in the much greater reality* of the mission to which they are now *called*.[654]

Those who were stricken with fear are now, in addition to Peter, reassured, empowered, and sent out to proclaim the gospel, baptize believers, and make disciples in the *name* of Jesus. Here again, Jesus elevates those in a place of shame and gives them a place of honor as they are now personally commissioned to represent not a senator, local governor, or even the Emperor, but they are now proclaiming the King of Kings to whom "all authority in heaven and on the earth" belongs. This is honor unparalleled.

We turn the kaleidoscope to another facet and look briefly at the honor made available to and experienced by some of the Jewish authorities.

King, Savior, and Messiah: The Jewish Authorities and the Honor of Jesus

Though there were Jewish authorities who were involved in calling for the shaming and death of Jesus, we also have a couple of instances in which Jewish authorities came to faith in Jesus as King, Savior, and Messiah. For example, the progression of Nicodemus is unique to John's Gospel. At first, Nicodemus, "a ruler of the Jews" (John 3:1), converses with Jesus at "night." The next instance Nicodemus surfaces, he addresses his fellow Jewish leaders and questions them as they are pursuing putting Jesus on trial. Nicodemus asks, "Does our law judge a man without first giving him a hearing and learning what he does?" (7:51). Then, in Jesus' most shameful moment,

---

653 Hellerman, *Embracing*, 57.
654 France, *Matthew*, 1112, emphasis mine.

after the trials, torture, mocking, flogging, and crucifixion, Jesus hung naked and dead, exposed in utter shame, we read that Nicodemus emerges yet again, not amongst the Jewish leaders who shamed Jesus but as one who wished to honor his Messiah. John records,

> After these things Joseph of Arimathea, who was a disciple of Jesus, but secretly for fear of the Jews, asked Pilate that he might take away the body of Jesus, and Pilate gave him permission. So he came and took away his body. Nicodemus also, who earlier had come to Jesus by night, came bringing a mixture of myrrh and aloes, about seventy-five pounds in weight. So they took the body of Jesus and bound it in linen cloths with the spices, as is the burial custom of the Jews. Now in the place where he was crucified there was a garden, and in the garden a new tomb in which no one had yet been laid. So because of the Jewish day of Preparation, since the tomb was close at hand, they laid Jesus there (19:38-42).

King

The most famous conversion of a Jewish leader comes to us outside of the gospel records, and that person, of course, is the Apostle Paul. The Jews had long awaited their king who would rise up and sit on the throne of David. Recall the words of Nathan to David,

> "Moreover, the Lord declares to you that the Lord will make you a house. When your days are fulfilled and you lie down with your fathers, I will raise up your offspring after you, who shall come from your body, and I will establish his kingdom. He shall build a house for my name, and I will establish the throne of his kingdom forever. I will be to him a father, and he shall be to me a son. When he commits iniquity, I will discipline him with the rod of men, with the stripes of the sons of men, but my steadfast love will not depart from him, as I took it from Saul, whom I put away from before you. And your house and your kingdom shall be made sure forever before me. Your throne shall be established forever." In accordance with all these words, and in accordance with all this vision, Nathan spoke to David (2 Sam. 7:11-17).

The trajectory had been set and the Jews had longed for this day. Though many spurned and shamed Jesus, some received him. Because space does not allow for a further discussion, attention will be called to one passage in which Paul who formerly *persecuted* Jesus and his people, now boldly proclaims not only the "kingdom of God" but the "King" himself. In Acts 8:3 we read that Saul "was ravaging the church, and entering house after house, he dragged off men and women and committed them to prison." Paul was keenly aware that what had transpired in his conversion moved him from a place of hostility with God to being truly one of God's children by grace and through faith. To Timothy he writes, "The saying is trustworthy and deserving of full acceptance, that Christ Jesus came into the world to save sinners, of whom I am the foremost" (1 Tim. 1:15). He then charges Timothy in this way,

I charge you in the presence of God, who gives life to all things, and of Christ Jesus, who in his testimony before Pontius Pilate made the good confession, to keep the commandment unstained and free from reproach until the appearing of our Lord Jesus Christ, which he will display at the proper time—he who is the blessed and only Sovereign, the King of kings and Lord of lords, who alone has immortality, who dwells in unapproachable light, whom no one has ever seen or can see. To him be honor and eternal dominion. Amen (6:13-16).

For Paul to move from persecutor of Christ to ambassador of the "King" is nothing less than God's grace bestowing honor where shame once ruled.

Savior

It is not uncommon throughout the Old Testament to find YHWH referred to as the "Savior" (see 2 Sam. 22:3; Ps. 17:7, 106:21; Isa. 43:3, 11, 45:15, 21; Hosea 13:4). Upon opening Matthew's Gospel we find the angel, speaking to Joseph about Jesus who was to be born, says of Mary, "She will bear a son, and you shall call his name Jesus, for he will save his people from their sins" (Matt. 1:21).

This "saving" work that Jesus will accomplish is specifically addressing his people's "sins." Hence, the penal model of the atonement is at work even here in the *naming* of the Son. At the Last Supper, this theme of saving and forgiveness of sins reaches its climax when Jesus "... took a cup, and when he had given thanks he gave it to them, saying, 'Drink of it, all of you, for this is my blood of the covenant, which is poured out for many for the forgiveness of sins'" (26:27-28).

Indeed, Luke's gospel records that this *Savior* even prayed for the *forgiveness* of those who crucified him and those Jewish leaders who "scoffed" at him, mocking his Kingship and ability to "save!" Luke writes,

And when they came to the place that is called The Skull, there they crucified him, and the criminals, one on his right and one on his left. And Jesus said, "Father, forgive them, for they know not what they do." And they cast lots to divide his garments. And the people stood by, watching, but the rulers scoffed at him, saying, "He saved others; let him save himself, if he is the Christ of God, his Chosen One!" (Luke 23:33-35).

To every scoffer in the crowd who would receive the forgiveness of Christ, that one no longer stands under the condemnation of sin but is "saved." We now turn to the last facet of this segment of the kaleidoscope to see the honorable position offered to those who receive Jesus as the Messiah of God.

Messiah

While before the Jewish authorities, including high priest, Matthew records that Jesus remained silent. And the high priest said to him, "I adjure you by the living God, tell us if you are the Christ, the Son of God" (Matt. 26:63). Everything was riding on the next words to proceed out of Jesus' mouth about his claim. Was he in fact the *"Messiah?"* Guthrie rightly notes that

In the Old Testament much is said, especially in the prophets about the coming messianic age which offered bright prospects to people of God (cf. Isa. 26-29; 40ff.; Ezek. 40-48; Dan. 12; Joel 2:28-3:21) but little is said about the Messiah. The title is nowhere used of the coming deliverer. Indeed, the agent for inaugurating the coming age was God himself. But although the absolute use of the term "Messiah" does not occur, there are various uses of the word in a qualified way, such as the Lord's Messiah (i.e., anointed one).[655]

Jesus then completely seals his fate with his reply. "Jesus said to him, 'You have said so. But I tell you, from now on you will see the Son of Man seated at the right hand of Power and coming on the clouds of heaven'" (26:64).

After Jesus' triumphant resurrection, ascension, and sending of the Holy Spirit into the world, the Apostle Paul teases out the implications of the gospel and expresses not only a rejection of what many Jews still believed but proclaimed that the Messiah is the end of the law! He writes in Romans 10:

Brothers, my heart's desire and prayer to God for them is that they may be saved. For I bear them witness that they have a zeal for God, but not according to knowledge. For, being ignorant of the righteousness of God, and seeking to establish their own, they did not submit to God's righteousness. For Christ is the end of the law for righteousness to everyone who believes (Rom. 10:1-4).

Indeed, for those who had rejected to now come to receive the righteousness of God's Messiah, is again the message of grace proclaimed. Those deserving the wage of death for sin receive eternal life (Rom. 3:23, 6:23). Such is the position of honor for God's children. The Jewish leaders who *shamed* Jesus through mockings, beatings, and sought to erase him from history subsequently found that he was, in fact, the long-awaited King of Israel, Savior-God, and Messiah; for those who would repent and trust him they found themselves *honored.*

We now turn to the final full facet of the kaleidoscope, and briefly examine the honor Christ extends to the Romans and how it is *intrinsic* to some of their own sociological values, though articulated in Kingdom of God vernacular.

Lord, Glory, and Status: The Romans and the Honor of Jesus

Lord

Though the language of *"lordship"* is uncommon in today's Western context, the ancient Romans were well-acquainted with the term. Guthrie points out that "the word 'lord' was used as a title of respect in the world of the NT period. It was a title of courtesy when addressing a superior. An extended use of it was in addressing the

---

[655] Guthrie, New Testament Theology, 237.

Roman emperor or pagan deity (such as Sarapsis or Isis). It was therefore widely used in the Gentile world."[656]

However, the word *"lord"* was not merely lifted out of the Roman context and "recycled" in light of the death and resurrection of Jesus in order to combat emperor worship. Rather, the Roman emperor cult worship did not surface until the second century AD.[657] Thus, for Jesus to be proclaimed all throughout the Roman Empire amongst peasants and kings as "Lord" thus preemptively invited all who would come into the second century an opportunity to yield to his saving grace and receive eternal life rather than be crushed into submission of the "lord Caesar" which was typical Roman protocol. Indeed, people from every Roman class were welcome to dwell with the Lord Jesus (for example, Gal. 3:24-27) whereas only a very few elites would ever have the ear of the Emperor. Because Jesus is exalted above the Emperor, this too, speaks profoundly to the honor extended to every citizen of Rome; they were provided the opportunity to become citizens of heaven. We now turn to our attention to the glory of Rome and the glory of Christ in the Church.

Glory

The idea of "glory" permeated the entire Roman Empire. From childhood on through life, the glory of Rome was the heartbeat of every citizen. By the second century, Rome had approximately 65 million in population. Rome covered about one point five million square kilometers and built impressive cities throughout. Glory was everywhere. Roman historian, Livy once commented,

> It is not without good reason that gods and men chose this place to build our city: these hills with their pure air; this convenient river by which crops may be floated down from the interior and foreign commodities brought up; a sea handy to our needs, but far enough away to guard us from foreign fleets; our situation in the very centre of Italy. All these advantages shape this most favoured of sites into a city destined for glory.[658]

There are multiple places in which the concept of glory is spoken of as being in the church. However, because of space restrictions, we will limit ourselves to just one instance. The Apostle Peter, writing from "Babylon" (1 Pet. 5:13), addresses several regions in the Roman Empire. He opens his letter mentioning the specific areas: "To those who are elect exiles of the Dispersion in Pontus, Galatia, Cappadocia, Asia, and Bithynia" (1:1). In writing to Roman citizens, Peter first reminds them that they were not merely born into the empire and thus a "citizen" of Rome but that they were "elect," chosen by God, caused to "be born again to a living hope through the resurrection of Jesus Christ from the dead, to an inheritance that is imperishable, undefiled, and

---

[656] Guthrie, New Testament Theology, 291.

[657] L. W. Hurtado. "Lord," in *Dictionary of Paul and His Letters* (Downers Grove: IVP, 1993), 561.

[658] Livy, *Roman History* (V.54.4).

unfading, kept in heaven for you, who by God's power are being guarded through faith for a salvation ready to be revealed in the last time" (vv.4-5).

Such was the incredible statement of one's identity and status. It must not be omitted that they were not merely counted among the elect at no expense to God. Before speaking of the glory, he speaks of the penal sacrifice of Christ on the cross: "For Christ also suffered once for sins, the righteous for the unrighteous, that he might bring us to God, being put to death in the flesh but made alive in the spirit" (3:18).

However, the recipients of 1 Peter were suffering severe persecution from the Empire. Though while they were prized by God (honor), they were despised in the world (shame). Because they had refused to pursue the glory of Rome and rather the glory of God, Peter admonishes the churches, "But rejoice insofar as you share Christ's sufferings, that you may also rejoice and be glad when his glory is revealed. If you are insulted for the name of Christ, you are blessed, because the Spirit of glory and of God rests upon you" (4:13-14). The "spirit of glory and of God rests upon you" is strong wording from the Apostle. This indicates an unusual fullness of the presence of the Holy Spirit to bless, to strengthen and to give a foretaste of heavenly glory.[659] Interestingly, when Peter speaks of the spirit and glory of God resting upon his people, it did not carry with it typical triumphalist overtones as was so common to Rome. Rather,

> This experience of the Spirit of God is what Jesus promised in Matthew 10:19-20, "when they deliver you up ... for what you are to say will be given you in that hour; for it is not you who speak, but the Spirit of your Father speaking through you" (Mark 13:11; Luke 12:11-12). Stephen experienced the glory of God in his martyrdom (Acts 7:55; he was, of course, a man full of the Spirit, 6:15), and so would other martyrs later (Mart. Pol. 2:2; Pss. Perp. and Fel. 1:3; Eusebius, *Eccl. Hist.* 5.1.34-35). Thus those suffering for Christ experience through the Spirit now the glory they are promised in the future (1 Pet. 1:7, 5:4; cf. 1 Cor. 4:17; Col. 3:4). Indeed, their very suffering is a sign that the reputation (glory) of God is seen in them, that the Spirit rests upon them. They indeed count themselves as blessed.[660]

We now turn the kaleidoscope one last time to see how Jesus extends glory to Romans in elevating one's status to being "co-heirs with Christ."

Status

As mentioned above, the Roman world was strictly divided into two classes, the Elites, and the Non-Elites. Within those respective categories, there were varying degrees of honor (for the elites) and dishonor (for the non-elites). Because identity in the Roman world was ascribed by birth (and achieved by accomplishments), the lines were drawn for one's entire life with the extremely rare exception of one rising out of non-elite status. As has been covered thoroughly in chapter four under "propitiation,"

---

[659] Grudem, Wayne A. *An Introduction and Commentary: Tyndale New Testament Commentaries,* vol. 17, *1 Peter* (Downers Grove, IL: InterVarsity Press, 1988).

[660] P. H. Davids, *NICNT: The First Epistle of Peter* (Grand Rapids, MI: William B. Eerdmans Publishing, 1990), 167-168.

Paul spoke to the Romans very plainly about the wrath of God in the death of Christ. Furthermore, we discussed throughout the vertical paradigm and usage of the kaleidoscope that each member of the Trinity now relates to each "child of God" on a familial level (*Abba*, Brother, Comforter). This speaks volumes to those who come from collectivist societies (honor-shame).

Paul writes,

> For you did not receive the spirit of slavery to fall back into fear, but you have received the Spirit of adoption as sons, by whom we cry, "*Abba*! Father!" The Spirit himself bears witness with our spirit that we are children of God, and if children, then heirs—heirs of God and fellow heirs with Christ, provided we suffer with him in order that we may also be glorified with him (8:15-17).

For a Roman citizen to hear that he or she is a child of God and fellow heir with Christ, regardless of family origin or accomplishments in life would sound utterly foreign. Such is the grace of God. The status of being a *"fellow heir"* communicates "that Christians inherit the blessings of God's kingdom only through, and in, Christ. We, 'the sons of God,' are such by virtue of our union with the one who is *the* heir of all God's promises (see Mark 12:10-12; Gl. 3:18-19; Heb. 1:2)."[661]

Thus, what we have briefly examined throughout this chapter is that through the penal sacrifice of Jesus and his triumphal resurrection, he bestows unique honors intrinsic to the sociological contexts that shamed him to death. Such is grace. Such is the work of our loving *Abba*, Triumphant Older Brother, and Powerful Holy Spirit.

Summary

In this chapter, attempts have been made to integrate the doctrine of PSA with the topic of "honor and shame" by discussions on several related themes. Below are two tables, published in Chinese by Enoch Wan in 1999, that can sum up our discussion well.

---

[661] Moo, *Romans*, 505.

Figure 14 - Honor and Shame[662]

Honor and Shame	The Son	Mankind
Glory/honor (prior to the fall of man)	— Pre-incarnation with honor (John 17:1-5)	— Created in God's image (Gen. 1:26-28; 2:7) — crowned with honor and glory (Ps. 8:4-5) — Designated dominion (Gen. 1:26-28; Ps. 8:6) — Naked but not ashamed (Gen. 2:25)
Shame (post-fall)	— Incarnation: self-emptying (kenosis), suffered shameful death at the cross (Phil. 2:5-8) — Cursed for mankind (Deut. 21:23; 2 Cor. 5:21; Gal. 3:13) — Forsaken by the Father (Matt. 27:46; Mark 15:34)	— Shamefully hiding from God (Gen. 3:8-10 — Corrupted humanity (total depravity), (Gen. 6:5-6) — Cursed and punished (Gen. 3:15-19; 6:7) — God clothed man with leather to cover his shame (Gen. 3:21)
Glory/honor (post-reconciliation)	Glory/honor: — Exalted...name above all names...to the glory of God the Father (Phil. 2:9-11) — Seated at the right hand of the Father (Mark 16:19; Eph. 1:20) — Superior to angels (Heb. 1:4) — Judge all (Acts 17:31)	— in Christ – image of God restored (Eph. 4:24) — in Christ – a new creation (2 Cor. 5:17) — transforming by H.S. (Rom. 12:1-2) — Reconciled with God, glory to judge angels (1 Cor. 6:3)

Figure 15 - Relational theology:

The reconciliation of the created order with the Triune God (Wan 1999:124-126)

---

[662] Enoch Wan, *Sino-theology* (Canada: Christian Witness Press 1999 [in Chinese]).

RECONCIL-IATION	HUMANITY	NATURAL ORDER
Necessity	At enmity with God by sin (Rom. 5:1-11; Col. 1:21) Under the wrath of God (Rom. 5:9)	Groaning... redemption (Rom. 8:18-23)
Way	By God's grace in Christ (objective) (2 Cor. 5:19), and self (subjective) (2 Cor. 5:20) By the atoning death of the Son (Rom 5:10; Col. 1:21-22 By the cross...enmity...reconciled (Eph. 2:16; Col. 1:20)	The Son at the cross reconciling all (Col. 1:20)
Consequence	Reconciled to be citizens of heaven (Phil. 3:20), children of God's household and at peace with one another (Eph. 2:11-22) Reconciled with the ministry of reconciliation ... Gospel of peace (2 Cor. 5:18-19) Reconciled to be holy and blameless (Col. 1:21-22)	Salvation (already-but-not yet) (Rom. 8:22-25)

CHAPTER 8

PRACTICAL IMPLICATIONS FOR CHRISTIAN MINISTRY IN NORTH AMERICAN CONTEXT

Introduction: Relational and Practical Implications for Christian Ministry

Applying the doctrine of PSA to a relational paradigm carries with it many effects for Christian thought and ministry in the 21st century. It has been repeatedly shown throughout the book that there are indeed both *vertical* and *horizontal* implications surrounding the doctrine of PSA when properly understood biblically, historically, theologically, hermeneutically, and relationally. The metaphor of a kaleidoscope has served to integrate several Scriptural-relational truths while employing the "anchoring color" of PSA. Because PSA belongs to Systematic Theology and is relational in both essence and functionality, the image of a kaleidoscope's movement and interaction with other facets and colors has served to keep multiple Scriptural-relational concepts present in the mind of the thinker.

Practical Implications for Christian Ministry: Thinking About and Relating to the Triune God (Vertical)

The doctrine of PSA implies that Christians need to better understand both the attributes of God (i.e., wrath, holiness, and love) and the actions of the Father specifically in the death of Jesus "who was delivered up for our trespasses and raised for our justification" (Rom. 4:25). Scripture is overwhelmingly clear that God does exercise his just *wrath* and the Biblical authors do not seek to hide this reality out of shame or embarrassment, nor do they attempt to make the gospel message more palatable to a broader audience by presenting a God without wrath. Instead, repentance of sin is preached to God's image bearers, who "remain under the wrath of God" (John 3:36) and therefore the coming wrath of God serves as a motivation for missions and evangelism. For example, Jesus' forerunner, John the Baptizer, rebuked the Pharisees and warned them "to flee the wrath to come!" (Matt. 3:7; Luke 3:7).

Equally true, throughout Scripture we find that God loves passionately and pardons sinners graciously. These truths about God the Father are in neither competition nor contradiction but are *complimentary* as both are present in the nature and character of the Triune God (see above: the *cooperation* between the Father and Son working together to accomplish redemption). Practically speaking, how a Christian thinks about the God that he or she worships impacts not only one's theology but ontology as well as sociological relationships. The Protestant preacher of the 1960s, A. W. Tozer wrote, "What comes into our minds when we think about God is the most important thing about us."[663] Though our knowledge of God is limited we must not conclude that God is unknowable. Rather, by grace, through faith,

---

[663] Tozer, Knowledge of the Holy, 1.

empowered by the indwelling Holy Spirit, Christians no longer stand before the Father, Son, and Holy Spirit as Judge; due to what is accomplished in the aversion of wrath in PSA, the enemies of God now become the children of God and relate to each member of the Trinity in radically new ways (vertical). Believers now are tenderly and graciously adopted and embraced by God and approach him as their wise, "*Abba*, Father" (Rom. 8:15; Gal. 4:6). Because of what PSA accomplishes, the children of God now relate to Jesus the Son as our older Brother who is sympathetic towards us, advocates on our behalf, and loves us unconditionally. The third vertical relationship that changes is how believers relate to the Holy Spirit; namely, that he is the Comforter, who is present, guides, and empowers the children of God.

Practical Implications for Christian Ministry: Thinking About and Relating to Oneself (Horizontal)

The doctrine of PSA applied through the relational paradigm also implies how Christians think about and relate to themselves as individuals. Feelings of guilt, shame, and fear all must be understood in light of the fact that though once enemies of God, the children of God are no longer under God's just wrath rather are now coheirs with Christ. This carries tremendous implications on how one understands his or her fundamental identity. This is ever so important given our current climate in North American culture as one's *identity* is constantly undergoing challenges – from sexuality, to politics, to financial stability believers must constantly remain grounded in our identity as those who were once enemies of God **now** are the children of God by, in, and through Jesus and sealed by the Holy Spirit.

Practical Implications for Christian Ministry: Thinking About and Relating to the Church (Horizontal)

From God, to self, the doctrine of PSA applied relationally also impacts how one views the local Church. Throughout Scripture familial language is used to describe these relationships and, therefore, fellow believers are not merely people who coldly confess the same creedal affirmations about who God is and what he has done and will do but are to truly relate to one another as children of *Abba*, Jesus' younger siblings, and recipients of the Comfort of the Holy Spirit. The community therefore practices the "ministry of reconciliation" and seeks to express itself doxologically, in servitude, and forgiveness.

Practical Implications for Christian Ministry: Thinking About and Relating to Unbelievers (Horizontal)

Because the doctrine of PSA calls attention to the reality that the "wrath of God remains" on unbelievers (John 3:36), this ought to create in followers of Christ hearts of compassion and an urgency to proclaim the gospel of God's saving grace extended toward fallen image bearers and admonish them to "Flee the wrath to come." (Matt. 3:7; Luke 3:7). As the Westminster Catechism reminds us, "the chief end of man is to glorify God and enjoy him forever." God's grace reveals his glory and thus the motive for engaging unbelievers with this message of saving grace is grounded in the glory of God and joy of his people. Unbelievers are not merely projects to be maintained but image bearers to be redeemed by the God who sent his Son in the image and likeness of men to reconcile his people to himself. The consolation of the believer is to not only feel compassion towards his or her neighbor but to lovingly, winsomely, and intelligently communicate the gospel in a way that is both faithful to Scripture and contextualized to the hearer.

Practical Implications for Christian Ministry: Preaching (Horizontal)

The doctrine of PSA is present throughout both Old and New Testaments and should be present in the preaching of the gospel. Though this is obviously not the only model of the atonement, it is important that words like "wrath" and "holiness," "propitiation," "love," and "grace" be explained clearly in the public preaching of the gospel.

Practical Implications for Ministry: Pastoral Care (Horizontal)

Those entrusted with carrying out pastoral care in the local church greatly serve those who are suffering by not only being *familiar* with concepts of God's justice, judgment, wrath, grace, compassion, and love but know how to practically apply these truths relationally both vertically and horizontally **after** listening well to the hurting and distressed. Undoubtedly, the children of God must be instructed in their identity; only from that vantage point can we move into the horizontal ministry of reconciliation.

Practical Implications for Ministry: Worship (Vertical and Horizontal)

In three of the hymns included in the NT (Phil. 2:5-11, Col. 1:15-20, Heb. 1:1-3), we find the doctrine of PSA present in the context of doxological thinking and practice. Therefore, very practically, those responsible for leading congregations in worship would do well to remind the people of God in weekly worship that our identity as God's children is secure and that we may worship our God freely, boldly, and passionately because we are no longer under God's wrath, and are to come before his throne of grace boldly in worship.

Practical Implications for Ministry: Forgiving Community (Horizontal)

One very practical implication of the doctrine of PSA understood through the relational paradigm is the *kind* of community that is created, namely, that forgiveness amongst its members is more than something that sounds virtuous and moral, rather functions as a prerequisite for worship (Matt. 5:24), is to be ongoing amongst believers (Matt. 18:21-22), as it gives evidence of the presence of the Holy Spirit (Eph. 4:25-32).

Practical Implications for Ministry: Serving Community (Horizontal)

It can be argued that Christian servitude is grounded first and foremost in the atoning work of Jesus. In the well-known passage of Mark 10:35-45, the disciples are found arguing over who will be the greatest in the Kingdom of God. They then enter a discussion with Jesus wherein Jesus instructs them in the greatness found hidden in serving others. Christ then describes his ransoming death as the ultimate act of *serving* (10:45). Practically speaking, it genuinely follows that those who would come after Jesus as his disciples cultivate the posture and practice of servitude.

Therefore, the aim of this book has been to offer fresh theological research into Biblical doctrine and to tease out many relational implications for effective Christian witness and ministry in the 21st century.

Summary

In this chapter, we have summarized much research and discussed practical implications of PSA in a North American context, from the perspective of relational paradigm with both vertical and horizontal dimensions, including the Triune God, the Church, and unbelievers. Christian ministries such as preaching, pastoral care, worship, forgiving community, and serving community in the North American context would be well benefitted by thinking seriously about what has been presented.

CHAPTER 9

CONCLUSION

This book begins with the clearly stated purpose of taking the research of Alex Early for his doctoral dissertation and turning it into this present book. The purpose is two-fold: firstly, to help Christians think correctly and articulate themselves well regarding this precious aspect of the atonement; secondly, to take the doctrine of PSA from the academy to ministries on the mission field and local church by utilizing Enoch Wan's many years of missiological research and prior publications towards developing a more robust relational theology for the 21st century. Much of the motive for this is provided where we find ourselves in contemporary society as it pertains to relational lack. The phenomenal and explosive proliferation of social media over the last decade is strong evidence that modern human beings are in desperate need for genuine relational connection between God, self, and others. In a digital age that is more connected electronically than ever before, loneliness, anxiety, and a sense of estrangement is found across the globe. Beyond being relationally disconnected, issues surrounding ethnic discrimination, phobias of every sort, and the human conscience that consistently bears witness that something is terribly wrong are all addressed by the Holy Trinity in the redemption wrought by the Father, Son, and Holy Spirit.

It is our hope that the years of prayer, travel, research, and writing of the authors would be of help to you as you seek to grow as a disciple of Jesus, our older Brother, find comfort in the Holy Spirit, to the Glory of God our *Abba*, Father.

BIBLIOGRAPHY

Abbott, Thomas K. *A Critical and Exegetical Commentary on the Epistles to the Ephesians and to the Colossians.* Edinburgh, England: T&T Clark, 1969.

_____. *The Epistles to the Ephesians and to the Colossians: A Critical and Exegetical Commentary.* Edinburgh, England: T&T Clark, 1979.

Adamson, James. *NICNT: The Epistle of James.* Grand Rapids, MI: Eerdmans, 1976.

Alison, Dale. *Studies in Matthew: Interpretation Past and Present.* Grand Rapids, MI: Baker Books, 2012.

Allen, David. "The Authorship of Hebrews: Historical Survey of the Lukan Theory." *Criswell Theological Review* 8, no. 2 (Spring 2011): 3-18.

Anselm. *Cur Deus Homo: Why God Became Man.* Pickerington, OH: Beloved Publishing, 2014.

Aquinas, Thomas. *Summa Theologica.* Translated by Fathers of the English Dominican Province. New York, NY: Christian Classics, 1981.

Arnold, Clinton. *Power and Magic: The Concept of Power in Ephesians.* Eugene, OR: Wifp & Stock, 2001.

Attridge, Harold. *Hermeneia, A Critical and Historical Commentary on the Bible. Hebrews: A Commentary on the Epistle to the Hebrews.* Minneapolis, MN: Fortress Press, 1989.

Augustine. *On the Holy Trinity; Doctrinal Treatises; Moral Treatises.* Edited by Anthony Uyl. Woodstock, Ontario: Devoted Publishing, 2017.

Aune, David. *Word Biblical Commentary.* Vol. 52b, *Revelation 6-16.* Nashville, TN: Thomas Nelson Publishers, 1998.

Averbeck, Richard. *New International Dictionary of Old Testament Theology and Exegesis.* Vol. 2. Grand Rapids, MI: Zondervan, 2012.

Awad, Najib. *Persons in Relation: An Essay on the Trinity and Ontology.* Minneapolis, MN: Fortress Press, 2014.

Barabas, Steven. "Judgment." In *New International Bible Dictionary.* Grand Rapids, MI: Zondervan, 1999.

Barnett, Paul. *NICNT: 2 Corinthians.* Grand Rapids, MI: Eerdmans, 1997.

Barr, James. "Etymologies and Related Arguments." In *The Semantics of Biblical Language.* London, England: Oxford University Press, 1961.

Barrett, Charles Kingsley. *Black's New Testament Commentary: A Commentary on the Epistle to the Romans.* 1957. Reprint, New York, NY: Harper, 1991.

_____. *The Gospel According to St. John: An Introduction with Commentary and Notes on the Greek Text.* 2nd ed. London, England: SPCK, 1978.

_____. *Freedom and Obligation: A Study of the Epistle to the Galatians.* London, England: SPCK, 1985.

Barrick, William D. "Penal Substitution in the Old Testament." *TMSJ* 20, no. 2 (Fall 2009).

Barth, Karl B. *Church Dogmatics.* Vol. 1-4. Translated by G. W. Bromiley. Peabody, MA: Hendrickson Publishers, 2010.

_____. *Church Dogmatics: The Doctrine of Creation.* Vol. 3, bk. 1. Edinburgh, England: InterVarsity Press, 1972.

_____. *Church Dogmatics: The Doctrine of Reconciliation.* Vol. 4, bk. 1. Translated by G. W. Bromiley. Peabody, MA: Hendrickson Publishers, 2010.

_____. *Church Dogmatics: The Doctrine of Reconciliation.* Vol. 4, bk. 2. Edinburgh, England: T.&T. Clark, 1958.

_____. *Church Dogmatics: The Doctrine of the Word of God.* Vol. 1, bk. 1. Translated by G. T. Thomson. New York, NY: T&T Clark, 2004.

Bauckham, Richard. *The Bible in Politics: How to Read the Bible Politically.* Louisville, KY: Westminster, 1989.

Bauernfeind, Otto. "ἁπλῶς." In *Theological Dictionary of the New Testament,* edited by Gerhard Kittle. Translated by Geoffrey W. Bromiley. Vol. 1. Grand Rapids, MI: Eerdmans, 1965.

Beale, G. K. *NIGTC: The Book of Revelation.* Grand Rapids, MI: Eerdmans, 1999.

Beasley-Murray, George R. *Baptism in the New Testament.* Grand Rapids, MI: Eerdmans, 1973.

_____. *Word Biblical Commentary.* Vol. 36, *John.* 2nd ed. Nashville, TN: Thomas Nelson Publishers, 1990.

_____. *New Century Bible: The Book of Revelation.* London, England: Butler and Tanner, 1974.

Bediako, Kwame. *Jesus and the Gospel in Africa: History and Experience.* New York, NY: Orbis Books, 2004.

Belousek, Darrin. *Atonement, Justice, and Peace: The Message of the Cross and the Mission of the Church.* Grand Rapids, MI: Eerdmans, 2012.

Bennema, Cornelis. "The Giving of the Spirit in John 19-20: Another Round." In *The Spirit and Christ,* edited by I. H. Marshall, V. Rabens, and C. Bennema.

Berger, Peter. *The Sacred Canopy: Elements of a Sociological Theory of Religion.* New York, NY: Anchor, 1995.

Berkhof, Hendrikus. *The Doctrine of the Holy Spirit.* Louisville, KY: Westminster John Knox Press, 1986.

Best, Harold. *Ephesians: An Exegetical Commentary.* Grand Rapids, MI: Baker Academic, 2002.

Biederwolf, William Edward and William Moorehead. *A Help to the Study of the Holy Spirit.* Whitefish, MT: Literary Licensing, 2013.

Blench, J. W. *Preaching in England in the Late 15th and 16th Centuries.* Oxford, England: Basil Blackwell, 1964.

Blight, Richard. *An Exegetical Summary of 1 and 2 Thessalonians.* Dallas, TX: Summer Institute of Linguistics, 1989.

Blocher, Henri. "Atonement." In *Dictionary for Theological Interpretation of the Bible,* edited by Craig Bartholomew, Daniel Treier, and N. T. Wright, general editor Kevin Vanhoozer. London, England: SPCK, 2005.

_____. "Biblical Metaphors and the Doctrine of the Atonement." *JETS* 47, no. 4 (December 2004): 629-45.

Bloesch, Donald. *Jesus Christ: Savior and Lord.* Downers Grove, IL: IVP, 1997.

Blomberg, Craig. *Matthew.* Nashville, TN: Broadman Press, 1992.

Blomberg, Craig, Mariam Kamell, and Clinton Arnold, eds. *Zondervan Exegetical Commentary on the New Testament: James.* Grand Rapids, MI: Zondervan, 2008.

Boersma, Hans. *Violence, Hospitality, and the Cross: Appropriating the Atonement Tradition.* Grand Rapids, MI: Baker Academic, 2006.

Brown, Joanne Carlson and Carol R. Bohn, eds. "For God So Loved the World." In *Christianity, Patriarchy, and Abuse: A Feminist Critique.* New York, NY: Pilgrim Press, 1989.

Brown, Raymond. *The Gospel According to John 1–X11.* Anchor Bible Series, 29. New York, NY: Double Day, 1982.

Bruce, F. F. *NICNT: Acts.* Grand Rapids, MI: Eerdmans, 1988.

_____. *The Canon of Scripture.* Downers Grove, IL: InterVarsity Press, 1988.

_____. *NIGTC: The Epistle to the Galatians.* Grand Rapids, MI: Paternoster and William B. Eerdmans Publishing, 1988.

_____. *NICNT: The Epistle to the Hebrews.* Grand Rapids, MI: Eerdmans, 2012.

_____. *NICNT: The Epistles to the Colossians, to Philemon, and to the Ephesians.* Grand Rapids, MI: Eerdmans, 1984.

_____. *The Gospel and Epistles of John.* Grand Rapids, MI: Eerdmans, 1983.

Bruggemann, Walter. *Isaiah, 40-66.* Louisville, KY: John Knox Press, 1998.

_____. "The Human Person as Yahweh's Partner." In *Theology of the Old Testament: Testimony, Dispute, Advocacy.* Minneapolis, MN: Fortress Press, 1997.

Bruner, Frederick. *Matthew: A Commentary.* Vol. 2, *The Church Book: Matthew 13-18.* Grand Rapids, MI: William B. Eerdmans Publishing, 1990.

Brunner, Emil. *Dogmatics I: The Christian Name of God.* Translated by Olive Wyon. Cambridge, England: James Clarke Company Limited, n.d.

_____. *Man in Revolt.* New York, NY: Scribner's Press, 1939.

_____. *The Mediator: A Study of the Central Doctrine of the Christian Faith.* London, England: Lutterworth Press, 1949.

Budd, Phillip. *Word Biblical Commentary.* Vol. 5, *Numbers.* Waco, TX: Word Books Publisher, 1984.

Burge, Gary. *NIV Application Commentary: John.* Grand Rapids, MI: Zondervan, 2000.

Burke, Trevor. *Adopted into God's Family: Exploring a Pauline Metaphor.* Downers Grove, IL: IVP Academic, 2006.

Buschel, Fredrick. "*Hilaskomai.*" In *Theological Dictionary of the New Testament.* Vol. 3. Grand Rapids, MI: Eerdmans, 1965.

Calvin, John. *Commentary on II Corinthians.* Grand Rapids, MI: Baker Books, 1974.

_____. *A Commentary on Genesis.* Translated by J. King. London, England: Banner of Truth, 1965.

_____. *Institutes.* 2.17.3; 2.16.5 quoted in Martin Davie, "Dead to Sin and Alive to God," *SBET* 19, no. 2 (Autumn 2001): 158-94.

_____. *James.* Grand Rapids, MI: Baker Books, 1974.

Campbell, J. *The Nature of the Atonement.* Grand Rapids, MI: William B. Eerdmans Publishing, 1996.

Carson, Don A. *Expositor's Bible Commentary.* Vol. 8, *Matthew, Mark, and Luke.* Edited by Frank E. Gaebelein. Grand Rapids, MI: Zondervan, 1984-99.

_____. "Atonement in Romans 3:21-26: God Presented Him as a Propitiation." In *The Glory of the Atonement*, edited by C. Hill and F. James III.

_____. *Becoming Conversant with the Emerging Church: Understanding a Movement and Its Implications.* Grand Rapids, MI: Zondervan, 2005.

_____. "Is Faith in Christ Without Evidence Superior Faith? In *The Spirit and Christ,* edited by I. H. Marshall, V. Rabens, and C. Bennema.

_____. *The Difficult Doctrine of the Love of God.* Wheaton, IL: Crossway, 1999.

Carter, Charles, ed. "'Harmartiology': Evil, the Marrer of God's Creative Purpose and Work." In *A Contemporary Wesleyan Theology: Biblical, Systematic, and Practical.* 2 vols. Grand Rapids, MI: Zondervan, 1983.

Cassuto, Umberto. *A Commentary on the Book of Genesis.* Part 1, *From Adam to Noah.* Jerusalem, Israel: Magnes Press, 1961.

Chalke, Steve. "The Redemption of the Cross." In *The Atonement Debate,* edited by D. Tidball, D. Hilborn, and J. Thacker.

Chalke, Steve and Alan Mann. *The Lost Message of Jesus.* Grand Rapids, MI: Zondervan, 2003.

Childs, Brevard. *Isaiah: A Commentary.* Louisville, KY: Westminster John Knox Press, 2001.

Chrysostom. In *Ancient Christian Commentary on Scripture: 1-2 Corinthians,* edited by Thomas Oden. New York, NY: Routledge, 1999.

Chrysostom. "What Lowliness Accomplished." In *On the Incomprehensible Nature of God.* 8.46 – 47. Vol. 2 of *Mark: Ancient Christian Commentary*, edited by Thomas Oden and Christopher Hall. Downers Grove, IL: IVP, 2005.

Chubb, Thomas. *The True Gospel of Jesus Christ Vindicated and also a Vindication of the Author's Short Dissertation on Providence.* Gale ECCO, Print Editions, 2010.

Clarke, W. Norris, SJ. *The One and the Many: A Contemporary Thomistic Metaphysics.* Notre Dame, IN: University of Notre Dame Press, 2001.

Collinson, Sylvia Wilkey. *Making Disciples: The Significance of Jesus' Educational Methods for Today's Church.* Eugene, OR: Wipf & Stock Publishers, 2004.

Cranfield, C. E. *A Critical and Exegetical Commentary.* Vol. 1, *The Epistle to the Romans.* International Critical Commentary Series. Edinburgh, England: T&T Clark, 1979.

Crawford, Thomas. *Doctrine of the Holy Scripture.* Edinburgh, England: W. Blackwood, 1871.

Cresson, Bruce C. *Holman Illustrated Bible Dictionary.* Nashville, TN: Holman Reference, 2003.

Culpepper, R. *Interpreting the Atonement.* Grand Rapids, MI: Eerdmans, 1966.

Cyprian. *De dom. orat.* 23-24. In CSEL 3, edited by G. Hartel.

Cyprian. *De zel. et liv.* 17-18. In CCSL 3A, edited by M. Simonetti.

Dahl, N. A. "Cosmic Dimensions and Religious Knowledge (Ephesians 3:18)." In *Jesus and Paulus: Festschrift for Werner Georg Kümmel's 70th Birthday,* edited by E. E. Ellis and E. Grasser. Gottingen, Germany: Vandenhoeck und Ruprecht, 1975, 57-75.

Dale, R. W. *The Atonement.* London, England: Congregational Union of England and Wales, 1896.

Daniel, Stephen. "Postmodern Concepts of God and Edwards' Trinitarian Ontology." In *Edwards in Our Time: Jonathan Edwards and the Shaping of American Religion,* edited by Hyun Lee Sang and Allen C. Guelzo. Grand Rapids, MI: Eerdmans, 1999.

Danker, Frederick. "ὀργή." In *Greek-English Lexicon of the New Testament and Other Early Christian Literature.* 3rd ed (BDAG). Chicago, IL: The University of Chicago Press, 1957.

Davids, P. H. "Adoption." In *Evangelical Dictionary of Theology,* edited by Walter A. Elwell. Grand Rapids, MI: Baker Book House, 2004

———. *NICNT: The First Epistle of Peter.* Grand Rapids, MI: William B. Eerdmans Publishing, 1990.

Davie, Martin. "Dead to Sin and Alive to God," *SBET* 19, no. 2 (Autumn 2001): 158-94.

Davies, Oliver. *A Theology of Compassion.* Norwich, England: Hymns Ancient and Modern Ltd, 2001.

Dawkins, Richard. *The God Delusion.* New York, NY: Houghton Mifflin, 2006.

Deddo, Gary. *Karl Barth's Theology of Relations: Trinitarian, Christological, and Human: Towards an Ethic of the Family.* Eugene, OR: Wipf & Stock, 2015.

Demarest, Bruce A. and Gordon R. Lewis. *Integrative Theology: Historical, Biblical, Systematic, Apologetic, Practical: Three Volumes in One.* Vol. 2. Grand Rapids, MI: Zondervan, 1996.

DeSilva, David. *An Introduction to the New Testament: Contexts, Methods, and Ministry Formation.* Downers Grove, IL: IVP, 2018.

_____. _Honor, Patronage, Kinship, and Purity: Unlocking New Testament Culture._ Downers Grove, IL: IVP, 2000.

_____. _Perseverance in Gratitude: A Socio-Rhetorical Commentary on the Epistle "to the Hebrews."_ Grand Rapids, MI: Eerdmans, 2000.

Dictionary of Biblical Imagery: An Encyclopedic Exploration of the Images, Symbols, Motifs, Metaphors, Figures of Speech, and Literary Patterns of the Bible. Edited by Leland Ryken, James Wilhoit, and Tremper Longman III. Downers Grove, IL: IVP, 1998

Dodd, Charles H. _Epistle of Paul to the Romans._ New York, NY: Harper & Row, 1932.

_____. _The Moffatt New Testament Commentary._ Vol. 16, _The Johannine Epistles._ London, England: Hodder & Stoughton, 1946.

_____. "_Hilaskesthai_, its Cognates, Derivatives, and Synonyms, in the Septuagint." _Journal of Theological Studies_ 32, no. 128 (July 1931): 352-360.

Dowling, Melissa Barden. _Clemency and Cruelty in the Roman World._ Ann Arbor, MI: University of Michigan Press, 2006.

Driver, John. _Understanding the Atonement for the Mission of the Church._ Eugene, OR: Wipf & Stock, 2005.

Dunn, James. "The Body of Christ in Paul." In _Worship, Theology, and Ministry in the Early Church,_ edited by Michael J. Wilkins and Terence Paige. Sheffield, England: Sheffield Academic Press, 1992.

_____. _Black's New Testament Commentaries: The Epistle to the Galatians._ London, England: A & C Black, 1993.

_____. _Jesus and the Spirit: A Study of the Religious and Charismatic Experience of Jesus and the First Christians as Reflected in the New Testament._ London, England: SCM Press, 1975.

_____. "Paul's Understanding of the Death of Jesus." In _Reconciliation and Hope: New Testament Essays on Atonement and Eschatology._ Presented to L. L. Morris on his 60th birthday. Carlisle, PA: Paternoster Press, 1974.

_____. "Salvation Proclaimed: VI, Romans 6:1-11: Dead and Alive." _Evangelical Today_ 93 (1981-82).

Durham, John. _Word Biblical Commentary._ Vol. 3, _Exodus._ Waco, TX: Word Books, 1987.

Ebeling, Gerhard. _Luther: An Introduction to His Thought._ Philadelphia, PA: Fortress, 1972.

Eck, Diana. _A New Religious America: How a "Christian Country" Has Become the World's Most Religiously Diverse Nation._ New York, NY: Harper Collins, 2001.

Edwards, James R. "The Authority of Jesus in the Gospel of Mark." _JETS_ 37, no. 2 (June 1994): 217-233. Accessed October 14, 2015. http://www.etsjets.org/files/JETS-PDFs/37/37-2/JETS_37-2_217-233_Edwards.pdf.

_____. _The Gospel According to Mark._ Grand Rapids, MI: William B. Eerdmans Publishing, 2002.

_____. _Pillar New Testament Commentary: Mark._ Grand Rapids, MI: Eerdmans, 2002.

_____. *Sinners.* Accessed February 17, 2017. http://www.wwnorton.com/college/history/archive/resources/documents/ch03_03.htm.

Elgvin, Torleif. "The Messiah Who Was Cursed on the Tree." *themelios* 22, no.3 (October 1996).

Evans, Craigh A. *Word Biblical Commentary.* Vol. 34b, *Mark 8:27-16:20.* Nashville, TN: Thomas Nelson Publishers, 2001.

Fabella, Virginia. "Context." In *Dictionary of Third World Theologies,* edited by Virginia Fabella and R.S. Sugirtharajah. Maryknoll, PA: Orbis, 2000.

Fee, Gordon. *NICNT: The First Epistle to the Corinthians.* Grand Rapids, MI: Eerdmans Publishing, 1987.

_____. *NICNT: Paul's Letter to the Philippians.* Grand Rapids, MI: Eerdmans Publishing, 1995.

Feldman, Lewis H. and Meyer Reinhold, eds. *Jewish Life and Thought Among Greeks and Romans.* Minneapolis, MN: Augsburg Fortress Press, 1966.

Ferguson, Everett. *Backgrounds of Early Christianity.* Grand Rapids, MI: Eerdmans, 2003.

Ferguson, Sinclair B. "Image of God." In *New Dictionary of Theology,* edited by Sinclair B. Ferguson and David F. Wright. Downers Grove, IL: InterVarsity Press, 1988.

_____. *The Christian Life: A Doctrinal Introduction.* Edinburgh, England: Banner of Truth, 2013.

Fiddes, Paul. *Past Event and Present Salvation: The Christian Idea of Atonement.* London, England: Darton, Longman, and Todd, 1989.

Fiedler, Paul. *"Amartia."* In *Exegetical Dictionary of the New Testament,* vol. 1, Ἀαρών-Ἐνώχ, edited by H. Balz and G. Schneider. Grand Rapids, MI: William B. Eerdmans Publishing Company, 1980.

Fiering, Norman. *Jonathan Edwards's Moral Thought and Its British Context.* Wake Forrest, NC: University of North Carolina Press, 1981.

Filson, Floyd V. *Yesterday: A Study of Hebrews in Light of Chapter 13.* Studies in Biblical Theology, second series 4. London, England: SCM 1967.

Fish, Stanley. *Is there A Text in This Class?: The Authority of Interpretive Communities,* Cambridge, MA: Harvard University Press, 1982.

Fisher, Fred. *Commentary on 1 and 2 Corinthians.* Waco, TX: Word Books, 1975.

Forsyth, P. T. *Positive Preaching and the Modern Mind.* London, England: Hodder & Stoughton, 1909.

_____. *The Work of Christ.* London, England: Hodder & Stoughton, 1910.

Fox, Matthew. *Original Blessing: A Primer in Creation Spirituality Presented in Four Paths, Twenty-Six Themes, and Two Questions.* Santa Fe, NM: Bear & Company, 1983.

Frame, John M. *Doctrine of God: A Theology of Lordship* Grand Rapids, MI: Zondervan, 2002.

_____. *No Other God: A Response to Open Theism.* Phillipsburg, NJ: P&R Publishing, 2001.

France, Richard T. *NIGTC: The Gospel of Mark.* Grand Rapids, MI: William B. Eerdmans Publishing, 2002.

_____. *NICNT: The Gospel of Matthew.* Grand Rapids, MI: Eerdmans, 2007.

Fromm, Erich. *On Disobedience: And Other Essays.* New York, NY: Seabury Press, 1984.

Fung, Ronald. *NICNT: The Epistle to the Galatians.* Grand Rapids, MI: Eerdmans, 1988.

Gadamer, Hans-Georg "Reflections on My Philosophical Journey." In *The Philosophy of Hans-Georg Gadamer,* edited by Lewis Edwin Hahn. Chicago and LaSalle, IL: Open Court, 1997.

Gaffin, Richard B. Jr. "Atonement in the Pauline Corpus: 'The Scandal of the Cross.'" In *The Glory of the Atonement,* edited by C. Hill and F. James III.

Garland, David. *The New American Commentary.* Vol. 29, *2 Corinthians.* Nashville, TN: Broadman & Holman Publishers, 1999.

Garrett, James. *Systematic Theology: Biblical, Historical, and Evangelical.* Vol. 1. Grand Rapids, MI: William B. Eerdmans Publishing, 1990.

Geldenhuys, Norval. *Commentary on the Gospel of Luke.* London, England: Marshall, Morgan, and Scott, 1950.

George, Timothy. *The New American Commentary.* Vol. 30, *Galatians.* Nashville, TN: Broadman & Holman Publishers, 1994.

Georges, Jayson. "5 Types of Honor Shame Cultures." Accessed November 20, 2018. http://honorshame.com/types-honor-shame-cultures/.

_____. Home page: http://honorshame.com.

Girard, Rene. *Things Hidden Since the Foundation of the World.* Translated by Stephen Bann and Michael Metteer. United Kingdom: The Athlone Press, 1987.

Glancy, Jennifer A. "Boasting of Beatings (2 Corinthians 11:23-25)." *Journal of Biblical Literature* 123, no. 1 (March 2004): 99-135.

Godet, Frederic. *A Commentary on the Gospel of St. Luke.* Vol. 2. Edinburgh, England: T&T Clark, 1957.

Goldingay, John, ed. *Atonement Today: A Symposium at St. John's College, Nottingham.* London, England: SPCK, 1995.

_____. *Models for Interpretation of Scripture.* Grand Rapids, MI: Eerdmans, 2004.

_____. *Old Testament Theology.* Vol. 1, *Israel's Gospel.* Downers Grove, IL: IVP Academic, 2003.

_____. *Baker Commentary on the Old Testament Wisdom and Psalms.* Vol. 2, *Psalms 42-89.* Edited by Tremper Longman III. Grand Rapids, MI: Baker Academic, 2007.

_____. "Your Iniquities Have Made a Separation Between You and Your God." In *Atonement Today,* edited by J. Goldingay.

Green, Joel. "Kaleidoscopic View." In *The Nature of the Atonement: Four Views.* Downers Grove, IL: InterVarsity Press, 2006.

_____. "Must We Imagine the Atonement in Penal Substitutionary Terms?: Questions Caveats and a Plea." In *The Atonement Debate,* edited by D. Tidball, D. Hilborn, and J. Thacker.

_____. *NICNT: The Gospel of Luke.* Grand Rapids, MI: Eerdmans Publishing, 1997.

Green, Joel and Mark Baker. *Recovering the Scandal of the Cross: Atonement in New Testament and Contemporary Contexts.* Downers Grove, IL: InterVarsity Press, 2011.

Green, Joel, Scot McKnight, and Howard Marshall, eds. "God." In *Dictionary of Jesus and the Gospels.* Downers Grove, IL: IVP Academic, 1992.

Greenberg, Moshe. *The Anchor Yale Bible Commentaries: Ezekiel 1-20.* New Haven, CT: Yale University Press, 1983.

Greene, Colin. "Is the Message of the Cross Good News for the Twentieth Century?" In *Atonement Today,* edited by J. Goldingay.

Gregory of Nyssa. *To Abalabius, on "Not Three Gods."* Nicene and Post-Nicene Fathers, 2nd term.

Grenz, Stanley. *The Social God and the Relational Self: A Trinitarian Theology of the Imago Dei.* Louisville, KY: Westminster John Knox Press, 2001.

Grogan, Geoffrey. "The Atonement in the New Testament." In *The Atonement Debate,* edited by D. Tidball, D. Hilborn, and J. Thacker.

Groves, Alan. "Atonement in Isaiah 53: 'For He Bore the Sins of Many.'" In *The Glory of the Atonement,* edited by C. Hill and F. James III.

Grudem, Wayne A. *An Introduction and Commentary. Tyndale New Testament Commentaries.* Vol. 17, *1 Peter.* Downers Grove, IL: InterVarsity Press, 1988.

_____. *Systematic Theology: An Introduction to Biblical Doctrine.* Grand Rapids, MI: Zondervan 1994.

Gruenler, Royce. "Atonement in the Synoptic Gospels and Acts: Poured Out for the Forgiveness of Sins." In *The Glory of the Atonement,* edited by C. Hill and F. James III.

Grunlan, Stephen and Marvin Mayers. *Anthropology: A Christian Perspective.* Grand Rapids, MI: Zondervan, 1988)

Guelich, Robert. *Word Biblical Commentary.* Vol. 34a, *Mark 1-8:26.* Nashville, TN: Thomas Nelson, 1989.

Gulley, Norman. *Systematic Theology: God As Trinity.* Berrien Springs, MI: Andrews University Press, 2003.

Gundry-Volf, Judith. "Expiation, Propitiation, Mercy Seat." *DPL* (1993).

Gunton, Colin E. *Act and Being: Towards A Theology of the Divine Attributes.* Grand Rapids, MI: Eerdmans, 2003.

_____. *Actuality of Atonement: A Study of Metaphor, Rationality, and the Christian Tradition.* London, England: Bloomsbury Academic, 2003.

_____. *Father, Son, and Holy Spirit: Toward a Fully Trinitarian Theology.* New York, NY: T&T Clark, 2003.

_____. *Theology Through the Theologians: Selected Essays 1972-1995.* London, England: Bloomsbury Academic, 2003.

_____. *The Triune Creator: A Historical and Systematic Study.* Grand Rapids, MI: Eerdmans, 1997.

Guthrie, Donald. *New Testament Theology: A Thematic Study.* Downers Grove, IL: IVP, 2013.

Hagner, Donald. *Word Biblical Commentary: Matthew 1-13.* Grand Rapids, MI: Zondervan, 1995.

_____. *Word Biblical Commentary: Matthew 14-28.* Grand Rapids, MI: Zondervan, 1995.

Hamilton, Victor P. *The Book of Genesis: Chapters 1-17.* Grand Rapids, MI: Eerdmans, 1990.

Harris, H. A. "Should We Say that Personhood is Relational?" *Scottish Journal of Theology* 51, no. 2 (May 1998): 214-34.

Harris, M. J. *A Commentary on the Greek Text: The Second Epistle to the Corinthians.* Grand Rapids, MI: Eerdmans, 2005.

Harris, R. Larrid, ed. *Theological Wordbook of the Old Testament.* Vol. 2. Chicago, IL: Moody Press, 1981.

Hauwerwas, Stanley. *Matthew.* Grand Rapids, MI: Brazos Press, 2015.

Haya-Prats, Gonzalo. *Empowered Believers: The Holy Spirit in the Book of Acts.* Eugene, OR: Wipf & Stock, 2011.

Hellerman, Joseph H. *Embracing Shared Ministry: Power and Status in the Early Church and Why It Matters Today.* Grand Rapids, MI: Kregel Publishing, 2013.

Hendriksen, William. *New Testament Commentary: Galatians, Ephesians, Philippians, Colossians, and Philemon.* Grand Rapids, MI: Baker Books, 2002.

_____. *New Testament Commentary: Exposition of the Gospel of Luke.* Grand Rapids. MI: Baker Academic, 1980.

Heron, Alasdair. *The Holy Spirit: The Holy Spirit in the Bible, in the History of Christian Thought, and Recent Theology.* Louisville, KY: Westminster John Knox, 1963.

Heiron, Gary. "Wrath of God (OT)." In *Anchor Bible Dictionary,* vol. 6, edited by David Noel Freedman. New York, NY: Doubleday, 1992.

Hill, Charles. "Atonement in the Old and New Testaments." In *The Glory of the Atonement,* edited by C. Hill and F. James III.

Hill, Charles E. and Frank A. James III, eds. *The Glory of the Atonement: Biblical, Historical, and Practical Perspectives: Essays in Honor of Roger Nicole.* Downers Grove, IL: InterVarsity Press, 2004.

Hill, David. *Greek Words and Hebrew Meanings: Studies in the Semantics of Soteriological Terms.* Society for New Testament Studies Monograph Series. Cambridge, England: University Press, 1967.

Hill, Michael R. *Archival Strategies and Techniques.* Thousand Oaks, CA: Sage, 1993.

Hillyer, Norman. *New International Biblical Commentary: 1 and 2 Peter, Jude.* Grand Rapids, MI: Baker Books, 1991.

_____. "'The Lamb' in the Apocalypse." *Evangelical Quarterly* 39 (1967): 228-36.

Hoehner, Harold. *Ephesians: An Exegetical Commentary.* Grand Rapids, MI: Baker Academic, 2002.

Hofius, Otfried. "*Abba*." In *New International Dictionary of New Testament Theology,* edited by Colon Brown. Vol. 1. Grand Rapids, MI: Zondervan, 1986.

_____. "Ist Jesus der Messias? Thesen." In *Der Messias,* JBTh 8, edited by I. Baldermann. Neukirchen, Germany: Neukirchener Verlag, 1993.

_____. "The Fourth Servant Song in the New Testament Letters." In *The Suffering Servant: Isaiah 53 in Jewish and Christian Sources,* edited by Bernd Janowski and Peter Stuhlmacher, translated by Daniel P. Bailey. Grand Rapids, MI: Eerdmans, 2004.

Honor-shame cultures: Accessed November 20, 2018. http://honorshame.com/types-honor-shame-cultures/.

Honor-shame contexts and the gospel: Accessed October 12, 2018. http://honorshame.com/about/.

Honor-shame name: Accessed January 18, 2019. http://honorshame.com/biblically-what-is-your-name/.

Hooker, Morna D. *From Adam to Christ: Essays on St. Paul.* Cambridge, England: Cambridge University Press, 1990.

_____. "Interchange in Christ." *Journal of Theological Studies* 22, no. 2 (October 1971): 349-361.

_____. *The Gospel According to St. Mark.* Grand Rapids, MI: Baker Academic, 1991.

Horton, Michael. *The Christian Faith: A Systematic Theology for Pilgrims on the Way.* Grand Rapids, MI: Zondervan, 2011.

House, Paul R. "Creation in Old Testament Theology." *The Southern Baptist Journal of Theology: Genesis* 5, no. 3 (Fall 2001): 4-17.

_____. "Sin in the Law." In *Fallen: A Theology of Sin,* edited by C. W. Morgan and R. A. Peterson. Wheaton, IL: Crossway, 2013.

Hughes, Phillip. *Hebrews.* Grand Rapids, MI: Eerdmans, 1987.

Hurtado, L. W. "Lord." In *Dictionary of Paul and His Letters.* Downers Grove, IL: IVP, 1993.

Japhet, Sara. *I & II Chronicles: A Commentary.* London, England: SCM Press, 1993.

Jeanrond, Werner. *Text and Interpretation as Categories of Theological Thinking.* Eugene, OR: Wipf & Stock, 2005.

Jeffery, Steve, Michael Ovey, and Andrew Sach. *Pierced for Our Transgressions: Rediscovering the Glory of Penal Substitution.* Nottingham, England: IVP, 2007.

Jeremias, Joachim. *The Central Message of the New Testament.* London, England: SCM, 1965.

_____. *The Parables of Jesus.* London, England: SCM Press, 2003.

Jersak, Brad. "Nonviolent Identification and the Victory of Christ." In *Stricken by God?* edited by B. Jersak and M. Hardin, 18-53.

Jersak, Brad and Michael Hardin, eds. *Stricken by God?: Nonviolent Identification and the Victory of Christ.* Grand Rapids, MI: William B. Eerdmans Publishing, 2007.

Jobes, Karen. *BECNT: 1 Peter.* Grand Rapids, MI: Baker Academic, 2005.

Jobling, David. "A Structural Analysis of Genesis 2:4b-3:24." *SBLSP* 1 (1978): 61-69.

Johnstone, William. "Exodus." In *Eerdmans Commentary on the Bible*, edited by James D. G. Dunn and John W. Rogerson. Grand Rapids, IL: Zondervan, 2003.

Karris, Robert. *A Symphony of New Testament Hymns.* Collegeville, MN: Liturgical Press, 1996.

Kasper, Walter. *The God of Jesus Christ.* Spring Valley, CA: Crossroad Publishing, 1986.

Keener, Craig. *A Socio-Rhetorical Commentary: The Gospel of Matthew.* Grand Rapids, MI: Eerdmans, 2009.

_____. *The IVP Bible Background Commentary: New Testament.* Grand Rapids, MI: Baker Academic, 1994.

Kennedy, George. *New Testament Interpretation Through Historical Criticism.* Chapel Hill, NC: University of North Carolina Press, 1984.

Kidner, Derek. *An Introduction and Commentary: Genesis.* Downers Grove, IL: InterVarsity Press, 1967.

_____. "Retribution and Punishment in the Old Testament, in Light of the New Testament." *Scottish Bulletin of Evangelical Theology* 1 (1983).

Kiel, C. F. and F. Delitzch. *Commentary on the Old Testament in Ten Volumes.* Vol. 1, *The Pentateuch.* Grand Rapids, MI: Eerdmans, 1978.

Kirk, Andrew. *The Mission of Theology and the Theology as Mission.* Leominster, England: Gracewing Publishing, 1997.

Kistemaker, Simon J. "Atonement in Hebrews: 'A Merciful and Faithful High Priest.'" In *The Glory of the Atonement,* edited by C. Hill and F. James III.

_____. *New Testament Commentary: James, Epistles of John, Peter, and Jude.* Grand Rapids, MI: Baker Books, 1996.

_____. *New Testament Commentary: Exposition of the Acts.* Grand Rapids, MI: Baker Books, 1990.

Koehler, L. and W. Baumgartner. *Lexicon in Veteris Testamenti Libros.* Leiden, Netherlands: Brill Academic Publishers, 1953.

Koester, Craig. *The Word of Life: A Theology of John's Gospel.* Grand Rapids, MI: Eerdmans, 2008.

Koester, Helmut. "Jesus the Victim." *JBL* 111, no. 1 (Spring, 1992): 3-15.

Kostenberger, Andreas. *A Theology of John's Gospel and Letters: The Word, the Christ, the Son of God.* Grand Rapids, MI: Zondervan, 2009.

Kostenberger, Andreas and Scott Swain. *New Studies in Biblical Theology.* Vol. 24, *Father, Son and Spirit: The Trinity and John's Gospel.* Edited by D. A. Carson. Downers Grove, IL: Intervarsity Press, 2008.

Kraus, Norman. "From Biblical Intentions to Theological Conceptions: Response to Thomas N. Finger." *Conrad Grebel Review* 8 (Winter 1990): 218-19.

Kruse, Colin. *Pillar New Testament Commentary: The Letters of John.* Grand Rapids, MI: William B. Eerdmans Publishing, 2000.

Kubo, Sakae, ed. of Floyd V. Filson. *Studies in Biblical Theology.* Vol. 4, *"Yesterday": A Study of Hebrews in Light of Chapter 13.* London: SCM 1967. *Andrews University Seminary Studies Book Review.* 1967: 80-82.

Ladd, George. *A Theology of the New Testament.* Grand Rapids, MI: Eerdmans, 1993.

Lampe, G. *The Seal of the Spirit: A Study of Baptism and Confirmation in the New Testament and the Fathers.* London, England: Longmans Green, 1951.

Lane, William L. *Word Biblical Commentary.* Vol. 47a, *Hebrews 1-8.* Nashville, TN: Thomas Nelson Publishers, 1991.

_____. *NICNT: The Gospel of Mark.* Grand Rapids, MI: Eerdmans Publishing, 1974.

Lausanne Committee for World Evangelization. "The Willowbank Report: Gospel and Culture." Wheaton, IL. *Lausanne Occasional Papers* 2 (1978): 7.

Lé, Dan. *The Naked Christ: An Atonement Model for a Body Obsessed Culture.* Eugene, OR: Wipf & Stock, 2012.

Lennox, John. *Gunning for God: Why the New Atheists Are Missing the Target.* Oxford, England: Lion Hudson, 2011.

Leupold, H. P. *Exposition of Genesis.* Vol. 1, *Chapters 1-19.* Grand Rapids, MI: Baker Book House, 1942.

Levine, Baruch. *The JPS Torah Commentary: Leviticus.* New York, NY: The Jewish Publication Society, 1989.

Lewis, C. S. *The Four Loves.* New York, NY: Mariner Books, 1971.

Lewis, Gordon and Bruce Demarest. *Integrative Theology: Historical, Biblical, Systematic, Apologetic, Practical.* Vol. 2, *Our Primary Need: Christ's Atoning Provisions.* Grand Rapids, MI Zondervan Publishing House, 1990.

Lincoln, Andrew and Alexander Wedderburn. *The Theology of the Later Pauline Letters.* Cambridge, England: Cambridge University Press, 1993.

Lincoln, A. T. "From Wrath to Justification." In *Pauline Theology.* Vol. 3, *Romans,* edited by David Hay and Elizabeth Johnson. Minneapolis, MN: Fortress, 1995.

_____. *World Biblical Commentary.* Vol. 42, *Ephesians.* Nashville, TN: Thomas Nelson, 1990.

Link, H. G. "Reconciliation, Restoration, Propitiation, Atonement." In *New International Dictionary of New Testament Theology.* Vol. 3. Grand Rapids, MI: Zondervan, 1986.

Louw, J. P. and Eugene Nida, *Greek-English Lexicon of the New Testament: Based on Semantic Domains.* 2nd ed. Vol. 1. New York, NY: United Bible Societies, 1996. Logos Bible Software, for Mac.

Luther, Martin. *W.A.*, 42:356. In Emil Brunner, *Dogmatics I: The Christian Name of God.* Translated by Olive Wyon. Cambridge, England: James Clarke Company Limited, n.d.

Luz, Ulrich. *The Theology of the Gospel of Matthew.* Cambridge, England: Cambridge University Press, 1995.

Manson, T. W. *The Teachings of Jesus: Studies in its Form and Content.* Cambridge, England: Cambridge University Press, 1959.

Marshall, I. Howard. *An Introduction and Commentary.* Vol. 5, *Acts.* Downers Grove, IL: IVP 1980.

_____. *Aspects of the Atonement: Cross and Resurrection in the Reconciling of God and Humanity.* London, England: Paternoster, 2007.

_____. *IVP New Testament Commentary: 1 Peter.* Downers Grove, IL: IVP, 2011.

_____. *New Testament Theology: Many Witnesses, One Gospel.* Downers Grove, IL: IVP, 2014.

_____. *NICNT: The Epistles of John.* Grand Rapids, MI: Eerdmans, 1976.

Marshall, I. Howard, Volker Rabens, and Cornelis Bennema, eds. *The Spirit and Christ in the New Testament and Christian Theology.* Grand Rapids, MI: Eerdmans, 2012.

Martin, Ralph. *Tyndale New Testament Commentaries: Philippians.* Downers Grove, IL: IVP, 2008.

_____. *Word Biblical Commentary.* Vol. 40, *2 Corinthians.* Nashville, TN: Thomas Nelson, 1985.

Matthews, Kenneth A. *The New American Commentary.* Vol. 1a, *Genesis 1-11:26.* Nashville, TN: Broadman & Holman Publishers, 1996.

McCurdy, Leslie. *Attributes and Atonement: The Holy Love of God in the Theology of P. T. Forsyth.* Carlisle, PA: Paternoster, 1999.

McFarlane, Graham. "Towards a Theology of Togetherness." In *The Spirit and Christ,* edited by I. H. Marshall, V. Rabens, and C. Bennema.

_____. *Why Do You Believe What You Believe About the Holy Spirit?* Eugene, OR: Wipf & Stock, 2009.

McGrath, Alister. *Christian Theology: An Introduction,* 3rd ed. Oxford, England: Blackwell Publishers, 2001.

McIntyre, John. *The Shape of Pneumatology: Studies in the Doctrine of the Holy Spirit.* Edinburgh, England: T&T Clark, 2004.

_____. *The Shape of Soteriology: Studies in the Doctrine of the Death of Christ.* Edinburgh, England: T&T Clark, 1992.

McKnight, Scot. *1 Peter.* Grand Rapids, MI: Zondervan, 1996.

_____. *A Community Called Atonement.* Nashville, TN: Abingdon Press, 2007.

_____. *Jesus and His Death: Historiography, the Historical Jesus, and Atonement Theory.* Waco, TX: Baylor University Press, 2005.

McKnight, Scot and Joseph B. Modica. *Jesus is Lord, Caesar is Not: Evaluating Empire in New Testament Studies.* Downers Grove, IL: IVP, 2013.

McLaren, Brian. *The Story We Find Ourselves in: Further Adventures of a New Kind of Christian.* San Francisco, CA: Jossey-Bass, 2003.

Melick, Richard. *The New American Commentary.* Vol. 32, *Philippians, Colossians, Philemon.* Nashville, TN: Broadman & Holman Publishers, 1991.

Melito of Sardis and Alistair Stewart-Sykes. *On Pascha: With the Fragments of Melito and Other Material Related to the Quatrodecimans.* Yonkers, NY: St. Vladamir's Seminary Press, 2001.

Menoud, P. *"La Mort d'Ananias et de Saphira* (Acts 5: 1–11)." In *Aux Sources de la Tradition Chrétienne: Melanges offerts à M. Maurice Goguel.* Neuchatel, Germany: Delachaux et Niestlé, 1950. In John Polhill. *Acts.*

Michaels, J. Ramsey. *Word Biblical Commentary.* Vol. 49, *1 Peter.* Waco, TX: Word Books Publisher, 1988.

Milbank, John. *Being Reconciled: Ontology and Pardon.* London, England: Routledge, 2003.

Milgrom, Jacob. *Anchor Yale Bible Commentary.* Vol. 3, *Leviticus 1-16.* New York, NY: Doubleday, 1991.

Miller, Alice. *The Untouched Key: Tracing Childhood Trauma in Creativity and Destructiveness.* Translated by Hildegarde and Hunter Hannum. London, England: Virago Press, 1990.

Mody, Rohintan. "Penal Substitutionary Atonement in Paul: An Exegetical Study of Romans 3:25-26." In *The Atonement Debate,* edited by D. Tidball, D. Hilborn, and J. Thacker.

Moltmann, Jürgen. *The Crucified God: The Cross of Christ as the Foundation and Criticism of Christian Theology.* Translated by John Bowden and R. A. Wilson. Minneapolis, MN: Augsburg Fortress Publishing, 1993.

———. *Trinity and the Kingdom.* Minneapolis, MN: Fortress Press, 1993.

Moo, Douglas. *NICNT: The Epistle to the Romans.* Grand Rapids, MI: Eerdmans, 1996.

———. *Pillar New Testament Commentary: The Letter of James.* Grand Rapids, MI: Eerdmans, 2000.

Morgan, Robert and John Barton. *Biblical Interpretation.* Oxford, England: Oxford University Press, 1988.

Morhlang, Roger. *Matthew and Paul: A Comparison of Ethical Perspectives.* Cambridge, England: Cambridge University Press, 2004.

Moroney, Stephen. "Calvin's Teachings on Reason and the Noetic Effects of Sin." In *The Noetic Effects of Sin: A Historical and Contemporary Exploration of How Sin Affects Our Thinking.* Lanham, MD: Lexington Books, 1995.

Morris, Leon L. *Bible Study Commentary: Hebrews.* Grand Rapids, MI: Zondervan Publishing, 1983.

_____. *Jesus is the Christ: Studies in the Theology of John.* Grand Rapids, MI: Eerdmans, 1989.

_____. *NICNT: The Gospel According to John.* Grand Rapids, MI: William B. Eerdmans Publishing, 1995.

_____. *The Apostolic Preaching of the Cross.* London, England: Tyndale, 1955.

_____. "The Day of Atonement." In *The Atonement: Its Meaning and Significance.* Downers Grove, IL: IVP, 1983.

_____. "The use of *Hilaskethai* etc. in Biblical Greek." *Expository Times* 62, no. 8 (May 1951): 227-233.

Mounce, Robert. *NICNT: The Book of Revelation.* Grand Rapids, MI: Eerdmans Publishing, 1998.

Moxnes, Halvor. "Honor and Shame." In *The Social Sciences and New Testament Interpretation,* edited by Richard Rohrbaugh. Grand Rapids, MI: Baker Academic, 1996.

Murray, John. *Systematic Theology.* Vol. 2, *Collected Writings of John Murray.* Reprint, London, England: Banner of Truth, 1991.

_____. Quoted in Jeong Koo Jeon. *Covenant Theology: John Murray's and Meredith G. Kline's Response to the Historical Development of Federal Theology in Reformed Thought.* Rev. ed., paperback ver. Lanham, MD: UPA, 2004.

Neuhaus, Richard. *Death On A Friday Afternoon: Meditations on the Last Words of Jesus From the Cross.* New York, NY: Basic Books, 2000.

Newbigin, Leslie. *Proper Confidence: Faith, Doubt, and Certainty in Christian Discipleship.* Grand Rapids, IL: Eerdmans, 1995.

_____. *The Light Has Come: An Exposition of the Fourth Gospel.* Grand Rapids, MI: Eerdmans, 1987.

_____. *The Open Secret: An Introduction to the Theology of Mission.* Grand Rapids, IL: Eerdmans, 1995.

Nichols, Greg. "Doctrine of Man." Class Lectures from Trinity Ministerial Academy. Privately Printed, 1982.

Nicole, Emile "Atonement in the Pentateuch: 'It Is the Blood that Makes Atonement for One's Life.'" In *The Glory of the Atonement,* edited by C. Hill and F. James III.

Nicole, Roger. "C. H. Dodd and the Doctrine of Propitiation." *WTJ* 17, no. 2 (May 1955): 117-57.

_____. "Postscript on Penal Substitution," In *The Glory of the Atonement,* edited by C. Hill and F. James III.

_____. "Propitiation." *Christianity Today,* April 15, 1957.

Nineham, Dennis. *The Use and Abuse of the Bible: A Study of the Bible in an Age of Rapid Cultural Change.* London, England: SPCK, 1978.

Nolland, John. *Word Biblical Commentary.* Vol. 35a, *Luke 1:1-9:20.* Nashville, TN: Thomas Nelson, 1989.

_____. *Word Biblical Commentary.* Vol. 35c, *Luke 18:35-24:53.* Nashville, TN: Thomas Nelson, 1989.

Northey, Wayne. "The Cross: God's Peace Work Towards A Restorative Peace Making Understanding of the Atonement." In *Stricken by God?* edited by B. Jersak and M. Hardin, 356-77.

O'Brien, Peter Thomas. *NIGTC: The Epistle to the Philippians.* Grand Rapids, MI: Eerdmans, 1991.

_____. *Pillar New Testament Commentary: The Letter to the Ephesians.* Grand Rapids, MI: Eerdmans, 1999.

_____. *Pillar New Testament Commentary: The Letter to the Hebrews.* Grand Rapids, MI: Eerdmans, 2010.

_____. *Word Biblical Commentary.* Vol. 44, *Colossians, Philemon.* Nashville, TN: Thomas Nelson, 1982.

Oden, Thomas, ed. "Chrysostom." In *Ancient Christian Commentary on Scripture: 1-2 Corinthians.* New York, NY: Routledge, 1999.

Oden, Thomas and Christopher Hall, eds. *Ancient Christian Commentary.* Vol. 2, *Mark.* Downers Grove: IVP, 2005.

Orlinsky, Harry. *Supplements to Vetus Testamentum, Studies on the Second Part of the Book of Isaiah: The So-Called "Servant of the Lord" and "Suffering Servant" in Second Isaiah.* Leiden, Netherlands: E. J. Brill, 1967.

Oswalt, John N. "1948." In *New International Dictionary of Old Testament Theology and Exegesis,* edited by Willem A. VanGemeren. Vol. 1. Grand Rapids, MI: Zondervan, 1997.

_____. *NICOT: The Book of Isaiah, Chapters 40-66.* Grand Rapids, MI: Eerdmans, 1998.

Packer, J. I. *God Has Spoken: Revelation and the Bible.* Grand Rapids, MI: Baker Books, 1994.

_____. *In My Place Condemned He Stood: Celebrating the Glory of the Atonement.* Wheaton, IL: Crossway, 2007.

_____. *Knowing God.* Downers Grove, IL: IVP, 1993.

_____. "What Did the Cross Achieve?: The Logic of Penal Substitution," *Tyndale Bulletin* 25 (1974):17.

Pannenberg, Wolfhart. *Anthropology in Theological Perspective.* Edinburgh, England: T&T Clark, 1985.

_____. *Basic Questions in Theology.* Minneapolis, MN: Augsburg Fortress Publishers, 2008.

Parratt, John ed. *An Introduction to Third World Theologies.* Cambridge, England: Cambridge University Press, 2004.

Pattison, Stephen. "'Suffer the Little Children': The Challenge of Child Abuse and Neglect to Theology." *TCJCSTS (Theology and Sexuality)* 4, no. 9 (September 1998).

Paul, Robert. *The Atonement and the Sacraments: The Relation of the Atonement to the Sacraments of Baptism and the Lord's Supper.* Eugene. OR: Wipf & Stock, 1992.

Payne, J. B. and W. Möller. "Atonement, Day of." In *The International Standard Bible Encyclopedia.* rev. ed., vol. 1, edited by G. W. Bromiley. Grand Rapids, MI: Wm. B. Eerdmans, 1988.

Peterson, David. "Atonement in the New Testament." In *Where Wrath and Mercy Meet: Proclaiming the Atonement Today.* Carlisle, PA: Paternoster, 2001.

_____. *Hebrews and Perfection: An Examination of the Concept of Perfection in the Epistle to the Hebrews.* Cambridge, England: Cambridge University Press, 1995.

Pillhofer, Peter. *Philippi, Band 1: Die erest christliche Gemeinde Europas,* WUNT. Tubingen, Germany: J.C.B. Mohr, 1995. In *Embracing Shared Ministry.* Translated by Joseph Hellerman. Grand Rapids, MI: Kregel Ministry, 2013.

Placher, William. "Christ Takes Our Place: Rethinking Atonement." *Interpretation* 53, no. 1 (January 1999).

Polhill, John. *The New American Commentary.* Vol. 26, *Acts.* Nashville, TN: Broadman Press, 1992.

Poythress, Vern. *Symphonic Theology: The Validity of Multiple Perspectives in Theology.* Phillipsburg, NJ: P&R Publishing, 2001.

Rabens, Volker. "Power from In Between: The Relational Experience of the Holy Spirit and Spiritual Gifts in Paul's Churches." In *The Spirit and Christ,* edited by I. H. Marshall, V. Rabens, and C. Bennema, 138-155.

Rayment-Pickard, Hugh. "Atonement." In *50 Key Concepts in Theology.* London, England: Darton, Longman, and Todd, 2007.

Ridderbos, Herman. *The Gospel of John: A Theological Commentary.* Translated by J. Vriend. Grand Rapids, MI: William B. Eerdmans Publishing, 1997.

Rohrbaugh, Richard. *The Social Sciences and New Testament Interpretation.* Grand Rapids: Baker Academic, 2003.

Rupp, Gordon. *The Righteousness of God: Luther Studies.* London, England: Hodder & Stoughton, 1953.

Russell, Jeffery. *Satan: The Early Christian Tradition.* Ithaca, NY: Cornell University Press, 1987.

Rutledge, Flemming. *The Crucifixion: Understanding the Death of Jesus Christ.* Grand Rapids, MI: Eerdmans, 2015.

Ryken, Leland, James Wilhoit, and Tremper Longman III, eds. "Comfort," "Fear of God," "Right, Right Hand," "Sin." In *Dictionary of Biblical Imagery: An Encyclopedic Exploration of the Images, Symbols, Motifs, Metaphors, Figures of Speech, and Literary Patterns of the Bible.* Downers Grove, IL: IVP, 1998.

Sabourin, L. *L'Evangile selon saint Matthieu et ses principaux paralleles.* Rome, Italy: Biblical Institute Press, 1978.

Sanders, Jack. *The New Testament Christological Hymns: Their Historical Religious Background.* Cambridge, England: Cambridge University Press, 1971.

Sarna, Nahum M. *The JPS Torah Commentary: Genesis, בראשית.* New York, NY: The Jewish Publication Society, 1989.

_____. *The JPS Torah Commentary: Exodus*. New York, NY: The Jewish Publication Society, 1991.

Schabb, Gloria. "Feminist Theological Methodology: A Kaleidoscopic Model." *Theological Studies* 62, no. 2 (May 2001): 341-365.

Schaff, Phillip, ed. *Nicene, and Post-Nicene Fathers*. Vol. 3, *St. Augustine, On the Trinity*. First Series. New York, NY: Cosimo Classics, 2005.

Schemiechen, Peter. *Saving Power: Theories of Atonement and Forms of the Church*. Grand Rapids, MI: Eerdmans, Publishing, 2005.

Schleiermacher, Friedrich. *The Christian Faith*. Translated by H. Mackintosh and J. Stewart. Edinburgh, England: T&T Clark, 1976.

Schnackenberg, Rudolph. *The Epistle to the Ephesians*. Edinburgh, England: T&T Clark, 2001.

Schnakenberg, Robert. *Matthew*. Grand Rapids, MI: Eerdmans, 2002.

Schneider, Benjamin. "A Certain Kind of Trinity: Dependence, Substance, and Explanation." *Philosophical Studies* 129, no. 2 (May 2006): 393-419.

Schreiner, Thomas. "Penal Substitution Response." In *The Nature of the Atonement*. Downers Grove, IL: IVP, 2006.

_____. "Penal Substitution View." In *The Nature of the Atonement*. Downers Grove, IL: IVP, 2006.

_____. *BECNT: Romans*. Grand Rapids, MI: Baker Books, 1998.

Sefrid, Mark. *New Studies in Biblical Theology. Christ, Our Righteousness: Paul's Theology of Justification*. Leicester, England: Apollos, 2000.

Sexton, Jason. "The *Imago Dei* Once Again: Stanley Grenz's Journey toward a Theological Interpretation of Genesis 1:26-27." *Journal of Theological Interpretation* 4, no. 2 (Fall: 2010).

Sherman, Robert. *King, Priest, and Prophet: A Trinitarian Theology of Atonement*. Edinburgh, England: T&T Clark, 2004.

Silver, Alan. *Jews, Myth, and History: A Critical Exploration of Contemporary Jewish Belief*. Leicester, England: Troubador Publishing, 2008.

Simon, Bud. "Shame and Secularization: A Collateral Rise in American Society with Implications for Evangelism." *Evangelical Missiological Society*. National Conference, Dallas, Texas, 2018. https://www.emsweb.org/conference.

Simonetti, Marlio. *Ancient Christian Commentary*. New Testament 1a, *Matthew 1-13*. Downers Grove, IL: IVP Academic, 2001.

Smail, Tom "Can One Man Die for the People?" In *Atonement Today*, edited by J. Goldingay.

_____. *Once and For All: A Confession of the Cross*. London, England: Darton, Longman, and Todd, 1998.

Smalley, Stephen. *The Revelation to John: A Commentary on the Greek Text of the Apocalypse*. Downers Grove, IL: IVP, 2005.

      . *Thunder and Love: John's Revelation and John's Community.* Franklin, TN: Authentic Lifestyle, 1994.

Snaith, N. H. "The Meaning of 'the Paraclete.'" *Expository Times* 57, no. 2 (1945-6): 47-50.

So, Damon W. K. *Jesus' Revelation of His Father: A Narrative-Conceptual Study of the Trinity with Special Reference to Karl Barth.* Carlisle, PA: Paternoster Press, 2006.

Socinus, Faustus. *De Iesu Christo Servatore*, in *Opera Omnia.* Vols. 1-2. *Bibliotheca Fratrum Polonorum Quos Unitarios Vocant.* 8 vols. Irenopoli: post, 1656.

Stein, Stephen. *Jonathan Edwards's Writings: Text, Context, Interpretation.* Bloomington, IN: Indiana University Press, 1996.

Stewart, James. *A Man in Christ: The Vital Elements of St. Paul's Religion.* New York, NY: Harper & Row, 1938.

Stott, John. *The Cross of Christ.* Leicester, England: IVP, 1989.

      . *The Cross of Christ.* 2nd ed. Downers Grove, IL: IVP, 2006.

      . *The Message of Acts: To the Ends of the Earth.* Leicester, England: InterVarsity Press, 1990.

      . *The Message of the Sermon on the Mount (Matthew 5-7, Christian Counter Culture).* Downers Grove, IL: IVP, 1985.

Strecker, Georg. *Hermeneia: A Critical and Historical Commentary on the Bible. The Johannine Letters: A Commentary on 1, 2, and 3 John.* Minneapolis, MN: Fortress Press, 1996.

Stuart, Douglas K. *The New American Commentary.* Vol. 2, *Exodus.* Nashville, TN: Broadman & Holman Publishers, 2006.

Stuhlmacher, P. *Gerechtigkeit Gottes bei Paulus.* Gottingen, Germany: Vandenhoeck und Ruprecht, 1965.

Tenney, Douglas. "Advocate." In *New International Bible Dictionary.* Grand Rapids, MI: Zondervan, 1999.

Tenney, Merrill C. *The Expositor's Bible Commentary.* Vol. 9, *John-Acts.* Edited by Frank E. Gaebelein. Grand Rapids, MI: Zondervan, 1984.

Terry, Milton. *Biblical Hermeneutics: A Treatise on the Interpretation of the Old and New Testaments.* New York, NY: Great Christian Books, 2014.

Thiselton, Anthony. *1 Corinthians: A Shorter Exegetical and Pastoral Commentary.* Grand Rapids, MI: William B. Eerdmans Publishing, 2006.

      . *Hermeneutics of Doctrine.* Grand Rapids, MI: Eerdmans, 2007.

      . *New Horizons in Hermeneutics.* Grand Rapids, MI: Zondervan, 1997.

      . *The Holy Spirit In Biblical Teaching, Through the Centuries, and Today.* Grand Rapids, MI: Eerdmans, 2013.

Thomas, W. H. Griffith. *The Holy Spirit of God.* London, England: Longmans, 1913.

Thompson, James. *Paideia Commentaries on the New Testament: Hebrews.* Grand Rapids, MI: Baker Academic, 2008.

Thompson, Leonard. *Abingdon New Testament Commentaries: Revelation.* Nashville, TN: Abingdon Press, 1998.

Thornton, Gerald. "Propitiation or Expiation? *Hilasterion* and *Hilasmos* in Romans and 1 John." *Evangelical Theology* 80 (1968-9): 54-55.

Tidball, Derek, David Hilborn, and Jeffery Thacker, eds. *The Atonement Debate: Papers from the London Symposium on the Theology of Atonement.* Grand Rapids, MI: Zondervan, 2008.

Tidball, Derek. "Penal Substitution: A Pastoral Apologetic." In *The Atonement Debate,* edited by D. Tidball, D. Hilborn, and J. Thacker.

Tienou, Tite. "Christian Theology in an Era of World Christianity." In *Globalizing Theology: Belief and Practice in an Era of World Christianity.* Grand Rapids, MI: Baker Academic, 2006.

Tigay, Jeffery. *The JPS Torah Commentary: Deuteronomy.* Philadelphia, PA: JPS, 1996.

Torrance, Thomas F. "The Christ Who Loves Us." In *A Passion for Christ: The Vision that Ignites Ministry,* edited by Gerrit Dawson and Jock Stein. Eugene, OR: Wipf & Stock, 2010.

———. *The Trinitarian Faith: The Evangelical Theology of the Ancient Catholic Faith.* New York, NY: T&T Clark, 1997.

Tozer, A. W. *Knowledge of the Holy.* Glendale, CA: Bibliotech Press, 2016.

Tracy, David. *Plurality and Ambiguity: Hermeneutics, Religion, Hope.* Chicago, IL: University of Chicago Press, 1994.

Travis, Stephen. "Christ as Bearer of Divine Judgment in Paul's Thought about the Atonement." In *Jesus of Nazareth: Lord and Christ: Essays on the Historical Jesus and New Testament Christology,* edited by Joel Green and Max Turner. Grand Rapids, MI: Eerdmans, 1994.

Treat, Jeremy. "Atonement and Covenant." In *Locating Atonement: Explorations in Constructive Dogmatics,* edited by Oliver Crisp and Fred Sanders. Grand Rapids, MI: Zondervan, 2015.

Trumper, Tim J. R. "A Fresh Exposition of Adoption: I. An Outline." *SBET* 23, no. 1 (Spring 2005): 60-80.

Turner, Max. "Receiving Christ and Receiving the Spirit: In Dialogue with David Pawson." *Journal of Pentecostal Theology* 7, no. 15 (Winter 1999): 1-31.

———. *The Holy Spirit and Spiritual Gifts Then and Now.* Grand Rapids, MI: Baker Academic, 1997.

Turretin, Francis. *Institutes of Elenctic Theology.* Vol. 3, *Eighteenth Through Twentieth Topics.* Translated by James T. Dennison and George Musgrave Giger. Phillipsburg, NJ: P&R Publishing, 1997.

Tvarberg, Lois. "Biblically, What Is Your 'Name'?" Accessed January 18, 2019. http://honorshame.com/biblically-what-is-your-name/.

Tylor, Edward. *Primitive Culture: Researches Into the Development of Mythology, Philosophy, Religion, Language, Art, and Custom*. Vol. 1. Mineola, NY: Dover Publications, 2016.

Unger, Merrill F. *The New Unger's Bible Handbook*. Chicago, IL: Moody, 1984.

Van Engen, Charles. "The Glocal Church: Locality and Catholicity in a Globalizing World." In *Globalizing Theology: Belief and Practice in an Era of World Christianity*. Grand Rapids, MI: Baker Academic, 2006.

Vanhoozer, Kevin. *First Theology: God, Scripture, and Hermeneutics*. Downers Grove, IL: IVP, 2002.

_____. *Is There A Meaning in this Text?: The Bible, the Reader, and the Morality of Literary Knowledge*. Grand Rapids, MI: Zondervan, 1998.

_____. "'One Rule to Rule Them All?' Theological Method in an Era of World Christianity." In *Globalizing Theology: Belief and Practice in an Era of World Christianity*, edited by Craig Ott and Harold Netland. Grand Rapids, MI: Baker Academic, 2006.

_____. *Remythologizing Theology: Divine Action, Passion, and Authorship*. Cambridge, England: Cambridge University Press, 2010.

_____. "The Atonement in Postmodernity: Guilt, Goats, and Gifts." In *The Glory of the Atonement*, edited by C. Hill and F. James III.

Vine, W. E., Merrill F. Unger, and William White Jr. *Vine's Complete Expository Dictionary of Old and New Testament Words*. Nashville, TN: Thomas Nelson Publishers, 1970.

Volf, Mirslov. *After Our Likeness: The Church as the Image of the Trinity*. Grand Rapids, MI: Eerdmans, 1998.

Vos, Geerhardus. *Biblical Theology: Old and New Testaments*. Grand Rapids, MI: Eerdmans, 1997.

Walaskay, Paul. *Acts*. Louisville, KY: Westminster John Knox Press, 1998.

Wall, Robert. *New International Bible Commentary (NT): Revelation*. Carlisle, PA: Paternoster Press, 1995.

Walls, Andrew. "Old Athens and New Jerusalem: Some Signposts for Christian Scholarship in the Early History of Mission Studies." *International Bulletin of Missionary Research* 21, no. 4 (October 1997):146-153.

Waltke, Bruce. *An Old Testament Theology: An Exegetical, Canonical, and Thematic Approach*. Grand Rapids, MI: Zondervan, 2007.

Walton, John H., Victor H. Matthews, and Mark W. Chavalas, eds. *The IVP Bible Background Commentary: Old Testament*. Downers Grove, IL: InterVarsity Press, 2000.

_____. *The NIV Commentary: Genesis*. Grand Rapids, MI: Zondervan Publishing House, 2001.

Wan, Enoch ed. *Christian Witness in Pluralistic Contexts in the 21st Century*. Vol. 11, EMS Series. Pasadena, CA: William Carey Library Publishers, 2004.

_____. "Core values of Mission Organization in the Cultural Context of the 21st Century." *Global Missiology* (January 2009). www.GlobalMissiology.org.

_____. "Inter-disciplinary and integrative missiological research: the 'what,' 'why,' and 'how.'" *Global Missiology* (July 2017). www.GlobalMissiology.org.

_____. "Relational Theology and Relational Missiology." *EMS Occasional Bulletin* 21, no. 1 (Fall 2007): 1-8.

_____. *Sino-theology.* Canada: Christian Witness Press, 1999 (in Chinese).

_____. "The Paradigm of Relational Realism." *EMS Occasional Bulletin* 19, no. 2 (Spring 2006).

Weaver, James Denny. "Narrative *Christus Victor.*" In *Atonement and Violence: A Theological Conversation,* edited by John Sanders. Nashville, TN: Abingdon Press, 2006.

_____. *The Nonviolent Atonement.* Grand Rapids, MN: Eerdmans, 2001.

Wenham, Gordon J. *Word Biblical Commentary.* Vol. 1, *Genesis 1-15.* Waco: TX, Word Books, 1987.

_____. "The Theology of the Old Testament Sacrifice.' In *Sacrifice in the Bible,* edited by Roger Beckwith and Martin Selman. Eugene, OR: Wipf & Stock, 2004.

Westcott, B. F. *The Epistle to the Hebrews.* United Kingdom: Macmillan and Co., 1902; Logos Bible Software, for Mac, 2015.

Westermann, Claus. *Genesis 1-11: A Commentary.* Translated by John J. Scullion SJ. London, England: SPCK, 1974.

Whybray, Richard. "Thanksgiving for a Liberated Prophet: An Interpretation of Isaiah Chapter 53." In *Journal for the Study of the Old Testament Supplement Series.* Vol. 4. Sheffield, England: JSOT Press, 1978.

Wilcox, Max. "Upon the Tree - Deut. 21.22-23 in the New Testament." *JBL* 96, no. 1 (March 1977): 85-99. www.jstor.org/stable/3265329.

Williams, Gary. "Penal Substitution: A Response to Recent Criticisms." In *The Atonement Debate,* edited by D. Tidball, D. Hilborn, and J. Thacker.

Witherington III, Ben. *Revelation.* Cambridge, England: Cambridge University Press, 2003.

_____. *A Socio-Rhetorical Commentary: The Gospel of Mark.* Grand Rapids, MI: Eerdmans, 2001.

_____. *A Socio-Rhetorical Commentary: on the Captivity Epistles, The Letters to Philemon, the Colossians, and the Ephesians.* Grand Rapids, MI: Eerdmans, 2007.

Wright, Christopher. "Atonement in the Old Testament." In *The Atonement Debate,* edited by D. Tidball, D. Hilborn, and J. Thacker.

Wright, N. T. "Gay Marriage: Nature and Narrative Point to Complementarity." Accessed January 18, 2015. http://www.firstthings.com/blogs/firstthoughts/2014/06/n-t-wrights-argument-against-same-sex-marriage.

_____. *Jesus and the Victory of God: Christian Origins and the Question of God.* Minneapolis, MN: Fortress Press, 1996.

_____. "Romans and the Theology of Paul." In *Pauline Theology*, vol. 3, *Romans*, edited by David M. Hay and E. Elizabeth Johnson. Minneapolis, MN: Fortress Press, 1995.

_____. *The New Interpreter's Bible*. Vol. 10. *The Letter to the Romans: Introduction, Commentary, and Reflections*. Nashville, TN: Abingdon, 2002.

_____. "The Reasons for Jesus' Crucifixion." In *Stricken by God?* edited by B. Jersak and M. Hardin, 78-149.

Wright, Paul A. "Exodus 1-24 (A Canonical Study)." Unpublished Ph.D. diss., University of Vienna, Austria, March 1993.

Yarborough, Robert. "Atonement." In *New Dictionary of Biblical Theology*, edited by T. Alexander and B. Rosner. Downers Grove, IL: InterVarsity Press, 2000.

Youngblood, Ronald. "Judgment." In *Evangelical Dictionary of Theology.* 2nd ed. Grand Rapids, MI: Baker Book House, 1984.

Zodhiates, Spiros. *The Complete Word Study Dictionary: New Testament.* Logos Bible Software, for Mac. Chattanooga, TN: AMG Publishers, 2000.

www.ingramcontent.com/pod-product-compliance
Lightning Source LLC
Chambersburg PA
CBHW060012050426
42448CB00012B/2718